THOMAS MACKAY

THOMAS MACKAY

The Laird of Rideau Hall and
the Founding of Ottawa

by
Alastair Sweeny

University of Ottawa Press
2022

University of Ottawa **Press**
Les **Presses** de l'Université d'Ottawa

The University of Ottawa Press (UOP) is proud to be the oldest of the Francophone university presses in Canada as well as the oldest bilingual university publisher in North America. Since 1936, UOP has been enriching intellectual and cultural discourse by producing peer-reviewed and award-winning books in the humanities and social sciences, in French and in English.

www.press.uottawa.ca

Library and Archives Canada Cataloguing in Publication

Title: Thomas Mackay : the laird of Rideau Hall and the founding of Ottawa / by Alastair Sweeny.
Names: Sweeny, Alastair, author.
Description: Series statement: Regional studies | Includes bibliographical references.
Identifiers: Canadiana (print) 20200395297 | Canadiana (ebook) 20200395483 |
    ISBN 9780776636788 (softcover) |
    ISBN 9780776636795 (hardcover) |
    ISBN 9780776636801 (PDF) |
    ISBN 9780776636818 (EPUB) |
    ISBN 9780776636825 (Kindle)
Subjects LCSH: MacKay, Thomas, 1792-1855. | LCSH: Businesspeople—Ontario—Ottawa—Biography. | LCSH: Stonemasons—Ontario—Ottawa—Biography. | LCSH: Legislators—Ontario—Ottawa—Biography. | LCSH: Ottawa (Ont.)—Biography. | LCSH: Ottawa (Ont.)—History—19th century. | LCSH: Ottawa (Ont.)—Buildings, structures, etc. | LCGFT: Biographies.
Classification: LCC FC3096.26.M52 S94 2021 | DDC 971.3/8402092—dc23

Legal Deposit: First Quarter 2022
Library and Archives Canada

© University of Ottawa Press 2022
All rights reserved.

No part of this publication may be reproduced or transmitted in any form or by any means, or stored in a database and retrieval system, without prior permission.

Production Team
Copy editing — Susan James
Proofreading — James Warren and Tanina Drvar
Typesetting — Nord Compo
Cover design — Édiscript enr.

In the case of photocopying or any other reprographic copying, please secure licenses from:

Access Copyright
www.accesscopyright.ca
1-800-893-5777

Cover image
1827 Mackay and Colonel By at the Ottawa Locks, painting by C. W. Jefferys, Library and Archives Canada, C-073703. Modified for cover purposes.

For foreign rights and permissions:
www.iprlicense.com

The University of Ottawa Press gratefully acknowledges the support extended to its publishing list by the Government of Canada, the Canada Council for the Arts, the Ontario Arts Council, the Social Sciences and Humanities Research Council and the Canadian Federation for the Humanities and Social Sciences through the Awards to Scholarly Publications Program, and by the University of Ottawa.

 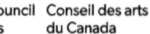 

Table of Contents

List of Figures vii
Acknowledgements xix
A Note on Images xxi
Other Books by Alastair Sweeny xxiii
Introduction 1

PART ONE

Lachine and the Rideau Canal

Chapter 1.	Early Ottawa	11
Chapter 2.	From Scotland to Montréal	25
Chapter 3.	Wellington's Generals	43
Chapter 4.	Enter Colonel John By	61
Chapter 5.	1826: The Founding of Bytown	69
Chapter 6.	1827: Canal Cornerstones	91
Chapter 7.	How to Build a Canal	107
Chapter 8.	Jones Falls, Malaria, and Black Powder ...	117
Chapter 9.	The Hog's Back Dam Disasters	125
Chapter 10.	1829: Handsome Profits	133
Chapter 11.	1831: Finishing the Work	139
Chapter 12.	1832: Colonel By's Recall	151

PART TWO
New Edinburgh and Rideau Hall

Chapter 13.	Militia, Politics, and Civics, 1830–1838	163
Chapter 14.	Miller Mackay, 1830–1849	179
Chapter 15.	Rideau Hall, 1838–1853	193
Chapter 16.	The Capital Idea, 1841–1849	205
Chapter 17.	Mackay a Legislative Councillor	213
Chapter 18.	Bust and Boom, 1840–1849	231
Chapter 19.	Annexation and Reciprocity, 1849–1854	241

PART THREE
Railway Mania

Chapter 20.	The Philosophy of Railroads, 1847–1853	259
Chapter 21.	The Bytown & Prescott, 1847–1853	269
Chapter 22.	The Keefers in Montréal, 1850–1859	285
Chapter 23.	The Queen Approves of Ottawa, 1853–1857	297

PART FOUR
Thomas Keefer and the Mackay Estate

Chapter 24.	The Thomas Keefer Regime, 1855–1865	315
Chapter 25.	The Sale of Rideau Hall	325
Chapter 26.	Keefer Develops Rockcliffe Park	341

Appendix A: Rockcliffe Arms	357
Appendix B: Lines on Thomas Mackay	359
Select Bibliography	365

List of Figures

Figure 1.	Thomas Mackay, 1830s	xviii
Figure 2.	Hope the bookseller, 1879	xx
Figure 3.	Commercial label of nephew Thomas McKay's flour mill	7
Figure 1.1.	Montréal from St. Helen's Island, 1830	9
Figure 1.2.	*Two Ottawa Chiefs Who with Others Lately Came Down from Michillimackinac on Lake Huron to Have a Talk with Their Great Father The King or His Representative* [likely Lord Dalhousie], circa 1812–1820	13
Figure 1.3.	*Algonquin Encampment at [Rideau] Falls* (Cornelius Krieghoff)	14
Figure 1.4.	*Indians [Algonquins] Paying Homage to the Spirit of the Chaudière*	15
Figure 1.5.	Coteau-du-Lac Canal, 1780	18
Figure 1.6.	Durham boats ascending the St. Lawrence	19
Figure 1.7.	Tiberius Wright on the family's first timber Raft, 1806	21
Figure 1.8.	*A View of the Mill and Tavern of Philemon Wright at the Chaudière Falls*, Hull, 1823	22

Figure 2.1.	Perth, Scotland, "City of stone"	26
Figure 2.2.	Clans of northern Scotland (note the town of Thurso at the top of the map)	27
Figure 2.3.	Emigrants bound for Québec	29
Figure 2.4.	Molson steamboat passing Île Ste-Hélène	30
Figure 2.5.	Thomas Mackay, c. 1827	32
Figure 2.6.	Major General Elias Walker Durnford, Royal Engineers	34
Figure 2.7.	Fort Lennox in 1886, showing barracks and officers' quarters	35
Figure 2.8.	Richardson and dignitaries inspecting the Lachine Canal	38
Figure 2.9.	Entrance to Lachine Canal at Windmill Point, Montréal, Quebec, 1826	41
Figure 2.10.	The Lachine Canal; Église Notre-Dame in the centre background	42
Figure 3.1.	Arthur Wellesley, 1st Duke of Wellington, detail, by Sir Thomas Lawrence, 1829	44
Figure 3.2.	HMS *St. Lawrence*, built at Kingston Royal Naval Dockyard	46
Figure 3.3.	A timber raft on the Ottawa, 1868	50
Figure 3.4.	The 4th Duke of Richmond and Lennox, 1823	51
Figure 3.5.	George Ramsay, 9th Earl of Dalhousie (1770–1838), Governor-in-Chief of Canada 1819–1828	55

List of Figures   ix

Figure 3.6. Fourteen voyageurs and four gentlemen in Dalhousie's Vice Regal canoe, 1821 58

Figure 3.7. Philemon Wright c. 1810 59

Figure 4.1. Lieutenant Colonel John By, 1832 64

Figure 4.2. *The First Camp Bytown,* 1826, by Lieutenant Colonel John By 65

Figure 5.1. Below the Chaudière Falls 69

Figure 5.2. Bytown, Nepean, and Richmond, 1830 71

Figure 5.3. Both banks of the Ottawa River and the Chaudière Falls, 1825 72

Figure 5.4. Wrightstown, 1830 73

Figure 5.5. One of Mackay's Union Bridge arches, built in 1825-26, surrounded by lumber, 1880s 80

Figure 5.6. The Ottawa Locks in 1869, showing part of the quarry on the east side where Mackay was able to extract superior seams of limestone 87

Figure 5.7. Colonel By's house, 1841 88

Figure 6.1. Log shanties along the canal, 1830 92

Figure 6.2. One of Mackay's buildings on Barrack Hill 95

Figure 6.3. Rideau Canal entrance with three barracks, 1833 96

Figure 6.4. Royal Sappers and Miners at work. 97

Figure 6.5. Mackay's Commissariat, Ottawa's oldest building 98

Figure 6.6.	Royal Engineers' chart of the Ottawa Locks with Mackay's Quarry, Commissariat, and Ordnance Office	99
Figure 6.7.	The Dalhousies arrive by fourteen-man rowing barge from Montréal, 1827	101
Figure 6.8.	Lady Dalhousie on the rope bridge, 1827.	102
Figure 6.9.	Sappers' Bridge, Lower Bytown from Barrack Hill, 1845	105
Figure 7.1.	An overdressed Mackay and Colonel By, 1826	108
Figure 7.2.	Colonel By's drawing of a lock gate.	109
Figure 7.3.	Rideau Canal crab	113
Figure 8.1.	Dam at Jones Falls from the west end	118
Figure 9.1.	Hog's Back Dam showing the 1830 breach and stonework	128
Figure 9.2.	Hog's Back [Prince of Wales] Falls and completed locks, 1832	129
Figure 9.3.	Hog's Back in 1845.	131
Figure 10.1.	Spanish four-real piece from the Mexican Mint	137
Figure 11.1.	*Blockhouse at Merrickville*, 1839	140
Figure 11.2.	Troops entering the Ottawa Locks in Durham boats, 1838	141
Figure 11.3.	Troops leaving the Jones Falls Locks in Durham boats, 1838	142
Figure 11.4.	Paddlewheel steamer *Pilot* on the Rideau Canal, August 3, 1844	143

Figure 11.5.	March 17, 1831, partners' agreement	146
Figure 11.6.	John Redpath, 1836.	147
Figure 11.7.	Montreal Telegraph Company logo.	148
Figure 11.8.	Redpath Sugar, Montréal	150
Figure 12.1.	Silver cup given to Mackay and Redpath	152
Figure 12.2.	*First Eight Locks of the Rideau Canal*, 1834	154
Figure 12.3.	Reputed image of Lieutenant Colonel John By	156
Figure 12.4.	Palace of Westminster destroyed by fire, 1834.	159
Figure 13.1.	Bytown waterscape, 1851, showing Mackay's stone arches and Keefer's suspension bridge	161
Figure 13.2.	Dalhousie Lodge by-laws. Mackay was a founding member of the Dalhousie Lodge of Freemasons	165
Figure 13.3.	Barrack Hill buildings, 1840s	167
Figure 13.4.	Volunteer militia, Montréal, 1850s	168
Figure 13.5.	View of Fort Henry, Kingston, Upper Canada	169
Figure 13.6.	Plan for a citadel by Colonels Durnford and By, May 17, 1831.	170
Figure 13.7.	Burrows's plan for the Ottawa Citadel, 1838	171
Figure 13.8.	Dr. Alexander James Christie	172
Figure 13.9.	Élisabeth Bruyère	173
Figure 13.10.	Upper Canada Parliament, Toronto, 1834	176

Figure 14.1.	Mackay's Lot O lease in black.	180
Figure 14.2.	Thomas Mackay, 1830s	181
Figure 14.3.	*Eastern and Greater Fall of the Rideau River,* 1830	182
Figure 14.4.	*Rideau Mills Complex,* 1840s	187
Figure 14.5.	*Mackay Mills,* 1851	189
Figure 14.6.	James Fraser's school announcement	190
Figure 14.7.	Old Fraser School House	191
Figure 15.1.	Mackay's original Rideau Hall, dwarfed by the current shaded structure.	193
Figure 15.2.	Plan of a typical Regency villa from Soane's 1798 volume	195
Figure 15.3.	Soane sketch for the Upper Canada Government House	196
Figure 15.4.	The original Rideau Hall.	197
Figure 15.5.	Rideau Hall, The Royal Bedroom, c. 1880	197
Figure 15.6.	Rideau Hall plans.	198
Figure 15.7.	Rideau Hall domain, with stables, cow barn, garden, and bowling green.	200
Figure 15.8.	Annie MacKinnon and Elizabeth Keefer, 1850s.	201
Figure 16.1.	*Bytown Council Shield*	206
Figure 16.2.	Dr. Alexander James Christie	208
Figure 16.3.	Bytown map, 1840s.	210

Figure 17.1.	Sir Charles Bagot	214
Figure 17.2.	*Samuel Keefer's Union Suspension Bridge, 1844*	216
Figure 17.3.	*Metcalfe Opening the Canadian Assembly, Montréal, 1845.*	218
Figure 17.4.	Grey Nuns' Mother House, St. Joseph's College, Cathedral, 1855	219
Figure 17.5.	Bishop Bruno Guigues	220
Figure 17.6.	Sir Charles Metcalfe, 1844	221
Figure 17.7.	Samuel Keefer, 1850s	223
Figure 17.8.	Lord Elgin, 1840s	224
Figure 17.9.	*The Stoney Monday Riot.*	228
Figure 18.1.	*The Arch Riot.*	232
Figure 18.2.	John and Annie MacKinnon	233
Figure 18.3.	Mackay's Mills, 1845; Rideau Hall back centre right	235
Figure 18.4.	Bytown map, 1842	236
Figure 19.1.	*Burning of Parliament,* Montréal, 1849	244
Figure 19.2.	John Redpath	245
Figure 19.3.	Anti-annexation cartoon in *Punch in Canada,* 1849	247
Figure 19.4.	Peter McGill (colourized)	249
Figure 19.5.	James Bruce, Earl of Elgin, 1855.	251

Figure 19.6a.	Mackay's silver New Edinburgh Shintie Club medallion, face, 1852	253
Figure 19.6b.	Mackay's silver New Edinburgh Shintie Club medallion, verso, 1852.	253
Figure 19.7.	*Scots on Ice—Curling on the St. Lawrence at Montréal*	254
Figure 19.8.	*Canada at the 1878 Paris Exposition*	255
Figure 20.1.	*Montreal and Lachine Railroad First Train, 19 November 1847*	257
Figure 20.2.	James Ferrier, 1866	261
Figure 20.3.	Montreal & Lachine Railroad token	262
Figure 20.4.	St. Lawrence & Ottawa Grand Junction Railway	264
Figure 20.5.	*Opening of the Welland Canal.*	266
Figure 20.6.	Elizabeth Mackay Keefer, 1869	268
Figure 21.1.	Lower Town market building	272
Figure 21.2.	The Bytown & Prescott	275
Figure 21.3.	Richard W. Scott and grandchild	277
Figure 21.4.	Ottawa & Prescott share certificate with corporate seal and Bell and MacKinnon signatures	278
Figure 21.5.	Ottawa & Prescott locomotive, "the Ottawa," 1861, Sussex Street Station	279
Figure 22.1.	Thomas Keefer, 1848	286

List of Figures   xv

Figure 22.2.   *Report on a Survey of the Railway Bridge over the St. Lawrence* 288

Figure 22.3.   Keefer's map showing the approach embankments and piers 289

Figure 22.4.   First version of the chart, with the names of Keefer and Young featured, top left 290

Figure 22.5.   Later chart missing "Hon. John Young, Chairman. Thomas C. Keefer, Engineer, 1851" .. 290

Figure 22.6.   Keefer's Fleet Street pumping station plaque 292

Figure 22.7.   *Enlargement of the Lachine Canal, 1840s* 293

Figure 23.1.   Mechanics' Institute lead cornerstone, 1853 299

Figure 23.2.   Edmund Walker Head 301

Figure 23.3.   *First City of Ottawa Crest* 302

Figure 23.4.   Samuel Keefer, 1860s 308

Figure 23.5.   Fuller and Jones design for Centre Block and Library, 1859 309

Figure 23.6.   *Prince of Wales Lays Cornerstone of Parliament* 310

Figure 23.7.   *The Lumberers' Regatta.* 311

Figure 24.1.   *Thomas Keefer, 1863* 313

Figure 24.2.   A world-weary Thomas Mackay in the 1850s 316

Figure 24.3.   Militia Corporal Charles Mackay 317

Figure 24.4.   Thomas Keefer, 1860s 319

Figure 24.5.	New Edinburgh, cloth and flour mills and brewery, 1864	320
Figure 24.6.	Lower Town and New Edinburgh, 1875, with the Ottawa & Prescott Railway and Maclaren Mills	322
Figure 25.1.	Anne Langton, *From Behind Rideau Hall*, 1870s	326
Figure 25.2.	Viscount Monck	327
Figure 25.3.	First photo of Rideau Hall, circa 1865	328
Figure 25.4.	Thomas Keefer and family at Birkenfels	329
Figure 25.5.	Rubidge plan of the Mackay Estate with the original villa, 1865.	331
Figure 25.6.	Lord Monck and family, Rideau Hall, 1866	332
Figure 25.7.	Rubidge addition, 1870s, with original Rideau Hall (left) and new greenhouses	333
Figure 25.8.	Old Rideau Hall entrance in 1889; to the right is the Tent Room built by Lord Dufferin in 1872	334
Figure 25.9.	Earnscliffe today	336
Figure 25.10.	Ann Crichton Mackay, 1873	339
Figure 26.1.	*Mackay Estate, West Side*, 1866, by T. C. Keefer	342
Figure 26.2.	*Mackay Estate, East Side*, 1866, by T. C. Keefer	293
Figure 26.3.	Thomas Keefer, *Mackay Estate Prospectus*, 1864	344
Figure 26.4.	Jessie Keefer	347

Figure 26.5.	Keefer's Ottawa City Passenger Railway Company, 1871	349
Figure 26.6.	OCPRC East	350
Figure 26.7.	OCPRC West	301
Figure 26.8.	Thomas Ahearn, 1903	352
Figure 26.9.	Thomas Coltrin Keefer, c. 1910	355
Figure C.1.	Granted May 31, 1994, to the Corporation of the Village of Rockcliffe Park	357
Figure C.2.	Mackay-Keefer graves, Beechwood Cemetery, Ottawa	361
Figure C.3.	Mackay French plaque	363

Figure 1. Thomas Mackay, 1830s.
Source: Library and Archives Canada, C-2846 Topley Studio.

Acknowledgements

Many thanks to Ken W. Watson of Info-Rideau, Randy Boswell of the Historical Society of Ottawa and Carleton University, Grant Vogl of the Bytown Museum, the staff of Library and Archives Canada (Cédric Lafontaine), the Ottawa Room of the Ottawa Public Library, and the Archives of the City of Ottawa. Also the National Capital Commission, Rideau Hall (Fabienne Fusade), McGill University, McCord Museum (Heather McNabb, Anne-Frédérique Beaulieu-Plamondon and Christian Vachon), Parks Canada (Fort Lennox, Lachine Canal, The Rideau Canal), and Friends of the Rideau.

And at the University of Ottawa Press, Caroline Boudreau, Lara Mainville, Susan James, Marie-Hélène Lowe, Maryse Cloutier Pierre Anctil, Damien-Claude Bélanger, and Michel Prévost. Thanks as well to Gaëtane Lemay, Sophie LeBlanc, Martha Edmond, Janet Uren, and Joan Mason.

Figure 2. Hope the bookseller, 1879.
Source: McGill University Digital Atlas Project.

A Note on Images

Image titles are given under each item, along with an image number, if applicable. For the source of the image, please see the Imagery section after the Bibliography. Images without a source are either Public Domain (PD) or courtesy of Mediawiki Commons (MWC), which may or may not have a source. You must verify copyright for anything other than personal use. The author has made reasonable efforts to locate the copyright owners, but has been unable to do so in some cases.

For readers of the ebook edition, I recommend the use of ePub readers such as Adobe Digital Editions, or Apple Books, which lets you click-to-expand images.

I am building and will maintain an archive of my research on the founding of Ottawa, and welcome any additional findings made by readers that can be added to a publicly available collection for future scholars and authors.

Contact: alastairsweeny@icloud.com

Other Books by Alastair Sweeny

George Étienne Cartier: A Biography (McClelland & Stewart, 1976)
"This is very much a life of Cartier: vivid, spirited and dramatic."
—Prof. W. L. Morton

BlackBerry Planet (Wiley, 2009)
"The book details the interesting story of RIM and how it started. I needed the book to find out about RIM's marketing strategies and it contained it as well as many other things." — M. Eldawi

Fire Along the Frontier: Great Battles of the War of 1812 (Dundurn, 2012)
"Best history of the War of 1812—I learned more in this one book about what led up to the War of 1812, and the men who fought it, than I had in all the bits and pieces I had studied over my long years in school. What a delight to learn the details of this mysterious war! Alastair Sweeny deserves an A++ or 100% on this." — A. Lewis

Introduction

Mackay's World

No one can look upon the geographical position of the Ottawa without becoming convinced that unless there be some positive disqualification, it is a district which ought not and cannot much longer remain a wilderness.

Those who have had such glimpses of it as a trip up some of its beautiful tributaries afford, can certify that when opened it will be second to no other part of Canada in the healthy character of its climate, the fertility of its innumerable and well-watered valleys, the transparent purity of its trout-filled lakes and gravelly brooks; or in the magnificent panorama which is presented by mountain, flood, and plain—decked out with evergreen and hardwood furring the sloping banks of her golden lakes, and affording under the influence of the autumnal frost one of the most gorgeous spectacles under the sun.

Nor can the day be far distant when those valleys will be filled with their teeming thousands, and the sheep and cattle on a thousand hills shall every where indicate peace and progress—the happy homes of a people whose mission it is to wage war only upon the rugged soil and the gloomy forest, to cause the now silent valleys to shout and sing, and to make the wilderness blossom like the rose.

—Thomas Keefer, "On the Ottawa,"
Lecture to the Montreal Mechanics' Institute, 1854

Why a Biography of Mackay?

In diving into the past, and coming up with this book, I wanted to correct a glaring deficiency in Canadian history—the lack of a work detailing Thomas Mackay's unique role in transforming a wilderness construction camp run by the British Army into the national capital of Canada.

In 1932, University of Ottawa chief librarian Francis Audet wrote in the *Canadian Historical Review* that it was "almost inconceivable that such a man should have found no biographer so far. For Thomas Mackay was a man of standing in society":

> It may be that Thomas Mackay was one of those unassuming Scotchmen who do things but are reluctant to have their photographs published or see their names on the front page of a newspaper, being satisfied with the approval of their own conscience. However that may be, he greatly contributed to the improvements of the town's business life and expansion and aided materially to the general prosperity of the country during more than thirty years.

Mackay was:
1827–1855 — One of the chief founders of Ottawa
1821–1822 — Principal contractor of Fort Lennox on Île-aux-Noix
1822–1825 — Principal contractor of Montréal's Lachine Canal
1824–1825 — Contractor on Notre-Dame Basilica and the île Ste-Hélène Armoury
1827–1831 — Builder of the Ottawa and Hog's Back locks on the Rideau Canal
    1827 — Builder of the Royal Engineers' Commissary, today's Bytown Museum, as well as Colonel By's house, and the barracks and hospital on the heights above called Barrack Hill
1827–1831 — Consultant to John Redpath's Jones Falls dam and the Grenville-Carillon Canal on the Ottawa River
    1828 — Builder of the first Presbyterian church in the capital, St. Andrews
    1828 — A member of Bytown's first municipal council
    1830 — Founder of the village of New Edinburgh
1830–1855 — Builder and owner of the Rideau Falls industrial complex

1831–1855 — Owner of the large tract of land that son-in-law Thomas Keefer developed into Rockcliffe Park

1838–1853 — Builder of the two best-known residences of Ottawa: Rideau Hall and Earnscliffe (1855), which later became respectively the residences of the governor general, and Canada's first prime minister, Sir John A. Macdonald, followed by the British High Commissioner

1834–1841 — A member of the Legislative Assembly for the county of Russell

1837–1855 — Colonel of the Russell and Carleton Militias

1841 — A founding trustee of Queen's University, Kingston

1841 — Founding president of the Bytown Emigration Society, to encourage immigration to Canada

1842–1855 — A member of the Legislative Council of Canada

1847 — Founding president of the Mechanics Institute, forerunner of the Ottawa Public Library

Son in law Keefer donated part of Mackay Estate lands for Beechwood Cemetery, and for city parkland to the north and east of the Village of Rockcliffe Park.

Keefer employed Mackay Estate capital to create the horse-drawn Ottawa City Passenger Railway Company, forerunner of OC Transpo. In 2016, the City of Ottawa proclaimed September 1 as "Thomas MacKay Day."

Thomas Mackay was born in 1792 in Perth, a handsome town along the Firth of Tay in Scotland. He apprenticed as a mason, working beside his father, learning the satisfaction of shaping stone to make it useful and good and even beautiful.

With his father's death at age 50, and with a commercial depression deepening, he and his mother, Christina, and wife, Ann Crichton, decided to make a break with old Scotland. They would emigrate to Canada, where, he heard, there were jobs to be had in Montréal.

He easily found work in the new land, and developed a sterling reputation, partnering with fellow mason John Redpath in building fortifications on St. Helen's Island and at Fort Lennox. Together, from 1823 to 1825, they built the stone locks of the first Lachine Canal—a work greatly admired by Governor General Lord Dalhousie.

Lured upriver to the site of Ottawa by Colonel John By of the Royal Engineers, the partnership of Mackay & Redpath was awarded the major contracts on the Rideau Canal in 1827. Redpath took on the central section around Jones Falls and Mackay the famous Ottawa Locks.

At the laying of the Canal's cornerstone, Governor Dalhousie predicted that Ottawa's magnificent site was worthy of a great empire. He shared this vision with Thomas Mackay, who became the major driver of the movement that led to the creation of Ottawa as the capital of Canada.

After completing his canal work, John Redpath returned to Montréal and invested his capital there—including building a large-scale sugar refinery. Thomas Mackay chose to stay on in Bytown, and used the handsome profits of his masonry work—equivalent to an estimated $60 million in today's currency, paid in Spanish silver coinage—to help create a community in the wilderness. In 1830, he founded a village he called New Edinburgh, and put his capital into creating a mill complex at Rideau Falls that eventually boasted a sawmill, brewery, grist mill, and cloth factory.

For a quarter-century, Mackay served as a member of the assembly, as executive councillor, and as militia colonel. He and his friends helped the town incorporate after the British military handed over their Bytown and Rideau Canal property to the Canadian government. Informed by Governor General Metcalfe's staff that Ottawa could not be considered as the capital without a rail connection, he also risked a substantial amount of his fortune on the Ottawa & Prescott Railway, a line that bled money and never made a profit.

Mackay died in 1855, at his beloved residence, Rideau Hall, content that the movement to declare Ottawa the capital would soon bear fruit.

Mackay and his wife had sixteen children. There were happy times, but their lives were marred by a series of heart-rending tragedies. Several of their children died of smallpox, others of tuberculosis, and three from drowning. After Mackay's death, their eldest son perished in the Indian Mutiny while serving in the British army.

Only four daughters survived to adulthood. One, Annie, married Mackay's bank manager, John MacKinnon, who as President of the Ottawa & Prescott sacrificed a large chunk of the Mackay fortune in bringing a railway to Ottawa. Another daughter, Elizabeth, married civil engineer Thomas Keefer. Keefer would become manager of the Mackay Estate, and arrange the sale of Rideau Hall to the government. He then turned the balance of a beautifully wooded domain known as "Mackay's Bush" into the planned village of Rockcliffe

Park. Today Rockcliffe is home to over seventy embassies and ambassadors' residences.

Thomas Mackay Papers

This book explores the life, career, and legacies of Thomas Mackay, as well as his vision for Ottawa as the capital of Canada. But *The Laird of Rideau Hall* is not just a biography of Mackay and a business history; it is at the same time a biography of Ottawa. By looking through the lens of one of its major founders, and through the lives of his family and friends, we can get a glimpse of the struggles and triumphs of the people who founded our capital city.

In the fifteen years I spent researching this book, first as a hobby and then as a passion, I found that Thomas Mackay had left very few personal or business papers from his Ottawa years, and apparently no correspondence apart from two years of letters to the Adjutant General of Militia. The main Mackay & Redpath business account books and correspondence—now in Montréal's McCord Museum—are a useful resource.

In spite of the dearth of letters, I was able gradually to put together a jigsaw puzzle of records, accounts, and threads that describe Mackay at work as a mason, as an amateur architect, and as a miller and civic leader. We also have more detailed records of the work of his son-in-law, the civil engineer Thomas Keefer, whom he entrusted with the execution and management of his estate. Indeed, the Mackay Estate and the creation of Rockcliffe Park is an important part of the story of the founding of Ottawa.

For accounts of the lives and achievements of Mackay and Keefer, please consult the Select Bibliography and Notes at the end of the book.

Appendices

Because this book is about Thomas Mackay *and* about the founding of Ottawa, I have extracted three sections from the manuscript, added material and made them into separate articles, so as to give the main narrative a smoother flow.

I believe that all three appendices can deepen our knowledge of the period and lead to further discoveries and research.

1. **Spanish Silver and the Rideau Canal** – I detail how the Duke of Wellington's Ordnance Department paid for the security of British North America after the War of 1812, including construction of the Lachine and Rideau canals, using Spanish silver coinage captured during the Peninsular War; and how Mackay's profits helped promote Ottawa as Canada's capital. I also examine how Mackay and partner contractors John Redpath and Robert Drummond invested their Rideau Canal capital for the benefit of Ottawa, Montréal, and Kingston.

2. **The Rideau Canal Debates** – I argue that the Earl Grey ministry, facing growing deficits and the need to pay the costs of the *Great Reform Bill*, convinced the War and Colonial Office to swallow the expenses of the Rideau Canal and not press for parliamentary subsidies. The canal had already been paid for with Spanish silver. I also suggest that blaming Colonel By for maladministration was a complete smokescreen, not to mention a cruel treatment meted out to a dedicated servant of the empire.

3. **A Post Mortem on Railways** – This appendix looks at the Bytown & Prescott Railway (B&P), and the involvement of Thomas Mackay in its creation. Also the financing of other lines and the creation of other railway charters connecting Ottawa and Montréal. It shows how Thomas Mackay risked his fortune in supporting the line, because he was told by Governor Metcalfe's staff that Ottawa could not be considered a contender for becoming the capital of Canada without a railway. It details how the money-losing B&P, later the Ottawa & Prescott Railway, seriously damaged the credit of the city of Ottawa and other investing municipalities. It also looks at Thomas Keefer's involvement in other rail lines, and in planning the Victoria Bridge in Montréal. It details his efforts, as manager of the Mackay Estate, to salvage the family's finances in the face of huge losses on Mackay's railway investments.

To access or download the appendices, please visit the *Thomas Mackay* page on The University of Ottawa Press website at https://press.uottawa.ca/thomas-mackay.html.

The Spelling of Mackay

The spelling of family names—especially Scottish and Irish names—was more fluid in the Victorian era. I have pages from the Mackay family bible that show births, deaths, and marriages, and the names of family members are spelled "McKay." The Dictionary of Canadian Biography uses "McKay."

In the family bible list of deaths, Thomas's name is spelled "Mackay." His good friend John Mactaggart used the "Mackay" spelling in his book *Three Years in Canada*. My grandmother, a descendant, spelled her middle name "MacKay." The thoroughfare running alongside Rideau Hall is called "MacKay Street." But Thomas Keefer's map of Rockcliffe Park spells it as the "Mackay Estate." And finally, Mackay's tombstone in Beechwood Cemetery carries the name "Mackay."

Figure 3. Commercial label of nephew Thomas McKay's flour mill.
Source: John Henry Walker, McCord Museum, M930.50.5.327.

Why Mackay? Perhaps because he also had a favourite nephew called Thomas McKay, and he wanted to prevent confusion. After the premature death of his brother William, Mackay helped the young man build a flour mill beside the Chaudière Falls.

As Mackay got older and more nostalgic, he grew more interested in the history of his clan. No doubt he had a copy of Robert Mackay's *History of the House and Clan of Mackay*, published in Edinburgh in 1829. "Mackay" was the original spelling of the clan chieftains, so "Mackay," not "McKay" is the version I have chosen to use.

One other thing. His name is pronounced "Mac-eye," not "Mak-eh."

PART ONE

Lachine and the Rideau Canal

Figure 1.1. Montréal from St. Helen's Island, 1830.
Source: R. A. Sproule, McCord Museum M21765.

CHAPTER 1

Early Ottawa

Ottawa-Ojibway Contact

Strange persons were living on the continent. Possibly spirits in the form of men or just extraordinary people. A council was called to discuss the information and an expedition was planned to seek out the new strangers. The expedition was led by a shaman. The Anishinabeg traveled east from the Great Lakes toward the territories of the Ottawa. It was here they discovered a clearing where the trees were cut cleanly and not from stone axes. Possible explanations for the felled trees was a huge beaver, but they also believed it may have been the work of the strange people they were seeking.

The Anishinabeg explored further down river and discovered the remains of a winter village that had been occupied by the strange men in the previous season. They were encouraged to search the river edge further and encountered a settlement. Strange people greeted them. The Anishinabeg likened the foreigners to squirrels because of the way they stored their goods. They did not dig holes in the ground like a squirrel, but they built up a wood case around their provisions in a hollow of a tree. They traded for cloth, metal axes, knives, flint, steel, beads, blankets, and firearms in exchange for furs.

Upon returning home the Anishinabeg explorers recounted their encounter with the strangers. The trade goods were prized and the Anishinabeg entered into a commercial initiative, establishing regular trade with the French.

—Andrew J. Blackbird,
History of the Ottawa and Chippewa Indians

Ottawa Rivers and the Fur Trade

London has its Thames, Paris its Seine, Washington its Potomac, Budapest its Danube, Cairo its Nile, and Delhi its Ganges. None of the capital cities of the world can boast a confluence of three rivers—the Ottawa, Gatineau, and Rideau—as magnificent as those of the capital of Canada.

Canada's capital also sports a fourth waterway—the Rideau Canal—that runs for eight kilometres through the city from Hog's Back Falls by Carleton University, skirting Dow's Lake, then through a cut along a straight channel to Parliament Hill and the Ottawa Locks. It's the oldest continuously operated canal in North America, and a UNESCO World Heritage Site.

The shoreline of the largest of these rivers—the Ottawa—is lined with Ordovician limestone laid down in shallow seas 400 million years ago. The river itself flowed through the Ottawa-Bonnechere Graben, a rift valley formed 175 million years ago.

Until 17,000 years ago, the Ottawa lay crushed under two kilometres of Laurentide ice. Then for 2,000 years after that, the great ice sheets rapidly melted, the oceans rose, and the Champlain Sea invaded the land, drowning it in salt water to a depth of 200 metres.

As the earth's crust rebounded from the weight of the massive North American glacier, the Ottawa River began to cut a 1,300-kilometre valley through northern granite. It then followed a limestone fault, along which are now the Chaudière Falls, Parliament Hill, the Rideau Canal entrance, and Rideau Falls.

The French named this river after the *Ottawa* (or *Outaouais*), a tribe of *Nipissing* people called the *Odawa*—meaning "traders"—who operated from as far away as Lake Michigan.

In 1610, the first Europeans to paddle up the waterway were two young missionary volunteers, Étienne Brûlé and Nicholas Vignau. Samuel de Champlain sent them to live with the Huron nation on Georgian Bay.

Champlain himself followed three years later. On June 4, 1613, he and his party paddled past the mouth of the Gatineau, the river of the Algonquins, making its way down from the gentle northern hills. Facing south across the river, he marvelled at the twin falls of another river, spilling into the Ottawa over a dramatic limestone ledge in twin walls of white spray. He was inspired to name them "Rideau," meaning "curtain" in French.

Figure 1.2. *Two Ottawa Chiefs Who with Others Lately Came Down from Michillimackinac on Lake Huron to Have a Talk with Their Great Father The King or His Representative* [likely Lord Dalhousie], circa 1812–1820.
Source: Joshua Jebb, Library and Archives Canada, C-114384.

Finally, arriving at the grand Ottawa amphitheatre, he reached the thunderous cataract called the Chaudière Falls:

> Here are many small islands which are nothing more than rough, steep rocks. At one place the water falls with such force upon a rock that with the lapse of time it has hollowed out a wide, deep basin. Herein the water whirls around to such an extent, and in the middle sends up such big swirls, that the Indians call it Asticou, which means "cauldron." This waterfall makes such a noise in this basin that it can be heard for more than two leagues away.

The Algonquin-speaking nations of the region regarded the Ottawa as a highway. They called it *Kitchesippi*, or the Grand River, and viewed the Chaudière Falls as a sacred spot designed by Manitou. But they also saw it as a place of dread, after ambushes and massacres by Iroquois raiding parties.

Figure 1.3. *Algonquin Encampment at [Rideau] Falls* (Cornelius Krieghoff).
Source: Cornelius Krieghoff, Library and Archives Canada, C-010693.

Champlain witnessed a ceremony where the Algonquins blessed the Chaudière's power with offerings of tobacco:

> After carrying their canoes to the foot of the Fall, they assembled in one spot, where one of them takes up a collection with a wooden plate, into which each one puts a bit of tobacco. The collection having been made, the plate is passed in the midst of the troupe, and all dance about it, singing after their style. Then one of the captains makes a harangue, setting forth that for a long time they have been accustomed to make this offering, by which means they are insured protection against their enemies, that otherwise misfortune would befall them, as they are convinced by the evil spirit; and they live on in this superstition, as in many others, as we have said in other places. This done, the maker of the harangue takes the plate, and throws the tobacco into the midst of the caldron, whereupon they all together raise a loud cry.

Jesuit priests Brébeuf and Lalemant followed Champlain up the valley, and were martyred in the wars with the Iroquois in 1649. Then came coureurs des bois, voyageurs, and merchants from the Company of New France. In the 1660s, free traders Radisson and Groseilliers

Figure 1.4. *Indians [Algonquins] Paying Homage to the Spirit of the Chaudière.*
Source: C. W. Jefferys, Library and Archives Canada, C-073549.

paddled farther west, searching for a great salt water bay. Then came the canoe flotillas of the La Vérendrye family, who built a chain of forts west in the 1730s, and battled on the Prairies with the Hudson's Bay Company.

After the English conquest in 1759, the Montréal-based Northwest Company, run by shrewd Scottish traders, took over the French fur trade.

These Nor'Westers—Alexander Henry, Joseph and Thomas Frobisher, Peter Pond, Simon McTavish, Alexander Mackenzie, Lord Selkirk, and John Franklin—all of them paddled these waters, and portaged the Chaudière Falls. In 1791, Alexander Mackenzie and his brigade of French-Canadian voyageurs reached up the Ottawa right across the continent to the Pacific.

Nicholas Garry, the founder of Fort Garry, now Winnipeg, marvelled at "the Chaudière in all its Wildness and Majesty. The imagination cannot picture anything so romantic."

Today, tamed by hydroelectric dynamos, the romance of the Chaudière Falls is diminished, only showing its awesome power during the massive spring runoff.

Yet some romance remains. Today, in Brébeuf Park, just west of the Chaudière, you can climb worn stone steps where these voyageurs portaged their canoes and packs around the Falls. Farther west upriver, they hacked out a small canoe canal, today overgrown, beside the Deschênes Rapids near Aylmer and the calm waters of Lac Deschênes.

In 1821, the Montréal fur trade went into rapid decline, as the Nor'Westers—members of the Beaver Club—sold out to the London-based Hudson's Bay Company. Changing fashions played a role—oiled silk umbrellas replaced felt beaver hats for protection against the rain. Tough competition from the American Fur Company of John Jacob Astor also factored in the decline. But even Astor abandoned the business and put all his capital into Manhattan real estate.

So the Ottawa Valley now lay silent, unused by fur brigades, and where voyageur songs once echoed from hill to hill, now only the chants of the Algonquin people of the Gatineau Valley remained.

The Wars Against America and France

Better to live under one tyrant a thousand miles away, than a thousand tyrants one mile away.
—Daniel Bliss, Loyalist

The American Revolutionary War ended with the Peace of Paris in 1783. Loyalist refugees moving to the province of Quebec soon petitioned the government to be allowed to use the British legal system they were used to in the American colonies.

In 1791, the British divided Quebec into Upper and Lower Canada, making the Ottawa River the boundary between the two new provinces. Over 30,000 loyal Americans, lured by the promise of land, moved to Upper Canada in the 1790s.

The wars against Revolutionary France, and then against Napoleon, marked a new beginning for the Ottawa Valley, as the British military were determined to protect and exploit the timber riches of the Upper St. Lawrence and Ottawa Rivers. The Royal Navy felt menaced by attempts by the French to control the Baltic Trade. They needed an alternate source of supply. Without oak and pine from Sweden, and hemp rope and canvas from Russia, a British naval frigate would be dead in the water within two years.

By 1806, Britain was buying 90 percent or more of its marine hemp from Russia. The thousand ships of the Royal Navy ran on

Russian hemp, as each British ship replaced fifty tons of hemp a year in sails, rope, rigging, and nets. France had its own hemp supply, but the British were almost completely dependent on Russian hemp. Russia was the low-cost producer because of its cheap serf labour.

The emperor Napoleon knew he had to force the czar to stop trading hemp to the British. He reckoned quite rightly that inside of three years, he could bring Britain to its knees. In 1810, he determined on a final solution to his problem—he would personally invade Russia, topple the czar, and stop the flow of hemp to Britain, while his Jeffersonian allies would invade Canada, capture Quebec, and stop the Royal Navy's prime source of timber.

The British also needed Loyalist leaders to exploit the country's natural resources, especially timber. In 1796, fur trader James McGill changed professions, and pioneered the export of squared timber, masts, and spars. In 1812, Isaac Brock marvelled at Britain's bustling trade at Québec—the harbours and quaysides packed with scores of freighters loading timber to feed the demands of the Royal Navy.

The early settlers in the St. Lawrence and Ottawa valleys found it difficult to meet British demand. They still suffered many hardships. They had to travel almost entirely by water, in dugout or bark canoes and flat-bottomed bateaux, or by sleighs over frozen rivers. The massive rapids of these great rivers also barred easy settlement.

The British Royal Engineers built a few simple canals to navigate around the rapids of the Ottawa and St. Lawrence, to speed up the provision of military supplies to Lake Ontario. The first canal in North America was built by William Twiss at Coteau-du-Lac, just below Lake St. Francis, in about 1780, followed by a series of little "ditches" at Cedars and the Cascades.

The Royal Engineer in charge of building a new canal at Cascades was a young lieutenant in his twenties named John By—more on him later.

On the St. Lawrence, the bateaux were soon replaced by larger Durham boats, which could carry several times more freight. This enabled a downstream export trade in flour and wheat, sent to Britain in growing amounts.

The Ottawa Valley and its riches now lay open to settler families and new entrepreneurs, drawn to the site by good land, water power, and timber.

Figure 1.5. Coteau-du-Lac Canal, 1780.
Source: © Rogers Communications Inc. Rex Woods, Confederation Life.

In 1783, Lieutenant Gershom French, an assistant engineer with the Corps of Loyal Rangers, travelled up the Ottawa with seven soldiers of the Provincial Corps, two French voyageurs, and an Algonquin guide. He was ordered to evaluate the quality of the land for settlement. Reaching Rideau Falls, the party turned south along the ancient Indigenous canoe route between the Ottawa River and the St. Lawrence at Gananoque.

Lt. French drew the first map of the future Rideau route. He took meticulous notes about the quality of the soil—"everywhere good"—and recommended that "a site of a town be laid off at the forks of the River Reddo" [Rideau].

Nothing was done in the way of settlement as a result of his report until 1790, when Richard Cartwright of Kingston, a prominent United Empire Loyalist, pressed Governor Sir Guy Carleton, Lord Dorchester, to consider building a town at the juncture of the Rideau and the Ottawa, with a connecting road and canal system south to the St. Lawrence.

Figure 1.6. Durham boats ascending the St. Lawrence.
Source: Thomas Conant, Mediawiki Commons, PD.

Finally, the British were inspired by Sir Alexander Mackenzie, the first man to cross the continent, who in 1801 urged the government to consider building canals up the St. Lawrence and Ottawa rivers to the Great Lakes.

Enter Philemon Wright

Upper Canada Governor John Graves Simcoe was determined to speed up settlement. In 1792, he issued a proclamation inviting Americans to come north, declare their loyalty to the king, and settle in Upper and Lower Canada.

Many New England farm families—the so-called late Loyalists—took up the offer, since good uncleared land was at a premium. Others were attracted by lower taxes north of the border.

One Woburn, Massachusetts, entrepreneur named Philemon Wright, a descendant of the Pilgrims who landed at Plymouth Rock, was intrigued by Simcoe's proclamation.

Wright had served as sergeant in the American Revolution, but as he told Governor Dalhousie, a lot of people in Boston were having serious second thoughts about the Declaration of Independence:

Many now repent & don't like the Independency. My father paid 10 dollars a year of taxes under the British Government; after that war the people never thought of the necessity consequent, to keep & pay an Army & Navy of their own, and I soon found after my father's death, when I succeeded to his property, that instead of 10 I had to pay 150 dollars, & so my Lord will excuse me when I did not no longer like the Independency.[1]

Wright, a charismatic leader, originally planned to lead his family, friends, and followers to the Eastern Townships of Lower Canada. When he found most of the good mill sites already taken, he decided to visit the isolated and unsettled area of the Ottawa Valley to look for sites for a colony. In 1798 he settled on a magnificent plot beside the Chaudière Falls that had abundant water power and decent soil.

On March 7, 1800, Wright's party of six families and twenty-five hired axemen arrived in Lower Canada with seven sleighs, fourteen horses, and eight oxen. After a thirty-three-day journey, including a ceremony in Montréal where they took the oath of loyalty to the Crown, they reached their new home on the north bank of the Ottawa beside the Chaudière Falls, guided over the dangerous river ice by an Algonquin trapper.

Wright first called his settlement "Columbia Falls Village." In 1801, it was officially named Wrightstown, and later Hull, after the English home town of the Wrights. Today part of the city of Gatineau, Wright's village was the first permanent settlement in the National Capital Region.

Within a few years of their arrival, Wright's settlers were reaping bumper crops of wheat and potatoes, building livestock herds, and cutting timber in the winter months. But by 1805 Wright had nearly exhausted his $30,000 in start-up capital.

British demand and the war against Napoleon came to his rescue. The Royal Navy let it be known that it was looking for an alternate source of timber for planks and masts and hemp for ropes and sails, since Napoleon's Continental System could cut off supplies from the Baltic and Russia.

Wright and his oldest son, Tiberius, decided to explore that market by building a timber raft and floating it to the port of Québec. Through the winter of 1805–06, Wright's axemen assembled the raft

---

[1] Wright to Dalhousie, in Marjory Whitelaw, ed., *Dalhousie Journals*, vol. 2 (Ottawa: Oberon Press, 1980).

they called *Columbo* on the ice at the mouth of the Gatineau River. They lashed together seven hundred pieces of squared oak and pine, nine hundred planks and beams, and a variety of other forest products, including six thousand oak barrel staves. In April 1806, they launched *Columbo* down the Ottawa River towards Québec.

The going was slow at first—it took them twenty-five days to drive to the Long-Sault Rapids past Carillon. But the Ottawa River rose rapidly in the spring melt. The *Columbo* passed Montréal on June 25, racing through the swollen Lachine Rapids. They reached Québec on August 12, but even then, they had to wait until the end of November to sell the timber raft—Wright needed to drive a hard bargain. Finally,

Figure 1.7. Tiberius Wright on the family's first timber raft, 1806.
Source: C. W. Jefferys, Library and Archives Canada.

his raft was broken up and loaded onto ships bound for Britain. So began the timber trade on the upper Ottawa River.

After an 1808 fire in Wrightstown, Wright was distraught, but his sons mobilized the settlement to rebuild. Soon the village was bustling with hemp and grist mills, a foundry, tannery, brewery, distillery, and limestone quarry for building-stone and lime cement.

British demand during the War of 1812 was good for Wright and his community, but Wrightstown lost ground during the depression that followed the War of 1812. The community had to import flour, pork, and salt fish. In 1816—"the year without a summer"—the eruptions of Mount Tambora in Indonesia caused temperatures around the world to fall by an average of one degree. In the Ottawa Valley, hard frosts and snow in June led to crops rotting in the fields. Farmers slaughtered cattle and pigs early because there was no vegetation to sustain them. People had to survive on fish, venison, porcupines, and groundhogs.

The ups and downs of the timber business worried Philemon, and he wanted to abandon it entirely in favour of farming. Debts were piling up, and there were threats at Québec to seize the family

Figure 1.8. *A View of the Mill and Tavern of Philemon Wright at the Chaudière Falls, Hull, 1823.* Source: Henry DuVernet, Library and Archive Canada, MIKAN 2836987.

rafts. Son-in-law Thomas Bingham wrote to Ruggles Wright, "We are destitute."

Salvation for the Wrights came from the Duke of Wellington, the victor of Waterloo, who was determined to protect the Canadas and stop any further American invasions aimed at Montréal. Part of his plan was to build a canal from the Ottawa River to Kingston, and to create a military settlement in Perth, Upper Canada, which the Wrights would help supply, starting in 1818.

Wrightstown began to thrive. By the 1820s, the village was home to over seven hundred people, and the Wrights were sending four or five rafts a year to Québec; in the 1830s, twice as many. Ship captains bringing settlers to Canada were more than happy to make the return trip with Ottawa Valley timber in their holds.

Meanwhile, events in Montréal were moving that would bring a bonanza of business to Wright and his sons.

CHAPTER 2

From Scotland to Montréal

City of Stone

Today's Perth, Scotland, population forty-five thousand, is a sleepy port city on the Firth of Tay, blessed with some fine stone terraces and quays. The River Tay is the longest river in Scotland at 190 kilometres and an estuary of the North Sea. It's one of the top five Scottish salmon rivers. Nearby Scone Palace is the site of the coronation of the Scottish kings. Perth is also where the Scottish Revolution began.

In May of 1559, religious reformer John Knox returned to Scotland from the Calvinist stronghold of Geneva, enraged by his years spent as a French galley slave. He found the country ruled by a French Catholic regent, Mary de Guise, second wife of James V and mother of Mary, Queen of Scots. She was backed by a small French army, but her grip on power was weakening.

When Mary's men tried to entrap Knox in Stirling Castle, he proceeded instead to Perth, then a walled town that could be defended in case of a siege. In the pulpit of the ancient Church of St. John, Knox preached a fiery sermon against the French. He so inflamed his followers that they rioted. They sacked two friaries in the town, looting their gold and silver and smashing their holy images of saints.

A month later, in July of 1559, Knox and the Protestant Lords of the Congregation occupied Edinburgh.

Mary de Guise had promised freedom of conscience, but when further French troops arrived, her supporters betrayed this promise. The Scottish nobility, now fed up with religious warring and insecurity, formally deposed Mary. With the signing of the Treaty of Edinburgh in 1560, French and English troops departed, and left Scotland free, and primarily Presbyterian.

Figure 2.1. Perth, Scotland, "City of stone."

The years that followed were kind to Perth. By the end of the eighteenth century, the population reached fifteen thousand and the town bustled with industry. From the Tayside wharves, ocean-going vessels sailed away, loaded with linen, leather, and whisky for customers on the European continent.

In about 1785, the growing wealth of the town attracted a young family of the clan Mackay from Caithness, in the far northwest of Scotland. The original Mackays were a warlike and powerful people, but after five centuries of dispute, and time and treasure wasted fighting European wars, they had lost most of their lands to the Dukes of Sutherland.

The estate managers of that aristocratic family had decided that sheep were more profitable than people. Starting in the 1790s, they began what were known as the Highland Clearances—an attempt to displace the growing population of the highlands to industries on the coast, or induce them to emigrate.

The Clearances peaked at about the time of the Napoleonic Wars, forcing many highland families off lands they had tilled for generations. From 1814 to 1819, tens of thousands of acres in Caithness were "cleared"—with houses, barns, mills, kilns, and every other structure destroyed. Sutherland agents drove almost six hundred families off the land to consolidate the family's holdings into five

Figure 2.2. Clans of northern Scotland (note the town of Thurso at the top of the map).

huge sheep farms. Faced with this disaster, tens of thousands of crofters and townsfolk were forced to emigrate to the Lowlands, and farther afield, to North America and Australia.

John and Christina Mackay were both townsfolk, born in Thurso, Caithness, the northernmost town on the British mainland. They married there in 1783, and left for Perth just before the Clearances made themselves felt. In that year, and the year following, cold and rainy weather caused harvests in Scotland to fail, and famine spread throughout the land.

John Mackay found masonry work on the Clyde and Tay Canal, funded by merchants in Glasgow, Dundee and Perth. The Scottish canals proved their worth during the famine of 1783 and 1784, when they played a large role in importing and distributing Baltic grain throughout the country.

Beginning in the Middle Ages, associations of stonemasons existed in Scotland, and by the late 1500s, there were at least thirteen established craft lodges across Scotland, from Edinburgh to Perth. John Mackay soon joined the local Perth lodge of Freemasons.

The Birth of Thomas Mackay

On September 1, 1792, in Perth, Christina gave birth to a son, Thomas, the subject of this book.

After attending the Perth Grammar School, founded in 1067 AD, Thomas Mackay was apprenticed to a stonemason, then worked alongside his father, John, and younger brother William. The family built stone bridges, wharves, and houses, or repaired the town walls. Thomas learned the tools of that ancient trade, tools little changed since the building of the pyramids. He mastered how to use a mallet, chisel, and straight edge to split and finish stone. He learned the use of lewis wedges, cranes, and the block-and-tackle used to hoist huge stones into place, and mastered how to handle a trowel to fill joints and point mortar. And like a true mason, he felt the satisfaction of shaping a stone to make it useful and good and even beautiful.

Thomas was also reared on the bagpipes by his Highland father.

He was just 19 years of age in March of 1811 when John Mackay died at the age of 50.

On June 26, 1813, Thomas married a "comely" young woman, a 19-year-old cousin of his mother named Ann Crichton, born in Auchtergaven, 12 kilometres north of Perth. Their first son, John, was born April 13, 1814, in Perth, followed by James, born April 12, 1816.

Thomas and Ann's first children were born during the economic depression that followed the Napoleonic Wars. The year 1816 was also known as "the year without a summer." Cold and damp plagued Scotland, slashing crop yields and bringing back famine, depression, and dangerous diseases—including epidemics of smallpox, tuberculosis, scarlet fever, and diphtheria.

Profits in the masonry business dried up, as the town of Perth had to provide charity to a flood of refugees from the Clearances. Thomas felt his hopes for a good life for his family were dashed. They needed to escape. But what to do?

On February 22, 1815, Lord Bathurst, Secretary for War and the Colonies, issued a proclamation in Edinburgh offering 100 acres of land to each family (and to male children over 21 years) willing to emigrate to the Ottawa Valley in Upper Canada. They would be given six to eight months-worth of rations, some equipment, and other aid as needed. Provision was also made for the services of ministers and teachers.

Thomas Mackay knew that several families of farmers and weavers had already left Perth in 1815. They were given passage to Upper Canada, where they received land and support around a "military settlement" called Perth, founded by half-pay soldiers and officers—mostly veterans of the War of 1812.

Mackay was not tempted by the offer, not being a farmer. But in late July of 1817, he learned there was masonry work to be had in Lower Canada on military projects. After a family conference with Ann and mother Christina, the Mackays decided to assemble their savings, pull up their roots, and emigrate. They took a stagecoach to Glasgow, bringing along their two babies, and took ship on the brig *James Montgomery* from Greenock.[1]

Tragedy struck a few weeks into the voyage, when 3-year-old John became ill with smallpox, and shortly after died. He was sewn into a weighted canvas shroud, and after the captain said a short prayer, he was given to the waves to the mournful wail of his father's bagpipes.

Figure 2.3. Emigrants bound for Québec.

---

[1] *The Ships List.* Ship Arrivals at the Ports of Quebec, 1817.

After ten weeks at sea, they sailed through the foggy Grand Banks, past Cape Breton, and up the St. Lawrence. After a few days in Québec finding their feet, they embarked on a crowded Molson's steamboat, packed with settlers like themselves, paying nine shillings apiece for steerage, and supplying their own victuals. They arrived in Montréal on September 9, 1817.

The young Mackays soon faced the second of many family tragedies—one-year-old James died of the same malady as his brother. Broken-hearted, they buried baby James in a local Protestant cemetery.

Smallpox hit many young families before inoculation became common in the 1820s. Minor outbreaks emerged every few years in Britain, but 1817–1819 were epidemic years in western Scotland and Northern Ireland. Most adults escaped—the disease conferred immunity on its survivors—but 75 percent of smallpox deaths were of children under the age of five.

The Montréal Years: 1817–1826

The Mackay family spent about a week in the King's Barracks, a temporary quarters for immigrants. While Thomas set out to find lodgings and work, Ann and mother Christina and their fellow passengers got to work finding food and cleaning their clothes and bedsheets, filthy after six weeks at sea.

Figure 2.4. Molson steamboat passing Île Ste-Hélène.
Source: Archives de la Ville de Montréal, CA M001 BM099-1-D1.

Thomas easily found work in the building trade, and the Mackays settled into a house at 29 Saint-Urbain Street near the corner of Saint-Antoine, two blocks north of the Place d'Armes in old Montréal. The house stood where today's Montréal Congress Centre (Palais des Congrès) is situated.

Montréal was booming in those days, and the population had grown to over sixteen thousand, about the same as Perth, Scotland. Many of its streets glowed at night by the light of whale oil lamps. John Molson's brewery was in operation, and his growing fleet of steamboats plied the St. Lawrence downstream to Québec.

Mackay and Ann, being devout Calvinists, would volunteer to help out in soup kitchens and serve the poor, especially in the bitter cold of winter. They were both active in St. Gabriel's Scotch Presbyterian Church, and Thomas served as precentor or choirmaster for a few years, until he had to resign due to public works outside Montréal and harvest work in the country during the summer.[2]

The couple would have fourteen more children in their new homeland. Ann gave birth to five more during the couple's Montréal years. Four survived childbirth:

- Alexander, born January 6, 1818, in Montréal—drowned in the Ottawa River in 1827 at age 9.
- Thomas, born November 18, 1821, in Montréal—died aged 15 in April 1837, possibly of tuberculosis.
- Anna, born December 24, 1823, in Montréal—outlived her mother.
- Christina, born September 5, 1825, in Montréal—outlived her mother.[3]

A pastel drawing of Mackay from the 1820s shows a formidable character—dressed in his Sunday best, with a coat and vest and loose velvet bow tie. He has a high forehead, dark blond hair, and muttonchop sideburns going grey. His eyes show hints of a toughness and a shrewdness that would serve him well during his career.

---

[2] Robert Campbell, *A History of the Scotch Presbyterian Church, St. Gabriel Street, Montreal*. 1887.
[3] Mackay Family Bible (MacKay United Church, New Edinburgh).

Figure 2.5. Thomas Mackay, c. 1827.
Source: Library and Archives Canada.

John Redpath

Mackay did not lack for work in the bustling city. He soon built a reputation for skill and integrity. He also assembled a team of master masons who were soon very much in demand. In the 1820s, he hired a Scottish mason, John Redpath, four years younger, but highly experienced.

Redpath was the son of a poor farm labourer. Born in 1796 in the village of Earlston, in the Scottish border county of Berwickshire, John was one of five brothers—with Robert, George, Peter, and James—and a sister, Elspeth. When both their parents died, he and his brothers moved to Edinburgh, where they apprenticed and trained as stonemasons under a building contractor and city councillor named George Drummond. When the post-Waterloo depression deepened in 1816, the five Redpath brothers and George Drummond's brother Robert decided to emigrate to Canada together, joining 1,250 other Scots who were abandoning their native land.[4]

The party got off the boat at Québec City in midsummer. Unable—or too thrifty—to pay the nine shillings for steerage passage on one of Molson's steamboats, they walked all the way to Montréal along the dusty King's Highway, a distance of 350 kilometres, sometimes shod, sometimes barefoot, to save wear on the only pair of shoes each of them had.[5]

John Redpath found work with a contractor by the name of Couvrette, repairing chimneys and constructing walls, brick arches, and foundations. He developed a growing reputation, building residences for elite clients like William McGillivray, the Molsons, Peter McGill, and John Torrance. Within four years, he had founded his own business, Riley & Redpath, and married Janet McPhee from Glengarry County, Upper Canada; they would have three daughters and two sons. Janet would assist her husband and his partnerships with accounts and correspondence when he was in the field.

In 1820, Thomas Mackay brought Redpath into two major masonry contracts, for defence projects recommended by the late Duke of Richmond. Their timing was serendipitous. Colonel Elias Durnford, head of the Royal Engineers in Upper and Lower Canada, and builder of the Québec Citadel, knew of Mackay's reputation, and engaged Mackay & Redpath to provide building stone and masonry—"construction materials and haulage"—for the new fort on St. Helen's Island, a major armoury and artillery depot of the Ordnance Department, the supply division of the British Army in Canada.[6]

The Master General of Ordnance, then the Duke of Wellington, commanded the Royal Artillery, Royal Engineers, and Royal Sappers and Miners, and held a seat in cabinet. This powerful body, manufactured, procured, and transported all war supplies, and built and maintained fortifications, storehouses and military buildings throughout the British Empire.

---

[4] In 1817, 6,800 British arrived in Canada; in 1818, 8,400; in 1819, 12,800.
[5] Cabin passage from Québec to Montréal cost £3.
[6] McCord Museum, John Redpath fonds (P085), 1822–1824.

Figure 2.6. Major General Elias Walker Durnford, Royal Engineers. *Source*: Mediawiki Commons, PD.

On March 15, 1821, Colonel Durnford also contracted Mackay to supply masonry and construction for the new stone barracks, officers' quarters, and fortifications at Fort Lennox, on Île-aux-Noix, an island in the Richelieu River, close to the US border and a bulwark against potential American invasion. Mackay's masons trained and were

Figure 2.7. Fort Lennox in 1886, showing barracks and officers' quarters. *Source*: Henry Bunnett, McCord Museum M872.

assisted by the hundred-man garrison in building a powder house (1820), guardhouse (1821), two storehouses (1821–1823), and casemates (1822–1827), before Mackay returned to Montréal to bid on the Lachine Canal locks. Redpath's brother-in-law Robert Drummond remained at Fort Lennox to build the drawbridge.[7]

The Lachine Canal

The Lachine rapids had stopped Jacques Carter in 1535—he bitterly called them "La Chine," as the rivers were supposed to lead to China. Over a century later, the French colonial government began to consider the need for a canal to bypass the treacherous rapids. Any merchant supplying goods upriver had to portage 14 kilometres from the port of Montréal to the village of Lachine, then embark upriver on another vessel.

---

[7] In 1840, the executors of the estate of one of their associates, Peter Rutherford, sued Mackay for additional funds from a profit-sharing agreement, but were not successful.

In 1680, François Dollier de Casson, first Superior of the Sulpiciens, the religious order who were the landowning seigneurs of Montréal, suggested that such a canal could supply water power to drive Montréal's mills, while at the same time promoting westbound navigation.

Their project lay dormant until the end of the War of 1812, when Captain Samuel Romilly of the Royal Engineers was engaged to report on the feasibility of building a canal. The Lachine rapids had been a major bottleneck in supplying the St. Lawrence and Upper Lakes during the war—transport costs had amounted to almost £1 million.

Governor Sir John Sherbrooke backed the Lachine project, and on December 30, 1817, he suggested to Colonial Secretary Lord Bathurst that "if the legislative authorities in Canada will make provision for one half of the expense attending the construction of this Canal, My Lords will not object to sanction the payment of the remainder out of the Army Extraordinaries."

The Lower Canada legislature didn't bite.

A growing concern to Montréal merchants like John Molson and Thomas McCord came from reports that the Americans were planning a waterway from Lake Erie to New York—the Erie Canal. The Montrealers argued that the Lachine and St. Lawrence canals had to be built to counter, "the injurious effects which the Great Western Canal of the United States of America is likely to produce on the trade of this province."

In 1819, Bank of Montreal cofounder and fur trade veteran John Richardson founded the Company of the Proprietors of the Lachine Canal, with seven Montréal businessmen. On the recommendation of British canal pioneer Thomas Telford, the Company hired a young engineer named Thomas Burnett to design and manage the project.

Richardson's efforts to finance the canal failed at first, but in 1821, the Assembly of Lower Canada voted $25,000 to support the project. The Sulpicians, owners of the Saint-Gabriel Farm and much of the property along the projected Canal route, also gave their enthusiastic support. And to back the Lachine Canal project, the British Ordnance came up with a first subsidy of £10,000, on condition that the canal gave free use to all boats of His Majesty's service—toll-free passage of military supplies in perpetuity.

Thinking Big

No canal with the dimensions of the Lachine had ever been built in Canada. Indeed, the only canals in the colony were the small works undertaken by the Royal Engineers, upriver at Coteau and the Cascades, between 1779 and 1783.

In fact, Burnett designed the Lachine Canal with size and solidity in mind. The locks were to be bigger than anywhere else in North America, or even Britain, with one exception—the Caledonian Canal in Scotland. Unlike the seventy-seven wooden post locks installed on the Erie Canal and the forty on the Welland, the seven locks on the Lachine Canal were to be built entirely of stone.

In 1821, the commissioners of the Lachine Canal invited Thomas Mackay to bid on the masonry and lock work. Redpath agreed to join the bid, and their estimate was accepted on January 21, 1822. On March 13, they signed a further contract for quarrying and delivering stone required "for the use of making and construction of the Lachine Canal locks."[8]

Excavators Andrew White and Thomas Philips, both known to Mackay and Redpath, began to clear the ground on July 19, but were soon slowed down by having to deal with underground springs. Still another contract followed in 1824, due to delays suffered while draining the trench and building towpaths, before Mackay and Redpath could begin masonry work on the seven locks.[9]

The groundbreaking ceremony for the canal took place on July 17, 1822, at picket No. 18, near Windmill Point at the foot of McGill Street. Present were John Richardson and his fellow canal commissioners, members of the Montréal business elite, engineer Thomas Burnett, masons Mackay and Redpath, as well as the excavators White and Phillips, some labourers, local landowners and others, along with the band of the 60th regiment.

Richardson turned the first sod, followed by each of the commissioners, then Thomas Mackay and his fellow contractors in turn. After the shovels were put away, John Richardson stepped up on a platform and signalled the band to stop playing. He then gave a short

---

[8] City of Ottawa Archives, typed records.
[9] Thomas Phillips was a member of the Company of the Proprietors of the Lachine Canal, and resigned to be able to bid on the excavation contracts with friend Andrew White.

Figure 2.8. Richardson and dignitaries inspecting the Lachine Canal.
Source: BMO Financial Group Corporate Archives.

speech, reminding everyone that the project had taken a long time to come to fruition. He told the "undertakers"—Mackay, Redpath, White, and Philips—that he "hoped the job would be as profitable to them as it would be advantageous, once completed, to Upper and Lower Canada alike."

While Richardson and his banker friends partook of a celebratory supper at nearby Connelly's Inn, Mackay and Redpath hosted a beer and roast beef barbecue for the workers, which ended in a friendly brawl among the Irish, Scotch, and French.[10]

The Lachine Canal was the largest public work in Canadian history to that date. Burnett assembled a five hundred-strong workforce of labourers—mainly Irish immigrants—assisted and managed by small groups of soldiers, to assist the "undertakers" in draining the route and handling the rubble that was packed behind the masonry walls.

Starting in 1822, and over a four-year period, as White and Philips completed their excavating, Mackay and Redpath set to work quarrying and installing seven superb stone locks between Montréal and the old fur trade village of Lachine. Each was 30 metres [98 feet] long, 6 metres [20 feet] wide, and 1.5 metres [4.9 feet] deep.

Mackay's French-Canadian quarrymen started cutting limestone over the winter, across the St. Lawrence at Caughnawaga. To make the rough blocks, they drilled holes in the stone and then

---

[10] *Le Canadien*, July 25, 1821.

poured in hot water. The expanding of the water as it turned to ice usually broke the stone cleanly. The blocks were then barged on rafts across the river to Lachine.

Mackay insisted on strict discipline, but one incident at Caughnawaga nearly caused a complete stoppage in stone work. When Sir John Johnson, Superintendent-General of Indian Affairs, got news that some of Mackay's employees had sold some of their rum ration to the Caughnawaga Iroquois, he threatened to withdraw quarrying privileges, unless this illicit traffic ceased. Mackay spoke to Johnson, and the incident quickly subsided without serious repercussions. The men continued to be given their essential rum ration, on condition that they drink it.

Once enough good stone had been cut, Mackay moved many of his workmen from Caughnawaga up to his lock works across the river. Masonry on the locks could only be executed during the frost-free months. Because of the short building season, the working day of the labourers lasted fourteen hours, from five in the morning until seven in the evening. After the first frost, the uncompleted stonework was carefully covered with straw bales to insulate it and keep out water until the following spring.

Off-Season Work

In the off season, starting in November 1823, Mackay and Redpath worked on supplying dressed stone for the Sulpicians' magnificent new Notre-Dame Basilica on the Place d'Armes.[11]

The stone for Notre-Dame came from the Tanneries quarry in Griffintown. Mackay and Redpath were also supplied with statute (free) labour by residents of various Montréal Island parishes, who transported the stone to the building site on wagons.

The main construction work, led by Redpath, took place between 1824 and 1829. The cornerstone was laid at Place d'Armes on September 1, 1824; in 1829, the church was dedicated; the sanctuary was finished in 1830; the first tower in 1841; the second in 1843. On its completion, the church was the largest in North America, with a seating capacity of ten thousand.

---

[11] In a receipt dated May 12, 1825, Redpath billed the Sulpicians for 5,527 feet of stone for Notre-Dame Church.

To speed up construction of the Lachine Canal—there were frustrating delays in excavation due to underground springs and a hard granite reef to break up with explosives—the British Ordnance came up with a much richer subsidy, granting the commissioners another £107,000 to complete the project. The money likely came from a hoard of Spanish silver bullion captured by the Royal Navy during the wars against France and Spain, and shipped by frigate to strongholds in the Citadels at Halifax and Québec, and later upriver by Molson's steamboat to the Ordnance depot on Saint Helen's Island in Montréal.[12]

The Lachine Canal handled its first freight in August 1824—the official launch was July 23, 1825—opening the Ottawa River and upper St. Lawrence to more direct navigation. No major repairs or alterations were necessary for the time being The Lachine Canal easily handled a growing volume of traffic to and from the Great Lakes region, as well as up the Ottawa River.

The canal changed the whole geography of Montréal. Attracted by lower shipping costs, the manufacturing centre of the city shifted west, as new industries sprang up in the Saint-Antoine ward as a direct outcome of the easier transport of goods. From 1825 to 1841, the number of boats using the canal increased fivefold. In the 1840s, the canal was deepened under the direction of Public Works Commissioner Samuel Keefer, to allow heavier ships and the new steamboats to pass through. Even after the second canal was completed in 1848, the old canal remained in service for barge traffic for several years. Today it is a recreational corridor under the management of Parks Canada.

Channels off the new canal also fed water power to mills that sprang up along the canal banks, and the bustling factories soon made Montréal the industrial metropolis of Canada. From 1825 to 1860, canal traffic grew from six hundred small vessels passing through each year to more than thirteen thousand large steamship passages.

According to his foreman, John Robertson, an old friend from Perth, Mackay earned a handsome £10,000 profit from contracts on the Lachine locks. John Redpath likely earned the same. Both men, while not rich, were rapidly becoming well-off in their adopted country.

The reputation of Mackay & Redpath let them expand into profitable new commercial projects. During and after the period of the

---

[12] See Chapter 10: Handsome Profits, and Appendix 1: Pieces of Eight, for further details.

Figure 2.9. Entrance to Lachine Canal at Windmill Point, Montréal, Québec, 1826.
Source: Unknown artist, McCord Museum, MP-1976.288.2.

Lachine Canal construction, Redpath continued his house-building work for many of Montréal's leading business families. For John Molson, he built a new Theatre Royal at the corner of St. Denis and St. Paul streets. He also demolished a large chimney and rebuilt it at John Molson & Sons brewery. And he did repair work for the Bank of Montreal, built a billiards room in the Free Masons Hall, repaired the Nelson's Column Memorial (for which he billed £543 for masonry), and built classrooms at McGill University.

In 1825, the partners also began work on the beautiful Écuries d'Youville (Youville Stables), built on land owned by the Grey Nuns. The building was used mainly for warehousing goods. Renovated in the 1960s, the Youville building today contains offices and a popular steakhouse, Gibby's.

In 1826, Redpath's sister Elspeth and her husband, Thomas Fairbairn, and their eight children, arrived from Edinburgh and joined John and Janet in their home on Dalhousie Square in Montréal. The Fairbairns would later move north of Kingston, Upper Canada, while Fairbairn worked with Redpath as foreman of the Jones Falls works on the Rideau Canal.

That year, the contractors began to hear rumours that a change was in the air. With the Duke of Wellington now in power in faraway Britain, events were conspiring to take Thomas Mackay, John Redpath, and Robert Drummond away from their Montréal labours and up the Ottawa River.

Figure 2.10. The Lachine Canal; Église Notre-Dame in the centre background.
Source: James Duncan, McCord Museum, M984.273.

CHAPTER 3

Wellington's Generals

All the business of war, and indeed all the business of life, is to endeavour to find out what you don't know by what you do; that's what I call "guessing what was at the other side of the hill."

—Arthur Wellesley, Duke of Wellington

Spanish Treasure

The Duke of Wellington never lost a battle in some sixty-odd engagements, although his 1815 victory at Waterloo was "damned close." The Duke was determined to win the fight for Canada, which he knew had not ended with the signing of the Peace of Utrecht.

Waterloo was a hinge point of history, and the climax of twenty-five years of warfare. The century that followed 1815 saw rapid technological innovation and global marketing, particularly by the British Empire and America. Britain and the US were flush with capital, and Canada benefited, with canal and then railway building. Indeed, as I will argue, the Rideau Canal and to a lesser extent the Lachine Canal were paid for almost entirely from the stores of silver booty taken by Royal Navy frigates during the wars against Napoleon.

After Waterloo and the disbanding of much of his army, Wellington still insisted on keeping under his control, and offshore, hundreds of millions of dollars in Spanish silver to spend on keeping the peace. In his dealings with Whitehall, his refrain was, "Better not to go to war if you have not the money to pay for it."

The Royal Navy and British privateers had feasted on Spanish treasure ships during the conflict with France, amassing a fortune in bullion, mined in South America and minted into coinage in Mexico.

Figure 3.1. Arthur Wellesley, 1st Duke of Wellington, detail, by Sir Thomas Lawrence, 1829. *Source*: © National Portrait Gallery, London.

The British army and Royal Navy spent a good chunk of this Spanish treasure on the invasion of Portugal and on backing Spanish guerrillas. They forked over at least £25 million fighting the War of 1812 in North America. A large slice of that paid for the naval arms race on Lake Ontario in the final years of the war.

Commodore Sir James Yeo built a warship at the Kingston naval yards that was bigger than Admiral Nelson's *Victory*. The *St. Lawrence*, bristling with 112 long-range guns, half of which were big 24- and 32-pounders, was in fact the largest ship in the Royal Navy. This single vessel cost over £500,000 to build, and was manned by hundreds of sailors from the Royal Navy's Halifax fleet. One reason the Americans capitulated in 1815 was that they knew they could never outspend the British on the Great Lakes.[1]

The American invasion of Upper and Lower Canada during the War of 1812 still infuriated the Duke. He regarded their attempt to take Canada, while his armies were dealing with Napoleon, as something of a brazen land grab.

Wellington was also furious at the Americans because of their support of privateers—by the summer of 1814, eight hundred British merchantmen had been sunk or captured by the Americans during the war, seriously disrupting British supply lines.

It became clear to the Duke that the Americans had conspired with the French to time the invasion of Canada to go off at the precise moment—October of 1812—that Napoleon was invading Russia. Indeed, the American Ambassador to France travelled with the army on its disastrous quest, and froze to death in a Polish village halfway back to Paris.

The Canadian front also tied up British regiments and naval power needed to protect crucial supply routes on the coast of Portugal and in the Baltic Sea.

Bonaparte's sole goal in the race to Moscow was to force Czar Alexander to stop selling hemp to the British. Without a two-year supply of hemp for naval sails and cordage, the Royal Navy would be dead in the water. But a large merchant fleet of over six hundred disaffected New England sea captains, escaping the Jeffersonian embargo, happily hauled hemp from Russia to England during most of the war, and gratefully accepted gold and silver in payment from the British Admiralty.[2] Of course, Bonaparte's winter expedition to Russia was a disaster—the humiliated Emperor abdicated, and was sent into exile on the island of Elba.

In North America, the American campaign to capture Montréal failed because of a drug-addled general and jealousy in the US Army command. The British/Canadian victories at Crysler's Farm and Chateauguay prevented the loss of Canada. But Wellington knew that, like the Battle of Waterloo, the American invasion was a "close run thing."

---

[1] In January 1832, Robert Drummond acquired the hull for £25.
[2] Alastair Sweeny, *Fire Along the Frontier.*

Figure 3.2. HMS *St. Lawrence*, built at Kingston Royal Naval Dockyard. *Source*: Mediawiki Commons.

His forces at Waterloo—only 24,000 of them were British regulars—had been dangerously weakened by the diversion of experienced troops to defend Canada. Only the arrival of the Germans saved him. The British wouldn't be so lucky next time.

A "next time" was not out of the question. Indeed, in a letter dated February 10, 1815, US Secretary of War James Monroe sent US General Jacob Brown a complete new plan of attack along the St. Lawrence to capture Montréal. After the signing of the Treaty of Ghent, Brown actually described this plan to his British counterpart in Canada, Major General Frederick Robinson, who duly forwarded it to the Duke of Wellington.

Wellington was determined to prevent this Yankee threat at all costs. Secretary of State for War and the Colonies Lord Bathurst asked General Sir Gordon Drummond to get "estimates of expense of the Lachine Canal, and of the Ottawa and Rideau being made navigable, in order that His Majesty's Government may decide as to the propriety of undertaking these works, either separately or simultaneously."

It was not just Canada that was at stake. The farseeing Wellington and his fellow imperialists were absolutely determined to build a military and economic system that would let the British Empire expand westward to Lord Selkirk's Red River Colony and on to the Pacific, where the Empire would require a future base for the Royal Navy. Canada was also crucially important for shipbuilding supplies in case any future conflict in Scandinavia or Russia closed the Baltic Sea.

Post Waterloo, with Bonaparte finally exiled to remote St. Helena in the South Atlantic, Wellington turned his attention to improving water access away from the St. Lawrence borderlands, "so that supplies and boats might be thrown into the upper part of the country, in case of need." During the War of 1812, it proved difficult, dangerous, and expensive—an estimated £1.1 million—to draw military stores up the rapids of the St. Lawrence and supply British forces on the Great Lakes.

Even with war officially concluded, the safety of British North America was still a concern to Wellington. Mindful of the vulnerability of the St. Lawrence route and the naval harbour at Kingston, he sent orders to the Royal Engineers in Canada to subsidize the canal at Lachine—in return for free military passage—and make a rough survey of a waterway linking Montréal with Kingston via the safer route along the Ottawa, Rideau, and Cataraqui rivers.

In 1816, Royal Engineer Lt. Joshua Jebb led a small party from Kingston, up the Cataraqui River to the Rideau Lakes and down the Rideau River to "where the River Rideau falls." Jebb submitted reports to his superiors in Montréal on July 14, and they were sent on to the Duke, now commander-in-chief of the British army.

After the Rush-Bagot agreement of 1818 curtailed armed vessels on the Great Lakes, the British Ordnance moved to dismantle the naval shipyards at Kingston. Instead, they started to plan a more impregnable Fort Henry, assisted the provinces in improving the

St. Lawrence system, completing the Welland Canal, and started planning canals on the Ottawa and Rideau rivers.

On December 26, 1818, the Tory government of Lord Liverpool invited Wellington to enter the cabinet as master-general of the Ordnance. This gave him complete charge of all of Britain's fortifications, canals, and other military projects, including those in the Canadas.

He was now able to send some of his best and most talented warriors, his friends and colleagues from the Peninsular War and Waterloo, to govern British North America.

The names of Bathurst, Richmond, Dalhousie, Sherbrooke, Aylmer, Kempt, Murray, Colborne, Bagot, Maitland, Lennox, FitzRoy, Drummond, Cathcart, and Arthur, all war office staff or civil or military governors, resonate today in the names of hundreds of Canadian towns, cities, counties, streets, schools, and universities. They were all Wellington's men.

Along with them came hundreds of his staff officers, including Colonel John By of the Royal Engineers.

A Loyal and Warlike Population

The first Wellingtonian to reach the Ottawa Valley was Governor General Charles Lennox, 4th Duke of Richmond, the brother-in-law of Lord Bathurst, Secretary of State for War and the Colonies. Before the Napoleonic Wars, the Duke of Wellington had served as secretary to Richmond, when he was lord lieutenant of Ireland.

The two remained close. In 1815, before the battle of Waterloo, Wellington put Richmond in command of a reserve force in Brussels to protect the city in case Napoleon was victorious. On June 15, the night before the battle, the Duchess of Richmond held a glittering ball in the city. At about 10:30 p.m., Wellington received a message that the French had pushed up the main Charleroi to Brussels road nearly as far as Quatre Bras, 110 kilometres to the south. Wellington and Richmond retired from the table to study a map, whereupon Wellington blurted out, "Napoleon has Humbugged me by God! He has gained 24 hours' March on me." He quickly sent out orders for his troops to retreat to Waterloo. All his officers at the ball had to leave with the utmost haste, dampening the most infamously disastrous ball in history, featured in films and in novels such as Thackeray's *Vanity Fair*.

In 1818, three years after Waterloo, Wellington appointed Richmond Governor-in-Chief of British North America (BNA), replacing the ailing Sir John Sherbrooke. Sherbrooke had served as one of Wellington's major generals in the Peninsular War from 1807 until 1812, when he was appointed commander of the forces in the Atlantic provinces. The War of 1812 was profitable for Nova Scotia, as Sherbrooke's commercial policies turned the Maritimes into a dynamo of trade. In 1816, he was appointed governor general of BNA, until forced to retire after a stroke.

Wellington and Richmond were of one mind, that it was absolutely necessary to harden the defences of British North America, and encourage the settlement of disbanded soldiers and other British emigrants in the BNA colonies.

They were keenly aware of the ongoing strategic importance of British North America. The Napoleonic Wars and Philemon Wright's timber rafts had made the Ottawa Valley an attractive source of oak planks, pine masts, and hemp ropes and sails for Royal Navy frigates. Expanding inland navigation on the Ottawa River was a high priority.

The Canadas also produced a modest supply of hemp, which could be promoted with subsidies.

Wellington's problem was no longer France, it was the United States. Everything had to be done, from diplomacy to money power to fortifications, to prevent the Americans from capturing British North America.

Wellington was also proceeding to downsize the British regular army—from a high of 226,000 in 1810 to a low of 106,000 in 1830. Emigration was a prime solution, and the intention of the two dukes was to offer free land, provisions, and tools to British veterans of the War of 1812 and the Napoleonic Wars who settled in the Canadas. They had one major goal, "to form a loyal and war-like population on the banks of the Rideau and Ottawa."

Richmond arrived at Québec on July 29, 1818, accompanied by Peregrine Maitland, his new son-in-law and the freshly minted lieutenant governor of Upper Canada. Maitland was another Wellington man. He had been a superstar in the Marylebone Cricket Club in his youth. At Waterloo, he commanded two battalions of the Grenadier Guards, and led them in repelling the final bloody assault of the French Imperial Guard. After Waterloo, covered in glory, Maitland eloped with and married the Duke of Richmond's daughter, Lady Sarah Lennox.

Figure 3.3. A timber raft on the Ottawa, 1868.
Source: Frances Anne Hopkins, Library and Archives Canada, C-150716.

Maitland's sterling reputation had also reached Paris. His character made a cameo appearance in Victor Hugo's novel *Les Misérables*, demanding General Cambronne's surrender of the Imperial Guard at Waterloo, and receiving the curt retort, *"Merde."*

After a week in Montréal, Maitland headed to York, the capital of Upper Canada, which was still recovering from the 1813 sacking and burning by the Americans.

At the same time, Governor General Richmond ordered two companies of the Royal Staff Corps to proceed up the Ottawa Valley to build settlement roads and plan the canalization of the Ottawa River from Montréal to the Chaudière Falls.

The troops portaged up the Long Sault rapids in late August, and landed below the Chaudière Falls on the south shore at a site they called Richmond Landing, to survey a road west to what are now the towns of Richmond and Perth, and acquire land title from the local Algonquins.

About 1,500 former soldiers and their families had already made it to Perth and surrounding townships in the summer of 1816, having trekked north from Brockville and down Rideau Lake.

Now, in September 1818, another four hundred disbanded soldiers and their families from Wellington's 99th and 100th regiments arrived from Québec to open the Richmond Trail and lay out the new settlement of Richmond on the banks of the Jock River. Led by Lieutenant-Colonel Francis Cockburn, the families landed under harsh conditions as the Canadian winter was descending. As the road was completed, storehouses were built, settlers' cabins erected, and the colonists provided with farm implements and rations.

Figure 3.4. The 4th Duke of Richmond and Lennox, 1823.
Source: Henry Collen, PD.

At the same time, the Duke of Richmond pulled together a colonial defence plan that eventually resulted in the construction of expanded fortifications at Québec (the Citadel), and at Lake Ontario's main naval yard at Kingston (Fort Henry), as well as Île Sainte-Hélène (St. Helen's Island) opposite Montréal, as a major logistic depot.

To counter a new American fort at Rouses Point, New York, he decided that Île-aux-Noix in the Richelieu River should be refitted, since the 1812–1814 fortifications were inadequate.

In a letter to Wellington of March 1, 1819, Richmond strongly backed developing an alternative to St. Lawrence River communications (the Rideau Canal) as a crucial alternative supply route to the St. Lawrence.

The upbound St. Lawrence route was slow and expensive. A twelve-day passage from Montréal to Kingston cost about £4 a ton for freight. Its commercial viability was threatened by the planned Champlain and Erie canals, designed to draw the trade of the St. Lawrence and Great Lakes southward through the ice-free port of New York.

Wellington gave him the go-ahead, and that summer, Richmond began an extensive tour of Upper and Lower Canada, starting at Québec. At Fort William Henry in Sorel, when he reached out to touch a soldier's pet fox, he was warned against it by the owner. "No, no," said his grace, "the little fellow will not bite me." The fox snapped, and drew blood. "Indeed, my friend, you bite very hard," said the Duke.

The injury seemed to have healed, and he continued his tour to Kingston, York, and Niagara, examining the state of military sites as far as Drummond Island in Lake Huron, before returning to Kingston. He then proceeded up to the Ottawa Valley, to inspect the military settlement of Perth. At that stage of his journey, he developed pains in his shoulders and throat, and a raging thirst, the first symptoms of advancing rabies.

The night before his death, the Duke slept at the "Masonic Arms," a tavern in Richmond, owned by Andrew Hill, former sergeant major of the 100th Regiment of Foot, and Maria Hill, his wife and a heroine of the War of 1812. On August 28, 1819, he died in agony in the log cabin of a settler named Chapman, on the Jock River, near Perth.

Maria Hill prepared his body, and the coffin was carried out over the Richmond Road in a wagon pulled by a team of four oxen driven by Philemon Wright. It was taken by canoe to Montréal and by steamer to Québec, where it was interred at a state funeral before the altar of Québec's Holy Trinity Anglican cathedral.

Shocked by the death of his old comrade, Wellington ordered the name of Fort Île-aux-Noix changed to Fort Lennox. He also recommended, as Richmond's replacement, George Ramsay, 9th Earl of Dalhousie, another one of his generals in the Peninsular War, then serving as governor of Nova Scotia, where he founded the Halifax university that bears his name.

Dalhousie was a capable though cautious warrior. In 1813, during the flight of Napoleon's brother, King Joseph of Spain, Dalhousie had commanded Wellington's left-centre column during a night crossing of the rugged mountain north-west of Vittoria, capital of the Basque provinces of Spain.[3]

The Erie and Welland Canals, 1817–1829

Wellington then turned his attention to the looming threat from the Americans—that they were starting to build a 600-kilometre-long canal from the Hudson River to Buffalo on Lake Erie, with a branch from Syracuse to Lake Ontario, directly opposite Kingston's Fort Henry.

The first stage of Erie Canal construction began July 4, 1817, at Rome, New York. In less than ten years, the Americans would complete ship canals from the Hudson River to Lake Champlain (opened in 1823), to Lake Ontario opposite Kingston (opened in 1824), and to Lake Erie at Buffalo (opened in 1825).

The battle was clearly becoming as much commercial as military. Upper Canadians soon woke up to the need for an alternate route to Montréal and Europe instead of seeing the province's produce shipped down the Erie Canal to New York.

There were major advantages in shipping down the St. Lawrence through Montréal. Draw a line over a globe—you will see that the route follows a straight line directly to the European continent. Indeed, Montréal was two days' sailing closer to Britain than New York.

The proposed Welland Canal, west of the Niagara River, also had a two-week advantage over the Erie Canal, the entrance of which was usually choked with Lake Erie ice flows for up to a month in the

---

[3] The Battle of Vittoria (also spelled Vitoria) gave its name to the street in Ottawa that runs in front of the Supreme Court.

early spring. Montréal's only disadvantage was its winter ice up, whereas the port of New York was ice-free all year round. However, the Erie Canal also suffered from winter freeze-up, so the battle lines were fairly equal.

Before the Erie Canal opened, most shipping traffic between Lake Ontario and Lake Erie used a portage road in Upper Canada along the Niagara River between Chippawa and Queenston—above and below Niagara Falls.

Building the first canal joining Lake Erie and Lake Ontario was a project of two mill owners, William Hamilton Merritt and George Keefer, who also intended to tap into the water power of the route.

The Welland Canal Company was incorporated by the Province of Upper Canada in 1824, after a petition by nine "freeholders of the District of Niagara." The Duke of Wellington lent his name to the project, and personally subscribed for twenty-five shares in the project. Lord Dalhousie was also a subscriber.

On November 30 of that year, company president George Keefer turned the first sod for the canal. Construction began the following spring. The entire canal was dug by hand, with only pick and shovel and the assistance of horse-drawn carts. It saw the first shipping in 1830.

The forty locks were originally made of driven logs, but due to deterioration and the increasing size of ships, the province subsidized a second Welland Canal, which used cut stone locks, just a few years later.

All this canal building strengthened the Duke of Wellington's determination to harden the defences of Upper and Lower Canada, and to get the Rideau Canal project under way, as an alternate route from Kingston to Montréal. His old battlefield colleague, the Earl of Dalhousie, was ordered to leave Halifax and proceed with all dispatch to Québec to begin the great work.

Lord Dalhousie Inspects the Ottawa River

Once settled in Lower Canada, Dalhousie decided to make his first tour of inspection of the military settlements at Perth and Richmond.

In mid-August 1820, he and his party reached Richmond Landing, beside the Chaudière Falls, where the settlers stockpiled the stores they brought upriver from Montréal. The Earl and party then followed the Richmond trail on horseback to inspect the progress of the new towns.

Figure 3.5. George Ramsay, 9th Earl of Dalhousie (1770–1838), Governor-in-Chief of Canada 1819–1828.
Source: John Elliott Woolford, Library and Archives Canada.

Dalhousie's main concern at this early date was to lock up land for the Ordnance, particularly sites like Richmond Landing that could be used during the building of the Rideau Canal and fortress, without having to pay outrageous sums to speculators. He met with the Superintendent of Settlers, who told him about an advertisement for land around Richmond Landing belonging to an absentee landlord, Robert Randal, which was available for a "trifling sum."

Whether by design or not, Dalhousie soon got embroiled in some of the land hunger that was starting to infect the local citizenry. At this point, one of the founding myths of the Rideau Canal began to play out on the stage.

Dinner at the Masonic Arms

On the evening of August 27, 1820, His Lordship held a dinner party at Sergeant Major Andrew Hill's Masonic Arms tavern in Richmond, with a group of retired army officers. Most were veterans of Wellington's campaigns against Napoleon. When discussion turned to the subject of the Rideau Canal, Dalhousie supposedly told his dinner companions in confidence that Richmond Landing would be the entrance to the soon-to-be-built canal.

One of the retired officers at the dinner was a Captain John Le Breton. Five years earlier, in March of 1815, Le Breton had petitioned for land in Upper Canada. In 1819, he was awarded a grant beside Richmond Landing, which he called Britannia and which was later known as Le Breton Flats. He built a storehouse that May, beside the property of one Robert Randal, a bankrupt Yankee speculator. Randal had tried to promote an ironworks at the Chaudière Falls, claiming to have found "an inexhaustible iron bank, a mountain of the richest & best quality rock ore," across the river in Hull Township. In March 1809, just after Randal had finally acquired title to his 400 acres, he was arrested for debt in Montréal and spent the next six and a half years in jail.

The Superintendent of Settlers may have tipped off Dalhousie that Le Breton was trying to buy or lease the Randal property. In December 1820, three months after Dalhousie's dinner party, Le Breton did acquire the property for £449 at a sheriff's sale in Brockville. His troubles began early in 1821 when the Ordnance asked to purchase it. Le Breton's price: £3,000.

Dalhousie feigned rage when he heard of the offer from Le Breton. As he recalled in 1827, "I asked him if he seriously proposed such a demand—he said he did—and justified himself. I forget in what terms. I, at once, and very angrily told him, I would not permit so scandalous an imposition on H.M. Government... From that one interview I formed an unfavourable opinion of Captain Le Breton, and I have seen no cause to alter it since."

Dalhousie accused Le Breton of acting on privileged information given at the dinner party, reputedly overheard at the dinner in Richmond the preceding August:

> Captain Le Breton was then present; heard my sentiments and in my ideas, as a Member of that settlement; as an officer and a Gentleman was in honour bound to give his assistance. He did not do so, he availed himself of the information and set about a speculative purchase to make a profitable bargain and then offer it to Government.

Le Breton held his ground, refusing to sell for less than £3,000. Cued by Dalhousie, who publicly questioned the legality of Le Breton's purchase, and called his behaviour "indecent and shameful," the Upper Canada government began to give Le Breton a rough ride, even though a number of the half-pay officers testified that no such news was discussed at the dinner. He was struck off the list of magistrates for Upper Canada, which hit him in the pocketbook. Complaints about the theft of timber from his land were ignored, and in 1823–1824, the government declined to press charges of trespass after he was assaulted by "plunderers and thugs."

Of course, Dalhousie may have been smoking out land speculators among the retired officers—and soon found out Le Breton was one.

Ever on the alert for malefactors, Dalhousie also had mixed feelings about Philemon Wright:

> Philemon is a strange character, of shrewd sense, deep cunning and Yankee manners—he is composed of qualities that at the same moment recommend and show him a person that must be constantly suspected of a desire to cheat.

It's possible Dalhousie's actions against Le Breton were an elaborate charade. As an experienced military man, and one of Wellington's chief colleagues, he knew the importance of a bluff. His soldier's eye told him that the most attractive canal entrance was, of course, not the indefensible site of Richmond Landing at all, but the one we see today, which could be protected by a very large fortress on what is now Parliament Hill, that would guard the northern terminus of the canal, just as a rebuilt Fort Henry would guard the southern end at Kingston.

Figure 3.6. Fourteen voyageurs and four gentlemen in Dalhousie's Vice Regal canoe, 1821.
Source: John Elliott Woolford, Library and Archives Canada.

Dalhousie clearly envisioned the Parliament Hill site as a potential castle site for a capital—an Edinburgh of the new world. Once, while looking admiringly at the hill from across the river in Hull, he remarked to a bystander, "Would you not be startled were I to say that on those heights some day will be the seat of government?"[4]

Dalhousie's Tour to the West

The following summer of 1821, Dalhousie determined to make a more challenging canoe tour of the Great Lakes and Ottawa Valley with two aides and his friend John Wolford, an artist. They started at Lachine and took a batteau up the St. Lawrence to Kingston, where they were met by their tour guide, Angus Shaw, an experienced North Wester. Dalhousie described the scene before departure:

> Our Canoe is one of the large Birch bark canoes, & manned with 14 of the engagés of the North West Company. The intelligence & activity of these fellows cannot be described or understood without seeing them. When we arrived, they were all asleep on the grass. In an instant, at the Pilot's voice,

[4] Hamnett Hill, *The Genesis of our Capital*.

they jumped up, ran to their canoe, had it on their shoulders and launched on the water, in less time than I could have said it.

At 4 PM we started, and the first shoot the canoe made felt as if we had fallen a rapid; the 2nd or 3rd so elastic as you see the bounds of a horse starting in a race—then the boatsong—much spirit, such joy & such exactness of time to the paddles.[5]

Figure 3.7. Philemon Wright c. 1810.
Source: John James fonds, Library and Archives Canada, C-011056.

---

5 Marjory Whitelaw, ed., *Dalhousie Journals*, vol. 2 (Ottawa: Oberon Press, 1980), 32.

During the voyage, Dalhousie sat under a protective awning, wearing a top hat and coat, followed by a separate canoe for his luggage and supplies.

The party travelled via portages to Lake Simcoe and Georgian Bay, as far as the entrance to Lake Superior. They returned down the Ottawa via by the French and Mattawa rivers, and bade farewell to Angus and his voyageurs, before boarding Philemon Wright's passenger boat, *The Packet*, propelled by sail and oars, for the trip to Montréal.

Dalhousie's Major Land Purchase

On June 18, 1823, Dalhousie put his real plan in motion. He very quietly bought from Hugh Fraser, a Three Rivers notary, for the trifling sum of £750, 150 acres occupying what is now known as Entrance Valley, the head of the Rideau Canal. The property had originally been granted to a Loyalist family, the Carmans, in 1802. Fraser's father had bought the property in 1812 for £12.

This land today is bounded on the north by the Ottawa River, on the east by the Rideau River, on the south by Wellington and Rideau streets, and on the west by Bronson Avenue, ending at LeBreton Flats. It includes Parliament Hill, a fine site for a fortress.

Indeed, the Royal Engineers and the Ordnance would soon develop blueprints for Dalhousie's proposed citadel. The Earl had in his mind's eye the experienced team of Thomas Mackay and John Redpath, now completing work on the Lachine Canal locks. They could be engaged to build barracks and fortifications similar to those at Fort Lennox, on part of the land that Dalhousie had already acquired and reserved for Crown use.

Now how much would this massive project cost?

CHAPTER 4

Enter Colonel John By

There is a lovely waterway in Old Ontario.

—Robert Legget, *Rideau Waterway*

In 1821, the Upper Canada legislature in York set up a commission to look into the building of canal routes in the province. Headed up by Captain John Macaulay of Kingston, it was concerned mainly with the commercial promise of the St. Lawrence and Welland canals.

Upper Canada was not at all interested in funding the Rideau Canal route. In 1822, the province voted the paltry sum of £1,000 for a survey of the several potential routes: one started at Belleville and ended at Pembroke; the other two started from Kingston, one arriving near Wendover through the Petite Nation River, and the other at the mouth of the Rideau River.

However, on November 2, 1822, anticipating settlement, canal building, and the need for clear title, agents of the Crown signed the Long Woods Purchase with the Anishinabeg Chiefs, who ceded 1,112,100 hectares of land in Hastings, Addington, Frontenac, Lanark, Carleton and Renfrew counties, up to Smiths Falls, and land along the Thames River, in return for a yearly annuity of £600.

The Ordnance, under its Master General, the Duke of Wellington, made half-hearted overtures to the governments of Upper and Lower Canada to help finance the Rideau Canal. Lower Canada refused outright, and the Upper Canada Assembly at York opted to upgrade the St. Lawrence and Welland canals, which would be half subsidized by the British Treasury.

In the end, Wellington decided that it was far simpler and more efficient to finance and control the whole Rideau enterprise solely as a military project. He and his strategists were more concerned with security than with commerce. With healthy reserves of Spanish silver at their command, packed in barrels in fortresses at Halifax, Québec, and Montréal, they could easily afford to create a back door or alternate route between Montréal and Lake Ontario in the event of American invasion.

As with the Lachine Canal, the lure of toll-free passage of military supplies was a strong determining factor in the decision to go it alone, without provincial interference. Indeed, transport costs up the St. Lawrence during the War of 1812 had amounted to almost a million pounds.

Another important factor in making the Rideau Canal an Ordnance project was the flood of British immigrants that were arriving every year at Québec. Many were disbanded soldiers, displaced farmers, or desperate paupers. These people needed help. In 1823, Dalhousie wrote to Colonial Secretary Bathurst that the population of Lower Canada was not coping well with the invasion, and that he had to promote public works.[1] Building the Rideau Canal, he knew, would need to absorb many labourers. Indeed, in 1829 alone, the canal gave work to 2,700 men, many of whom were Irish pauper immigrants.

Costing the Work

On April 1, 1824, after the Duke of Wellington accepted the Rideau River route, surveyor Samuel Clowes reported to Upper Canada Lt.-Governor Maitland with cost estimates: £62,258 to build a canal with small locks 4 feet [1.2 metres] deep; for a system with stone locks 100 feet [30 metres] long by 22 feet [6.7 metres] wide, £230,785.

The following April, Wellington asked his Waterloo colleague Sir James Carmichael Smyth of the Royal Engineers to report on the canal's defence needs. Early in 1826 the Duke officially authorized the great project, and in March, General Gother Mann, now inspector general of fortifications at the Board of Ordnance, charged his old friend and colleague, Colonel John By of the Royal Engineers, to return to Canada and build another much larger canal.

---

[1] Dalhousie to Bathurst, in Marjory Whitelaw, ed., *Dalhousie Journals*, vol. 2 (Ottawa: Oberon Press, 1980).

In the 1780s, Colonel By had cut his teeth on one of the earliest canals in North America—not much more than a little "ditch" at Cascades below Lake St. Francis.

Recalled to England in 1812, the Colonel had spent over a decade serving as the Royal Engineer officer in charge of gunpowder and barrel production at the Board of Ordnance. After managing a fireworks display with Sir William Congreve to celebrate the Peace of Paris in 1814, he was elevated to the rank of major. Seven years later, in 1821, General Mann, inspector general of fortifications, placed him on the retired list following the curtailment of operations after Waterloo.

After the death of his wife from cholera, Major By was living quietly on half pay on his estate in Sussex, and taking up farming with his new wife Esther, and two small daughters. His bucolic dream was shattered in March of 1826, when General Mann ordered him to return to active service, with the rank of lieutenant-colonel. His new duty—to go back to Canada and superintend the engineering of a canal with a minimum depth of five feet, linking the Ottawa River and Fort Henry on Lake Ontario by way of the Rideau and Cataraqui river systems.

Smyth specifically recommended that Colonel By carefully examine the Lachine Canal, "a truly valuable and magnificent undertaking (for a young country). He will find everything here extremely well executed, and in a much more substantial manner than the American canals, and will derive every information as to the price and cost of materials, workmanship and labour."

In other words, use Thomas Mackay as a resource when costing the Rideau Canal.

The Duke of Wellington was now adamant that the Rideau Canal had to be built forthwith and without interference, solely as a military work. The canal would also provide work for British soldiers, artisans, and labourers who could be induced to emigrate to the Canadas.

The Duke also knew that Canadian politicians could not afford such a project, burdened as they were by the need to pay for the Welland and St. Lawrence canals. So he changed his whole approach, and ordered the Rideau Canal to be constructed solely as a military work.

In a strict instruction by the Duke on June 15, 1826, he enjoined Colonel By not to have "any novel [new] relation towards the authorities in Canada."

Figure 4.1. Lieutenant Colonel John By, 1832.
Source: Unknown artist.

In other words, from now on, go ahead and build this strategic canal as you see fit. Indeed, ignore the local politicians and the British Treasury. Proceed without waiting for parliamentary approval. Make your own contracts and if you need lands, buy them under your own name. And don't worry—the Ordnance can afford it.

The By family landed at Québec on May 30, and headed to Montréal a few days later to make preparations to travel up the Ottawa River.

When Colonel By and his assistant, Captain Daniel Bolton of the Royal Engineers, both contracted typhus, By sent ahead engineer John Mactaggart, who had been appointed by the Ordnance in London to act as By's clerk of works.

The Royal Engineers Take Charge

Colonel By was well enough to travel up the Ottawa in July. He invited Thomas Mackay to join the party, to get his feel for the potential costs of the project, and estimate the quality of limestone available on or near the site. The party passed several weeks living under canvas on Nepean Point, overlooking what would become the Ottawa Locks site, before returning to Montréal.

On their return to Montréal, Colonel By met with Lord Dalhousie to take up his position as superintending engineer of the Rideau Canal. Relying on Mackay's estimates, he frankly reported to the Governor that the £169,000 estimate given by Smyth was too low, by a factor of four or five, based on the costs of building the Lachine Canal.

Figure 4.2. *The First Camp Bytown*, 1826, by Lieutenant Colonel John By.[1]
Source: John By, McCord Museum, M386.

---

[1] The tents of the Royal Engineers sported red arrow flashes. The image may show Colonel By at a camp table discussing canal matters with Thomas Mackay.

Also, instead of a canal where boats were pulled along a towpath by horses, as at Lachine, Colonel By knew that the canal locks had to be larger than estimated, to accommodate steamboats. Otherwise, the waterway would be useless for defensive purposes.

One of Colonel By's first decisions was to confirm Dalhousie's choice for the canal entrance and ultimate fortress.

Many true canal aficionados have bought into the narrative that Dalhousie's anger at Captain Le Breton changed his mind as to where to place the head of the Rideau Canal. At Dow's Great Swamp, the Rideau River divided into two parts, one branch going into the Ottawa above the Chaudière Falls and the other draining the swamp towards Nicholas St. into the Rideau.

They argue that it would have been preferable to dig the canal to make the entrance at Richmond Landing, below the Chaudière Falls. This route was only half the length of today's 7-kilometre passage through the city. They argue it would have allowed for a branch of the canal to connect the Ottawa River upstream from the Falls, and a Georgian Bay canal to open the upper Ottawa to water transport as far as Lake Huron.[2]

A fine fantasy, but there was very little good land for settlement farther up the Ottawa, and a canal would be useless in winter, unlike a railway. Such a scheme could not at that time be justified on economic grounds.

The Richmond Landing story is doubly doubtful, since the British Ordnance took control of the whole project from the beginning. Their focus on the Rideau Canal was first and foremost military. Richmond Landing was not particularly defensible, while Entrance Bay could have been readily defended from attack by gun batteries atop the cliffs that flanked the locks. Indeed, to protect the northern terminus of the canal, the Ordnance was already planning a fortress, a twin of Fort Henry in Kingston.

Thomas Mackay and Colonel By also discussed another, more practical, issue with the Richmond Landing option—how to maintain enough water to feed the entry locks, on the one hand, and where to drain excess water in the event of massive spring floods on the Rideau

---

[2] Mackay would later serve on an Upper Canada commission struck to examine the Georgian Bay option, and future son-in-law Thomas Keefer also consulted on the subject from an engineering perspective.

River. There was a strong risk that locks to Richmond Landing might fail and be washed out under hydraulic pressure.

Canal planners soon came up with another way to ease the spring flood, by diverting overflowing spring melt water from the Canal turn basin/reservoir back into the Rideau River. The "by wash" ran from what was originally a beaver meadow through present-day Lower Town, along Musgrove, George, Dalhousie, York, and King Edward streets, before it drained into the Rideau River at the end of Cathcart Street.

With the help of Thomas Mackay, Dow's Lake contractor Jean-Baptiste Saint-Louis soon built a rudimentary flour mill in Lower Town, powered by the Bywash.

From the Canal Basin, Colonel By's Sappers and Miners dug out what was called the Deep Cut, running in a straight line with the locks for about one kilometre, where it connected with the drain coming from the Exhibition Grounds near Hurdman's Bridge, formerly a portage used by the Algonquins. A few kilometres further on, they dug through a natural gully and built an embankment to maintain a consistent water level in Dow's Great Swamp—soon renamed Dow's Lake—to feed the entry locks downstream. Saint-Louis finally erected a berm—called the St. Louis Dam—at the north end to block any discharge from going into the Ottawa River at Richmond Landing above the Chaudière Falls.

The Richmond Landing canal option was certainly considered. According to Sir John Colborne, in February 1832, the Imperial government had examined building a branch to Lac Deschenes and a canal up the Ottawa to Lake Huron, but decided that was a project for another day.

Upper Canada was more interested in opening up another waterway in southern Ontario. In 1833, Thomas Mackay served on a commission, staffed by Samuel Keefer, that looked at building a Trent—Severn Waterway, to connect Lake Ontario with Georgian Bay. This 386-kilometre-long canal, after many fits and starts, was finally completed in 1920. Like the Rideau Canal, it has taken on new life as a recreational canal under the direction of Parks Canada.

Back in the Ottawa Valley, some initial canal cuts were later made upriver through hard granite at the Deschenes and Chats Rapids. But in the end, the idea was fatally wounded by the building of the CPR main line up the Ottawa Valley in 1881–1882. That's not to say a recreational canal to Georgian Bay would not be a wonderful project at some time in the future.[3]

As for Captain Le Breton, after Dalhousie's 1828 departure as governor, Le Breton's Richmond Landing title survived a court challenge, and he began to take his profits by selling lots on the property, Le Breton Flats, now adjacent to the recently named settlement of Bytown. While it was no longer considered as a realistic canal entrance, it would eventually become the site of the world's biggest woodyard.

---

[3] The Upper Ottawa can be navigated by boats up to 32 feet, using transfer trailers around hydro dams.

CHAPTER 5

1826: The Founding of Bytown

The village of Bytown was not, like other villages, created by private endeavour nor was it conceived and developed by any Canadian Government. The land on which it grew was owned at Whitehall. The division of the land into lots was made by a British officer. It is the one case in history where the British Government owned outright a little village in a colony of its Empire, and later selected it as the Capital City of a great possession of that Government.

—Hamnett Hill, *Bytown Gazette*

Figure 5.1. Below the Chaudière Falls.
Source: John Elliot Woolford, Library and Archives Canada.

In 1826, Ottawa began life as a company town—the company being the British Army Board of Ordnance, headquartered in the Tower of London.

Much of this young settlement, including the canal, barracks, land for a fortress and offices, and Lower Town lots for lease, would remain military property for the next quarter century.

Under the *Vesting Act* of 1821, passed by the British government, the Ordnance Department could hold legal title to all property needed for military purposes. Its mandate was to "act as custodian of the lands, depots and forts required for the defence of the realm and its overseas possessions, and as the supplier of munitions and equipment to both the Army and the Navy."

From 1787 on, the Royal Engineers (RE) branch of the Ordnance was put in charge of designing, building, and maintaining fortifications and other military installations. The RE also engaged in large-scale civilian projects, using a civilian corps of "artificers"—carpenters, stonemasons, bricklayers, and other labourers, later renamed the Royal Sappers and Miners.

Under the leadership of the Duke of Wellington, British forces had already spent billions of dollars in Spanish silver in the invasion of Portugal and Spain, and in fighting the War of 1812 in North America. After Waterloo, the Duke was prepared to spend whatever was needed on canals and fortifications to maintain a hold on Canada and its resources. He had considerable reserves of Spanish booty to make it happen, and access to "Army extraordinaries"—supplements voted by Parliament—as well as a platoon of unemployed generals to oversee the job.

Wellington's challenge to the Ordnance was simply this—quickly and efficiently build a canal from Kingston through wilderness to the Ottawa River, so in any future conflict, troops going to or from Montréal could bypass the vulnerable border along the St. Lawrence from Kingston to Cornwall.

Colonel By Gets His Orders

On September 7, 1826, the Commanding Royal Engineer in Canada, Colonel Durnford, received official instructions from the Ordnance for Colonel By to proceed with the building of the Rideau Canal. At the same time, he was to construct a toll bridge from Wrightstown to the south shore of the Ottawa River. Thomas Mackay, the lead Lachine

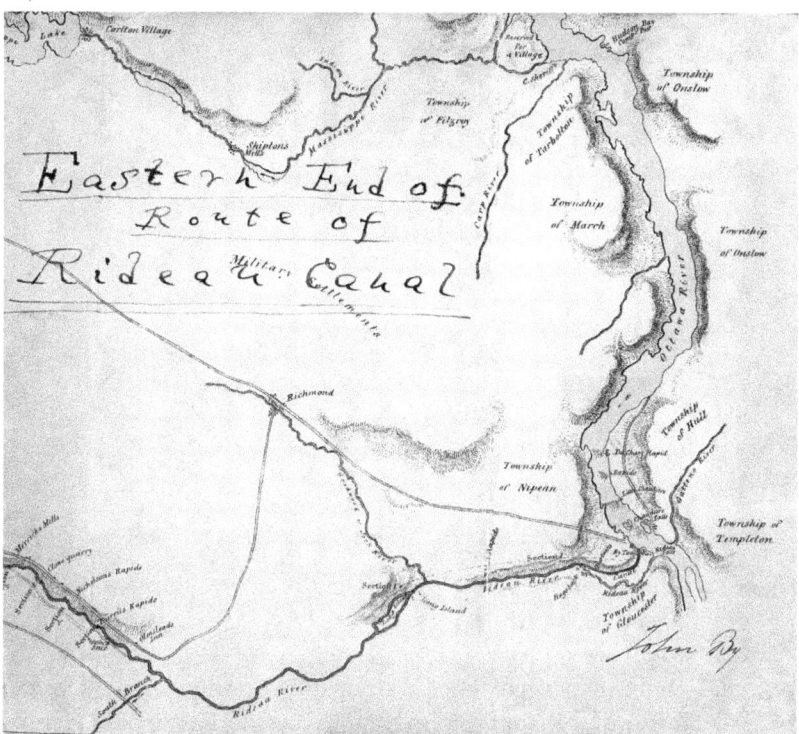

Figure 5.2. Bytown, Nepean, and Richmond, 1830.
Source: Map by John Burrows, Library and Archives Canada.

Canal contractor, was again assigned to travel up the Ottawa with Colonel By, and assist in building the bridge and choosing a site for the canal entrance.

Leaving Montréal on the 19th, and heading up the Ottawa, Colonel By's party reached the portage at Grenville and then embarked on Philemon Wright's new steamboat, *Union of the Ottawa*, for the twenty-four-hour trip to Wrightstown. In 1822, ever the entrepreneur, Wright had replaced his original passenger boat, *The Packet*, propelled by sail and oars, with a small steamer that could tow barges. By 1824, the steamboat was arriving every second day at Wright's Landing.

On the two-day journey up the Ottawa, Thomas Mackay gazed at the valley, and the low hills that bordered the river. He inhaled the piney scent of the forest, and the swampy smell of the big river. He marvelled at the deepening colours of the trees—the groves of yellow

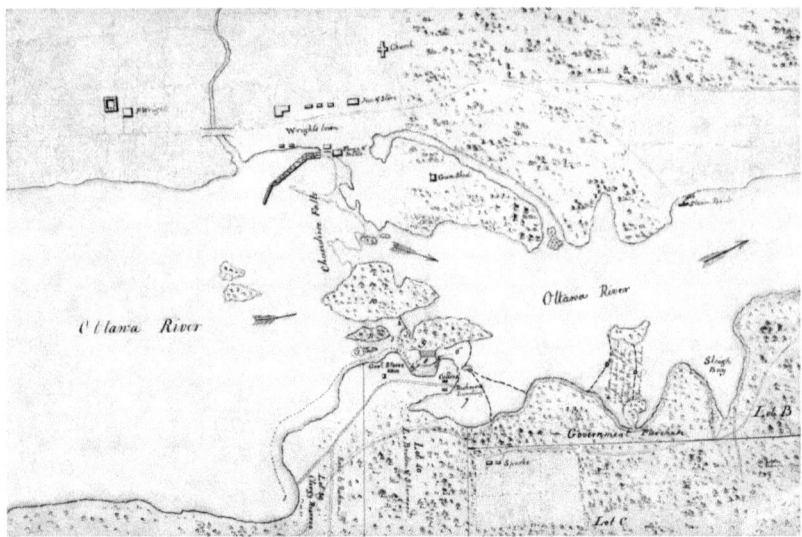

Figure 5.3. Both banks of the Ottawa River and the Chaudière Falls, 1825. *Source*: G. A. Elliot, Library and Archives Canada, MIKAN 4138620.

oak and flaming orange maples framed by stands of dark green pine—a far more brilliant autumn than in the Tay Valley of his native Scotland.

On September 21, nearing the Ottawa Basin, the travellers heard a roar and saw what looked like smoke rising in the distance. Looking to the left, they marvelled at the beautiful curtains of the Rideau Falls, named by Champlain, and on the right the wide Gatineau River coursing down from the hills to the north. Then, in between little islands, they glimpsed—felt—the thundering waters of the Chaudière Falls. The steamboat *Union of the Ottawa* then began to slow, turned towards the north shore and came alongside the Wrightstown wharf. The party disembarked, stretching their legs after the trip, while the crew loaded their baggage on a wagon. Then they took a short buggy ride to Philemon Wright's Columbia Hotel.

The following morning, one of the voyageurs rowed Mackay, Colonel By, and Lieutenant Pooley of the Royal Engineers across the Ottawa to Governor's Bay (just east of present-day 24 Sussex Drive, the prime minister's residence), which was one proposed alternative for the head locks of the canal. Major General Smyth had recommended this bay in a dispatch to the Duke of Wellington a year earlier. After walking the ground, Mackay advised Colonel By that the

Figure 5.4. Wrightstown, 1830.
Source: Thomas Burrowes fonds, Archives of Ontario, C 1-0-0-0-6.

high and steep limestone cliffs made this site unsuitable for a flight of locks.

The party then moved west to the next inlet, Sleigh Bay, later known as Entrance Bay, where a small stream trickled down through a cedar-choked gorge. They quickly concluded that Dalhousie's choice was the best site for the flight of the Ottawa Locks. It was also overlooked by a rocky height suitable for a potential military fortress. It was the central part of the property purchased by the Earl three years earlier.

Sleigh Bay got its name from the wedding of Tiberius Wright, Philemon's son, in the winter of 1819. He had arranged to be married in Hull by a justice of the peace from Perth. But the JP was not authorized to marry people in Lower Canada. So the wedding party decided to cross the frozen Ottawa River to a sheltered bay, where a charming marriage ceremony was performed surrounded by a ring of sleighs.

Mackay's foreman, John Robertson, brought several masons upriver from Lachine on September 24, with civilian engineer Thomas Burrowes, Colonel By's overseer of works. Burrowes was to labour on the canal until 1846, leaving us a wonderful visual heritage with his scores of watercolour paintings of the canal under construction and in operation.

Lord Dalhousie and his wife, accompanied by Colonel Durnford, the Commanding Royal Engineer in Canada, arrived on the steamboat two days later, after travelling part of the way from Lachine to Grenville coddled in a Hudson's Bay Company canoe, paddled by five crack voyageurs, donated to the cause by Sir George Simpson, "the Little Emperor," Governor-in-Chief of the HBC.

On the afternoon of September 26, Lord Dalhousie, his Countess, and Colonel By, crossed the river with Philemon Wright, Thomas Mackay, and others to engage in a ceremony on the heights above Sleigh Bay. With the Indian summer gloriously colouring the northern hills with shades of scarlet and yellow, and the Ottawa River with blue, the Countess of Dalhousie turned the first sod to mark the beginning of work on the Rideau Canal and the founding of a settlement on the Upper Canada side. The Earl then made an inspiring speech on the military project, also sharing his prophetic vision of the future value of this magnificent place, as if it were to be the seat of a new nation: "The public interest and the public prosperity will advance beyond the shortsighted views which any of us here can yet imagine."

After the ceremony, the participants repaired to Wright's Columbia Hotel for a sumptuous supper.

Dalhousie also enjoined Colonel By to consider the site as more than the northern terminus of a waterway, but the focal point of a significant new community. He handed the Colonel a letter with his instructions for the place:

> I take this opportunity of meeting you here to place in your hands a sketch Plan of several lots of land, which I thought it advantageous to purchase for the use of Government, where this Canal was spoken of, as likely to be carried into effect. These not only contain the site for the headlocks, but they offer a valuable locality for a considerable Village or Town, for the lodging of Artificers and other necessary Essentials, in so great a Work.
>
> I would propose that these be correctly surveyed, laid out in lots of 2 or so Acres, to be granted according to the means of settlers and to pay a Government rent of 2/6 per acre to the Crown annually. The locations to contain the positive condition of building a house within 12 months from date of the ticket, & to place the house on the line of street according to plan to be made of it.
>
> It will be highly desirable to encourage the half pay Officers & respectable people, should they offer to build on these town lots.

As the purchase was made by me for the public service, I place the whole in your hands for the purpose I have now explained.

Dalhousie[1]

The Chaudière Bridge Disaster

Back in Wrightstown, Dalhousie discussed with the engineers the need for a toll bridge to transport supplies and stone across the Ottawa River over the Chaudière Falls, a series of plunging cataracts as impressive as Niagara—indeed, a horizontal Niagara. Dalhousie felt that a bridge would lower the cost of building the canal, and the sum of £2,000 would be an appropriate amount to spend.

According to Burrowes, Dalhousie directed Colonel By "to commence the erection of a Chain of Bridges over the several chasms and rock Islands below the romantic Falls at this place… I was immediately ordered to measure the Gap or chasm at the north or Hull side of the River, and to draw a design for a bridge of rough stone to be thrown over the said chasm."

On October 18, John Mactaggart, Clerk of Works for the canal project, wrote a friend that:

> [T]he Governor and my commander, Colonel By, had laid me out plenty of work to superintend. What think ye of a bridge of stone over the Grand River,—a Union Bridge to connect Upper and Lower Canada? A more imposing situation for such a piece of architecture could nowhere be found. The arches are to curve between a chain of rocky islands, directly over the magnificent and splendid Falls of Chaudière! Behold but the scene, look at the mass of waters coming smoking over the shelving precipices, formed of the hardest horizontal strata of laminated limestone:— down they tumble, in some places more than one hundred feet [30 metres], into the cauldrons or kettles beneath; where, instead of their furiously driving, as you may imagine, down the channel, they in some instances vanish fairly, work their way through subterranean passages, and come up boiling white half a mile [.8 kilometre] down the river…

---

[1] Robert Legget, *Rideau Waterway*.

> This bridge, if we manage to build and finish it off as we ought, will surpass almost any other in the world as a wonderful piece of superstructure. It is to have eight arches; five of 60 feet [18 metres] span, two of 70 feet [21 metres], and one of 200 feet [60 metres] over the Big Kettle, where sounding-line hath not yet found a bottom at 300 feet [91 metres] deep. One of these bridges of 60 feet [18 metres] span, we are just finishing, and putting up centering for one of the 70 feet [21 metres] arches.
>
> Material are just for the lifting, of the best quality. Nature was never so kind. Plenty of timber, plenty of stone, good abutments—the truth is we build no abutments, but spring with the arches directly from the rocks themselves. The road-way will be about 30 feet [9 metres] wide; and as the spring floods of the Ottawa rise 24 feet [7 metres], we are obliged to raise the arches high to keep out of harm's way.[2]

Mactaggart engaged Thomas Mackay's fellow contractor Robert Drummond to design the bridge—he had already built the drawbridge at Fort Lennox, and a lock at Sainte-Anne's Rapids. Drummond hired carpenters and quarrymen in Wrightstown, to assist the Royal Engineers, while Mackay's masons got busy quarrying and squaring masonry for the first stone arches, jutting out towards the chasm from the north bank.

Colonel By invited Dalhousie to lay the foundation stone of the first arch of the Union Bridge before leaving the following day. As the Earl recalled:

> Accordingly all was prepared for the ceremony, which took place as we passed down to our Boats. We pointed out the line he had fixed upon, and Mackay the head mason on the Lachine Canal being there had an immense block of stone squared & ready. Some coins of the present reign [King William IV] were scattered in the bed of lime, then laid down the stone with three blows of the mall, and three times three reverberating cheers. A Royal salute from two field six pounders added grandly to the scene at that wild & romantic spot.

---

[2] Robert Haig, *Ottawa—City of the Big Ears* (Ottawa, 1969).

The viceregal pair then returned to Montréal, leaving behind a bustling amphitheatre of engineering activity.

Trial by Ice

After intensive measuring and planning, the Royal Engineers completed the necessary support scaffolding and a false wooden arch over the north channel to carry the weight of the stones and mortar to be laid by Mackay's masons.

The masons finished the first arch three weeks later, and Mackay and his men laid the keystones in place. Because the engineers feared that leaving the scaffolding in place over the winter might cause the bridge to be carried away by ice, they decided to remove the wooden support beams holding the false arch before freeze-up. But as they hammered out the wedges at the bottom, their timber supports suddenly began to shift. Suddenly, with a loud crack, they shattered, pulling the massive structure of mortared stone sideways as the broken arch collapsed before their eyes.

Recalled Burrowes:

> At the moment the Arch fell, Mr. John Mactaggart, Mr. Mackay, Mr. John Burrows and Self were standing upon a flat piece of rock immediately below the bridge, and not more than twelve feet [3.6 metres] from the side of it. Providentially, none of us were struck by the flying pieces of broken timber. The mortar that had fallen from the Arch made the water in the "Little Kettle" white as milk and the splash from it ruined our clothing.
>
> Whatever Mr. Mactaggart's real sentiments may have been, he appeared to make light of the matter; for, after we had wiped the mortar or grout off our faces, he exclaimed: "Egad, boys! We maun e'en big her up again." Doubtless he said this to cheer up Mr. Mackay, who stood appalled. We then returned to the Hotel for Breakfast, after which Mr. Mackay hastened to Montréal to impart the disastrous tiding to Lieut.-Col. By, who gave orders to have the work recommenced forthwith.[3]

---

[3] Brian S. Osborne, "Thomas Burrowes and the Rideau Corridor," unpublished, Parks Canada, 1982.

On Mackay's return, Mactaggart ordered the Royal Engineers to craft stronger false arches. Because of the approaching freeze-up, Mackay knew he would have to build classical keystone arches without mortar. As he and his masons began work in the increasing cold, they suffered through an early blizzard that howled down the Ottawa Valley.

Mackay doubled the rum ration, while Philemon Wright and his sons and farmhands assisted Mackay and his men with food and extra muscle. Lashed with frozen spray from the Chaudière Falls, the masons erected a screen of rough boards on the side of the bridge next to the falls and laid bundles of straw on the works every night. They finally finished carving the angled stones, and laid them over the false arches during a blessed thaw. On January 11, the supports were taken away, and Mackay's first section of the bridge held.

During the summer, Mackay's masons built a second stone arch, stretching over a cleft in the island south of the first bridge, and its centres were struck down in mid-August.

A passer-by called Mackay's twin arches

> one of the most beautiful specimens of rough masonry in the continent of America; it is built of stones hammer-dressed to the size of the arch; the work has been carried on in the depth of a Canadian winter, and during a season unusually severe,—an effort reflecting the highest credit on both the artificers and superintendents.[4]

At this point, the engineers decided that building stone arches right across the Chaudière was not yet practical, fearing the potential power of the spring flood waters. Colonel By also decided that the skills of Mackay's masons now had to be redirected to the Rideau Canal locks.

In the spring, the engineers completed a straight wooden platform bridge out to some small islands, then finally a 212-foot [65-metre] wooden truss and rope bridge built across the main Chaudière Falls chasm, using Philemon Wright's brass cannon to propel the rope over the raging torrent.

---

[4] One of Thomas Mackay's stone arches is still visible under the current Chaudière Bridge.

Built without loss of life, the Union Bridge was the first span to cross a major river in Canada and the first to connect Upper and Lower Canada.

The rope bridge was soon replaced by a wooden truss, to handle carriages, but it collapsed from rot on May 18, 1836. For the next seven years, until replaced by Canada's first suspension bridge, the major means of transportation across the Ottawa River was a ferry consisting of two small boats lashed together with paddle wheels powered by two horses walking on a treadle.

Colonel By had another Chaudière project in mind. He was impressed with the findings of Philemon Wright's son Ruggles, who had travelled to Norway and Sweden and brought back a new Scandinavian design of a "single-stick slide." This allowed timber rafts to travel down water slides without being disassembled. In 1829, Wright succeeded in building the first timber slide on the north shore, safely bypassing the Chaudière Falls. Colonel By copied his design and ordered the engineers to build a similar rafting channel on the south side of the falls, to prevent dangerous log jams and promote the timber trade.

Colonel By also put the engineers to work building proper steamboat landings at Richmond Landing and at the foot of Entrance Bay, for steamboats coming upriver from the Grenville Canal and Montréal.

That winter of 1826–1827, while Colonel By and his party and Thomas Mackay and his masons returned to Montréal, several small contractors were put to work along the canal route, taking advantage of the freeze to drain swampy areas and clear the trees and overburden down to at least 5 feet [1.5 metres] below water level, or to bedrock.

Completion of the Survey

Before returning to Montréal, Colonel By assigned civil engineer John Mactaggart and Clerk of Works Thomas Burrowes to check the route for conducting the Rideau River into the Ottawa by canal, from the entrance locks to the junction of the Rideau River at Hog's Back. Mactaggart had to survey most of the tract, 12 kilometres long by 6 kilometres wide, a region of dense forest and swamp.

The Royal Engineers went ahead to plan another bridge over the canal on the north side of what is now Confederation Square in

Figure 5.5. One of Mackay's Union Bridge arches, built in 1825-26, surrounded by lumber, 1880s.
Source: William James Topley, Library and Archives Canada, PA-012528.

downtown Ottawa. Designed to cross the canal and unite the upper and lower town, the Sappers' Bridge was built by the Sappers and Miners with the assistance of Mackay's skilled masons. The Sappers and Miners were also put to work clearing trees around Entrance Bay and up to what was first jokingly, and then conveniently, called "Bytown."[5]

In the spring of 1827, Colonel By and Samuel Clowes made a more extensive survey of the Rideau route from Kingston to Bytown. The Colonel wanted to see for himself the springtime swelling of the rivers, rapids, and waterfalls, and examine carefully the whole line of the canal, particularly the sites that would likely need potential dams and locks.

---

[5] According to army lore, the "town" was named after the Colonel in the course of a roisterous officers' banquet at Kingston, March 9, 1827.

At the same time, the Royal Engineers began to survey the townsite and divide it into lots. On his return, Colonel By named the town's major thoroughfares: Wellington Street, running west of Bank Street; Sparks and Rideau streets, on each side of Sappers' Bridge, from their proximity to the Locks; Sussex and York streets, beside a public market and above the wharf near Stirling's Brewery; and Daly Street and the neighbourhood of Sandy Hill, an area that the locals were now beginning to call Bytown, formerly the township of Nepean.

The Hull Mining Company

It was not all work and no play during the initial planning phase.

The local Algonquin people of the Gatineau Valley had been watching the arrival of the Rideau Canal builders with interest, and knew they were interested in minerals.

One day in 1826 an Algonquin hunter named Grey Bear told Philemon Wright's son Tiberius that there were valuable minerals, including iron, to be found north of Hull. He showed him some samples of reddish rock and said he would guide Tiberius to the site in exchange for a rifle.

An expedition was arranged, but it failed when the Algonquin women vigorously argued that showing the whites where to find precious rocks would cause the wildlife to flee from their territory. The Algonquins were already nervous about the Wrights' encroachment on their ancestral hunting grounds.

Philemon Wright scoffed at their concerns, and determined to search for the iron mine without the help of Grey Bear. So he persuaded some of the Rideau Canal team to join a prospecting expedition.

At a meeting that autumn in the Columbian Hotel, Thomas Mackay was elected head of the expedition, with Tiberius Wright, John Mactaggart—who had some training in geology—and fellow Scots Dr. Alexander Christie and Robert Drummond as partners. The men equipped themselves with food, tents, axes, and rock hammers, found another Algonquin guide, and mounted an exploratory expedition on horseback up the Gatineau River and into the bush.

It was not easy going in the thick forest. John Mactaggart had the worst of it, finding it was almost impossible to follow my companions, without getting myself bruised in all quarters, and perhaps some of my bones broken. They had got about a hundred yards before, and hallooed out to me to follow; I exerted myself to the utmost, but one of my legs getting into the cleft of a small tree, I was torn off my horse's back, and left among the briers again. Bawling out, they waited until I came up: none of them but Mr. Mackay, as good a Scotsman as lives, laughed, and I was almost inclined to curse him; the fellow being a good horseman, and used to the rough roads of Canada, could keep his seat on the saddle in a way, but the skin of his legs was partly peeled like my own, and his clothes torn in various places, but got lost in very deep brush, emerging with scratches and sprained ankles.

After travelling a great deal, riding but little, and being pulled down frequently as described, we got to a stream which the guide said had its origin in the iron-mountain. Proceeding up the stream to its source, we at last came upon the famous ore-bed; but through excessive fatigue, after having taken a little refreshment, I fell asleep, as did all my companions but one, the enterprising Lord of the Manor of Hull: he kindly let us take a nap for about an hour, when he roused us, much recovered. Traversing these wild mountains in all directions, we were much pleased with immense specimens of iron ore that everywhere appeared; and said to ourselves, that this place might be a muirkirk [a Scottish village where iron was smelted] at no very distant date.

Mr. Mackay wielded the hammer with Masonic skill, and laid the rich rocks open to inspection. These mountains seem to range over an extent of more than four miles [6.4 kilometres] square; at one place they are not more than two miles [3.2 kilometres] from the first Falls of the Gatineau, where a road might easily be constructed, and where machinery and engines could be erected at a very moderate rate, as waterpower may be had to any extent from the Falls.

The country all round is growing thickly with hard wood, particularly maple, which makes the best charcoal of any. From all I can think, this is the best place for an iron-manufactory in Canada.[6]

---

[6] John Mactaggart, *Three Years in Canada*. For more on the Forsyth Mine, see https://geo-outaouais.blogspot.com/2011/07/visite-guidee-de-la-mine-de-magnetite.html.

The expedition returned to Hull the following day, with a bag of samples that included minerals such as "iron feldspar, hornblende, native iron ore, granite of various colours, white, grey, and red, and a kind of stone very common in Canada, which we called Limestone granite; it being limestone that calcinates to powder, yet to all appearance by fracture granite. We also found marble blocks of great variety, white, green, and variegated."

Six weeks later, on December 28, Philemon Wright hosted a meeting in the Columbian Hotel to found an enterprise called the Hull Mining Company, to mine mine minerals from the iron, lead, marble, and granite in the surrounding mountains. Wright was appointed the president; Dr. A. J. Christie the secretary; Mr. John Mactaggart the engineer; and Thomas Mackay the managing director. Also joining the company were John Redpath, Tiberius Wright, Robert Drummond, John Burnett, James Gentle, and John Burrows.

The signed agreement recognized Wright's ownership of the land, and that the company would pay him 2 percent of the profits, and a bonus in the event that the company became productive.

The Hull Mining Company failed, even though the quality of the iron ore was excellent. The partners soon found that Montréal merchants, who imported a good deal of iron from England, would undercut the price of iron produced by the Company. So with the arrival of winter, the project went into permanent limbo.[7]

That was not the end of Ottawa Valley mining and prospecting. Philemon Wright's son Ruggles started to develop the site found by the 1826 expedition. The mine was a source of magnetite, an oxide of iron found in eulysite marble. In 1854, Ruggles sold the mine to Forsyth Company of Pittsburgh, Pennsylvania, as a source of iron for their smelters.

The operation of the Forsyth Mine was limited due to distance, but for a time the company shipped more than 2,000 tons of ore a year to Pittsburgh using Rideau Canal barges.

A grandson of Philemon Wright, Edward, also caught the mining bug, and in 1850 opened a silver-lead mine on the eastern shore of Lake Temiskaming. The Wright Mine produced some lead ore from a few tons of mineralization, but was soon abandoned.

---

[7] Joseph Tassé, *Philemon Wright, ou Colonisation et Commerce de Bois*, 50.

Fifty years later, Fred Rose, a railway blacksmith from Hull, discovered a silver deposit on the western shore of the lake that became one of the most prolific silver mining areas in the world. The Cobalt-Gowganda silver mining area—called "the birthplace of Canadian hard-rock mining"—would produce over 600 million troy ounces of silver, from veins "as wide as sidewalks."[8]

Contract Hassles

Thomas Mackay now had to turn his attention from mining speculation to negotiating the major contracts for canal masonry. The Ordnance was receptive—it was clear there was no one available in the Canadas who could match the all-weather skills, honesty, and experience of Mackay & Redpath.

Earlier in 1826, Major General Smyth wrote a memorandum to General Mann of the Ordnance stating his opinion that, "it will be found more economical and more expeditious to execute the greatest part, if not the whole, of the proposed Rideau Canal by contract"—as had been done with the Lachine Canal.

Indeed, inspired by the American experience on the Erie Canal, most of the Rideau Canal was eventually built by contractors. The basic engineering was performed by officers of the Royal Engineers, although sometimes they had to pitch in and get dirty. Colonel By and his colleagues were adamant that engineers trained at the Royal Military Academy were superior to civilian "civil" engineers.

This kind of assumption led Colonel Durnford in Montréal to make a bit of an amateur blunder. That December, he placed tender notices in the major Canadian and American newspapers. He noted that the canal would be divided into twenty-three sections, ranging in length from 1¾ miles to 29¼ miles (3 to 47 kilometres), each with its own contractor. No contractor was to be given more work than he was capable of completing in a two-year period.

The conditions were naive, and a recipe for disaster.

The Ordnance was clearly not used to public tendering, and expected to award contracts based on the lowest bids offered. When they received bids for the first eight entrance locks up from the Ottawa River, all of them were higher than Colonel By anticipated. They

---

[8] Potvin, *Sous le signe du quartz*, 51.

re-advertised the tender, and this time, an Erie Canal contractor, Walter Fenlon, of Montezuma, New York, submitted the lowest offer. Fenlon, whose experience consisted of damming mill ponds and digging channels in the Montezuma Swamp, described himself as a "civil engineer."

Colonel By was forced to follow the low-bid rule and recommend Fenlon to Dalhousie, but just as Dalhousie was about to sign with the Yankee, an exasperated Thomas Mackay submitted a lower bid, arguing quite correctly that Fenlon was not a masonry contractor, but simply an excavator.

By then wrote to Dalhousie of the change of plan, and urged Mackay to carry the letter to Québec City and present it to the Governor. His Lordship had personally inspected the Lachine Canal in May of 1826. He was particularly impressed with his fellow Scot Thomas Mackay's work—he called it "the finest masonry I ever saw."

Durnford was ordered to award the contract to the proven partnership of Mackay & Redpath, his favourites all along.

The first contract required Mackay to build eight entrance locks, rising 81 feet [24.6 metres] from the Ottawa River to a canal basin. The work was to be finished by 1829.

Mackay & Redpath were assisted by Redpath's wife, Janet McPhee, who stayed in Montréal preparing meticulous accounts of every penny spent by the partnership, which she forwarded to Colonel Durnford at the end of every month. Mackay would also forward his expenses to her and draw on cash reimbursements when needed.

Janet McPhee's contribution to the logistics of the Rideau Canal project was critical, since the Ordnance demanded strict listing of expenses. The account books show foodstuffs like salt pork and beef, tea, barley and sugar, tools like hammers and crowbars, mapping paper, horses, sleighs, soap, boots, gunpowder, ropes, chains, and such cold weather pick-me-ups as "Jamaican spirits" (rum) and "65 gallons of whisky."

Full Speed Ahead

In 1827, the Duke of Wellington was appointed commander-in-chief of the British Army. It was full speed ahead for the Rideau Canal.

Construction began at most stations in 1827, with major works at Entrance Bay; the highest point on Summit Lake (today's Big Rideau

Lake); and Kingston Mills. As far as possible, the work was done by contract.

A chastened Colonel By came to an understanding with Lord Dalhousie that henceforward they would consider each contract on its merits, not solely on cost. As for Redpath, his share of the contract was for the works at Jones Falls identified by the Royal Engineers. Their colleague Robert Drummond, who had built a lock at Sainte-Anne's Rapids and a drawbridge at Île-aux-Noix, was engaged in a separate contract for the Kingston Mills work. Mackay and Redpath also partnered on some work at Black Rapids and Long Island with Thomas Phillips and Andrew White, who had worked with them on the Lachine Canal.

Perhaps Colonel By's most unfortunate decision was to award a contract for a 40-foot-high [12-metre-high] dam and three locks at what is now Hog's Back Falls to the low bidder, Walter Fenlon. On May 4, 1827, he noted that, "Mr. Walter Fenlon's being much under all others, his tender has been accepted for all the said works, and he is to complete them in two years from the day of signing the contract."

As we shall see, awarding such a consolation prize to excavator Fenlon was not a wise move. Colonel By would narrowly escape death during the building of the dam, Fenlon would go bankrupt, and Thomas Mackay would have to be brought in to pick up the pieces.

In yet another bout of amateurism, the Ordnance constrained Colonel By with the initial order to build locks that everyone knew were too small to be practical. Colonel By argued rightly that to make the Rideau a route usable by military steamboats, the locks should be larger than 100 feet [30.5 metres] long by 22 feet [6.7 metres] wide. They had to be 150 feet [45.7 metres] long by 50 feet [15.2 metres] wide to accommodate boats up to 130 feet [40 metres] in length, as well as 10 feet [3 metres] deep (he later modified this to 5 feet [1.5 metres] deep).[9]

Clearing the Site of the Ottawa Locks

Still, the work had to proceed. Colonel By wanted to get the Ottawa Locks under way before winter, and ordered the Royal Engineers to clear the site of trees and rubble. French-Canadian axe men and

---

[9] According to Ken Watson, today's locks, at 134 feet long and 33 feet wide, can handle a maximum boat length of 113 feet (however, only boats 110 feet or less are allowed).

lumberjacks were the best at this sort of job, since many had cleared land for their own farms with axes and brute force.[10]

Mackay gladly complied with By's order to proceed with the initial stages of lock building, as he was itching to get at the work. He had already found good seams of limestone along the newly exposed cliff east of the valley. The Colonel approved without question his suggestion that it was as good as nearly identical stone floated across the river from Philemon Wright's quarry.

With contracts in hand, Mackay also acquired Lot 27 on newly surveyed Wellington Street and ordered his workmen to build him a frame house close to the lock site. He planned to bring his family upriver from Montréal in the spring.

Showing some talent as an amateur architect, Mackay also built for Colonel By and family a comfortable two-storey country house, on the heights behind the present Chateau Laurier Hotel in what is today Major's Hill Park, named after Colonel By's successor, Major Daniel Bolton, who moved into the house in 1832.

Figure 5.6. The Ottawa Locks in 1869, showing part of the quarry on the east side where Mackay was able to extract superior seams of limestone.
Source: William Notman, McCord Museum I-38066.

---

[10] Mactaggart, *Three Years in Canada*, vol. 2, 103–104.

Figure 5.7. Colonel By's house, 1841.
Source: Thomas Burrowes, Library and Archives Canada, MIKAN 2895237.

Mackay at times partook of Colonel By's hospitality in the house, as did his superior Colonel Durnford. Durnford's daughter Mary recalled that her father visited the Rideau Canal works every year, "affording Colonel By the benefit of his advice. They were on a scale of magnificence hitherto not attempted in Canada; which since that period has been so abounding in grand and varied provincial outlays. Colonel By enjoyed from his wife a handsome private income, and his showy hospitable mode of living made him universally popular and beloved."[11]

On November 17, 1826, Colonel By announced to Nicholas Sparks and others that he was vesting 88 acres [35.6 hectares] of land as necessary for the construction of the canal, 200 feet [61 metres] on each side of the waterway, as it was built south from the Ottawa Locks to Hog's Back Falls. Sparks, Philemon Wright's son-in-law, owned Lot C, comprising much of what is today downtown Ottawa.

Early in 1827, the Colonel attempted to purchase from Sparks a wider swath of land south of Barrack Hill (the steepest slope of which

---

[11] Mary Durnford, *Family Recollections of Lieut. General Elias Walker Durnford*.

actually extended as far as a midpoint between Queen and Albert streets). His plan was to excavate a moat facing a fortress on the Hill that would protect the canal's entrance.

Sparks demanded £600 an acre, a price Colonel By turned down as too high—he also knew he would soon be given authority to expropriate the land. Indeed, on February 17 of that year, the Upper Canada Assembly passed the *Rideau Canal Act*, giving the Ordnance the "power to take land for the needs and purposes of the Rideau Canal," and "empowering the officer in charge to take possession of or expropriate all such lands." In practice, if a mutual agreement could not be made, an arbitrated settlement would ensue after the completion of the canal.[12]

With that nuisance out of the way, Colonel By continued to urge the Ordnance to give him the go-ahead for a canal wide enough to accommodate steamboats, rather than the Durham boats, barges, and trade canoes then in use. To resolve the impasse, Dalhousie set up a committee headed by Lieutenant-General Sir James Kempt, Lieutenant Governor of Nova Scotia. They compromised on locks 134 feet [40.8 metres] long, by 33 feet [10.1 metres]) wide, with 5 feet [1.5 metres] of water over the sills.

Colonel By gave Mackay a green light to dismantle and widen the three nearly built masonry locks, started in 1827, in order to accommodate the greater width, length, and depth. The way was now clear to move forward with the great work of the Rideau Canal entry locks.

---

[12] Brault, *Ottawa Old and New*. Sparks was dispossessed of eighty-eight acres during the spring of 1827 without remuneration. It would be almost twenty years before he was able to get a satisfactory amount for his property, with the help of Thomas Mackay.

CHAPTER 6

1827: Canal Cornerstones

Our master mason is Mackay, from Montreal, he who built the locks of the Lachine Canal, from the plans of poor Burnett, the engineer. Mac is a good practical mason, and scorns to slim any work: this is to my liking, as I cannot suffer sliming and shuffling on any account.

—John Mactaggart, *Three Years in Canada*

Pushed into action by American moves to build a canal from Albany, New York, to Lake Erie and Lake Ontario, the Duke of Wellington was determined to set the Rideau project in motion without delay. His instructions were soon transmitted to the field.

That spring, Colonel By began advertising in newspapers, offering work for labourers, masons, and carpenters. William Lyon Mackenzie's *Colonial Advocate*, York, published this letter on April 12:

> I can offer constant work for four years, winter and summer, to stone cutters and miners; and that to such as have the means of building a house 30 feet [9 metres] square by 98 feet [30 metres] deep, I can give a village lot, 66 feet [20 metres] front by 198 feet [60 metres] deep; and to keep down the imposition of the neighbouring stores, the workman may take pork, flour, rum, gunpowder and tools out of the king's magazines, by paying the price they cost government.
>
> The miners I divide into small parties, and pay them by the cubic yard, according to the nature of the rock, which is in most parts grey limestone.

> The masons are paid by the superficial foot, & I conceive there is sufficient work on the Rideau Canal to employ at least 1000 miners, and the same number of stone cutters, as I have 50 locks to execute in four years. I shall also require a great number of labourers and excavators, but fear I cannot give them employment during the winter.
>
> As the work is already commenced at Nepean Point, near Hull on the Ottawa, men may obtain immediate work on their arrival there.[1]

Arriving back in Bytown, Colonel By found that people seeking work were pouring into the canal site daily. Many of the labourers lived in tents or built themselves rude log shanties, while the lucky ones found lodging in three newly constructed civilian barracks on George Street, built by the Ordnance.

Figure 6.1. Log shanties along the canal, 1830.
Source: James Pattison Cockburn, Library and Archives Canada.

---

[1] Before moving to York, William Lyon Mackenzie worked for a time with Dr. Christie on the *Montreal Herald*, and also for the Lachine Canal company.

Dr. Christie later had harsh words to say about the wooden barracks, calling them totally inadequate to meet the suffering faced by civilian labourers during their first harsh winter in Bytown. He argued that Colonel By proceeded too rashly with the canal, failed to engage competent workers, and enticed skilled tradesmen to the site without providing proper housing or advising them of the conditions they would encounter.

An Amphitheatre of Activity

Shortly after the ice broke in 1827, Thomas Mackay and John Redpath were back at Entrance Bay with a party of their own masons.

As the hot spring sun melted the remaining slush, the site for the Ottawa Locks came to life—an amphitheatre of bustle and activity—with the rasping of saws and the clanking of pickaxes and the high-pitched singing of chisels on stone.

Colonel By had entrusted excavation of the canal gorge to an Irish contractor named John Pennyfeather. After his labourers had removed trees and boulders, then 21,000 cubic feet [594 cubic metres] of clay to dam the Ottawa River from the lock works, he found that hidden springs were filling in the newly dug trenches in the gorge, causing their sides to collapse. When two workers tragically died during blasting operations, the unfortunate Pennyfeather quit the job and returned to Montréal.[2]

Absent Pennyfeather, Colonel By then contracted Mackay & Redpath to take on the work of excavating as well. Mackay's foreman John Robertson pulled together a new crew of navvies, who were soon fighting the constant springs and drainage from the beaver swamp above. One lock wall collapsed from the water pressure, but none of the workers were hurt. The crew eventually channelled the leaks into a drain through masonry arches underneath the lock bottoms.

While Mackay & Redpath were managing a chaotic construction site, Colonel By engaged Walter Fenlon to clear the section south of the beaver meadow, on the north side of Dow's Great Swamp, today's Dow's Lake. That job completed, Fenlon was sent to begin

---

[2] Pennyfeather was back in Bytown in 1829, and served on the committee charged with the construction of the first Catholic church.

work on the 41-foot-high [12.5-metre-high] Three Rock Rapid dam at Hog's Back, where the Rideau Canal was to diverge from the Rideau River, which flowed northeast to Rideau Falls.

Back in Montréal in late May, Colonel By's plans began to take shape. Samuel Clowes's original idea for a towpath along the canal was not at all practical. The only towpath that the Colonel built was from the Ottawa Locks to Hog's Back to move barges without the use of steam tugs in that easy section. And with only a few small hamlets from Bytown to Kingston, a canal suited for steamboats was essential.

By the summer, he had made a new reckoning of costs—£474,844—and estimated he would require about six thousand men for the canal enterprise.

Colonel By sent his report to England in the care of Lieutenant Henry Pooley, who travelled to London to present the plans for all Ordnance works at that time. Pooley also took with him the Colonel's formal request for larger locks to accommodate steamboats. His plans were reviewed by a board of senior officers, headed by Major-General Alexander Bryce. They were generally approved, with some minor modifications.

The Royal Sappers and Miners

To support the great work, the Duke of Wellington had already ordered a new company of the Royal Sappers and Miners (eighty-one men) to be raised in England, expressly for service on the Rideau Canal works. The 15th company arrived in Bytown June 1, 1827, and were put under the command of Captain Victor.

Colonel By was so pleased with the men, and found them so useful, that he petitioned the Ordnance for another company, the 7th, who arrived on September 17 and were placed under the command of Captain Savage. Both companies lived under canvas at Richmond Landing until Mackay completed three wood-frame residences for them on what became known as Barrack Hill, today's Parliament Hill.

The barracks were smaller than those at Fort Lennox, and partially wood frame instead of stone, since the soldiers were only expected to stay for three years. Costing £499 each, the buildings were completed by June. Each measured 108 feet by 70 feet [33 metres by 21 metres], and contained sixteen rooms on the ground floor and a long garret for single soldiers and families on the second floor, where privacy was created by hanging curtains. Over half of the two companies

Figure 6.2. One of Mackay's buildings on Barrack Hill.
Source: John By, Library and Archives Canada.

of 162 men were married, and between thirty and forty wives and numerous children accompanied the men.

To help pass the winter more agreeably, and to raise money for charity, the families of this outpost of empire later fitted a room in one of the barracks with a stage. On February 6, 1837, the birth of amateur theatre in Ottawa took place, as Bytownians flocked to see *The Village Lawyer*, a two-act farce first performed in 1795 in Drury Lane and at the Haymarket Theatre in London. The receipts were given out to various ministers and priests for the care of poor parishioners.

One of the barracks was first used as a twenty-bed hospital for Royal Ordnance and Commissariat employees. It could also be partitioned for use by canal labourers if needed. A stone officer's barrack was later added to the west for the Royal Engineers, with a brig for military miscreants.

When the barracks proved too small to house everyone, Colonel By ordered a cookhouse built at the front of each building, to free up space for additional rooms. He also engaged Mackay to construct two stone bakehouses, which were leased to local bakers to supply canal workers with bread at a low price.

One of the barracks was lost on January 5, 1832, when a fire broke out in the mess kitchen. It quickly spread to the entire building in a matter of minutes. It was not rebuilt.

Barrack Hill was encircled by a stockade of sharpened cedar posts 3.7 metres high, with a locked gate and guardpost close to the

Figure 6.3. Rideau Canal entrance with three barracks, 1833.
Source: Henry Pooley, Library and Archives Canada.

eastern edge of the cliff. A tall flagstaff signalled that the site was now a permanent military post. In the longer term, the Ordnance intended to install a star-shaped fortress to guard the entrance locks of the Rideau Canal.

The soldiers helped coordinate Mackay's canal work over a three-year period. They built paths and roads, finished the truss bridge linking Bytown and Hull, and laid out the Byward Market in Lower Town.

Shortly after their arrival, they were called upon to help fight a fire that broke out in Entrance Valley, and burned up some of the timber to be used for lock gates. The Sappers and Miners also acted as a police force, to keep some control over temporary labourers, as Thomas Mackay began construction of the first three Ottawa Locks.

The Commissariat

Colonel By also asked for bids from MacKay and Robert Drummond to build a commissary on the west side of the locks, and an office for the Royal Engineers on the east. Mackay's bid of £880 was accepted

Figure 6.4. Royal Sappers and Miners at work.

as lower than Drummond's. His Commissariat, which is still standing, today houses the Bytown Museum, Ottawa's oldest existing stone structure. It is still admired for the craftsmanship of the Scottish stonemasons. Mackay's crew erected it in only six months, using local timber and limestone from the surrounding cliffs. They built it like a stone barn, fastening the joints with wooden dowels, not nails. By June of 1827 the walls were up, and it was finished by August.

The Commissariat used the ground floor as storage space for provisions formerly stored in Hull. It was first filled with barrels of salt pork and rum, and sacks of peas and flour, as well as the hardware and blasting powder needed by Mackay's masons. The second floor housed offices for the tendering and letting of contracts, and the ordering of tools and materials. The Commissariat accountants and clerks occupied the third floor. In 1830, a vault with 3-foot-thick [1-metre-thick] stone walls was added to the south-west corner of the ground floor for security and safekeeping of the barrels of cash needed to pay the bills.

Figure 6.5. Mackay's Commissariat, Ottawa's oldest building.[3]
Source: Bytown Museum, under the licence Creative Commons Attribution-Share Alike 4.0 International license (https://creativecommons.org/licenses/by-sa/4.0/deed.en).

At the same time, Colonel By hired Robert Drummond to build a similar headquarters building on the east side of the locks to serve as offices for himself and the staff of the Royal Engineers and the Ordnance.[4]

Completed in 1828, the ground floor of this building, no longer standing, also served for a time as a workshop for carpenters, smiths,

---

[3] On June 27, 1952, the Women's Canadian Historical Society of Ottawa, who had founded the Bytown Historical Museum in 1917, took possession of the Commissariat as their new Bytown Museum.

[4] This building was later demolished to make way for railway tracks leading to a bridge to Hull.

1827: Canal Cornerstones   99

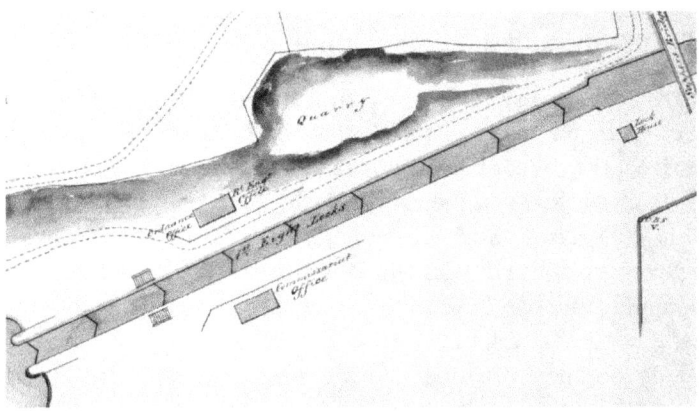

Figure 6.6. Royal Engineers' chart of the Ottawa Locks with Mackay's Quarry, Commissariat, and Ordnance Office.
Source: Library and Archives Canada.

and stonecutters working on the gates of the Ottawa Locks. With furnishings, the final cost of the two buildings came to £2,199.

By July of 1827, Mackay had prepared the ground for the masonry of the first eight locks. In mid-July, Colonel By invited Mackay, John Burrows, and John Mactaggart to accompany Lt. Froome on a military survey party on a birchbark canoe trip over the entire route of the Rideau canal system to Kingston. The trip was in company with fourteen officers, soldiers, and Indigenous canoemen.

Burrows kept a daily log of this adventure, running rock-strewn rapids, hacking out portages, and swatting mosquitoes. Here's a sample:

> July 23—At one o'clock we proceeded up the rapids of Long Island, which are three miles [4.8 kilometres] in length and have a rise of twenty-four feet [7.3 metres] in that distance.
> We had to wade through the rapids the whole distance. We arrived at the head of the rapids at 6 o'clock and there encamped for the night.
> July 27—To-day it came on to rain very heavy and the canoes began to fill with water. Mr. Burrows went to shift the rum keg and upset the canoe, and all of us got a ducking in the river.[5]

---

[5] Library and Archives Canada; John Burrows fonds; sketch book and diary.

The First Stone and the Cornerstone

By early August 1827, John Redpath and Robert Drummond were hard at work on their contracts at Jones Falls and Kingston Mills. Thomas Mackay went back to his lock building at Bytown, where he and the Colonel awaited the visit of Royal Navy Captain John Franklin and his colleague, naval surgeon John Richardson. The explorers were voyaging down the Ottawa after a three-year expedition to chart the Coppermine River and over 3,000 kilometres of previously unmapped coast along the North-West Passage.

Late on the 15th, in blistering August heat, Franklin's party landed at the newly built wharf in Entrance Bay. Colonel By escorted them up to Barrack Hill, where they were wined and dined and spent the night.

The following morning, while Mackay's crew prepared a two-ton block of limestone, Colonel By showed Franklin the progress of works as far as Hog's Back, and visited Rideau Falls. After lunch, they descended the path to the canal workings, where at 3:10 p.m., Captain Franklin performed a Masonic ceremony and laid the first foundation stone of the Rideau Canal entrance locks.

At the moment the stone was lowering into its bed—in the trough of the inverted arch at the third lock from the river—black powder explosions were set off on the heights, to imitate artillery, and then Mackay's foreman John Robertson broached a puncheon of rum, which was given to the workmen.

A *Montreal Herald* reporter was on the scene, and breathlessly wrote:

> I have this evening to communicate to you one of the most important events that ever occurred in the Canadas—an event which will doubtless form an era in the history of this country for ages to come. It was no less than the depositing of the first stone of the locks of the Rideau Canal ... to the tap of Mackay's trowel young Capt. Franklin put the one-and-one-quarter ton stone to bed while the garrison band played and loud "huzzas" went up from the excavation in a strange and wild setting.

The following month, Governor-in-Chief Lord Dalhousie, performed an even more moving ceremony—the laying of the cornerstone of the Ottawa Locks.

Figure 6.7. The Dalhousies arrive by fourteen-man rowing barge from Montréal, 1827.[6]
Source: John Crawford Young, Library and Archives Canada.

On a warm Indian Summer evening of September 26, 1827, Dalhousie and his countess arrived at Wrightstown on a magnificently decked out batteau propelled by fourteen oarsmen.

After this splendid entrance, with flags flying, the Dalhousies were given a grand reception and their usual best bed in Philemon Wright's inn. The next day they inspected the progress of the works,

---

[6] Capt. John Crawford Young of the 79th regiment was aide-de-camp to Lord Dalhousie from October 1826 to June 1827.

and also bravely navigated the seven spans over the Chaudière Falls, including the new "Swing Bridge" made of ropes stretched across the Great Cauldron.

As Dalhousie recalled:

> Lady Dalhousie did walk across the rope bridge on that day—even that trembling and nervous part of it, the Suspension Bridge—which in fact Col. By himself had not ventured to do, until Lady D. called me back to accompany her over. I admit it was a bold thing for a Lady, but I was satisfied before of the safety of it.

Dalhousie also inspected the progress of the span across the canal, later called Sappers' Bridge, that was to link Rideau Street in Lower Town with the footpath (now Sparks Street) that led around the base of Barrack Hill to Upper Town. Aided by Thomas Mackay's masons, the bridge was finished that December.

Dalhousie and Colonel By then toured the canal works on horseback from the entrance locks to Black Rapids, 10 kilometres upstream from the Hog's Back Falls. The next morning, the Governor discussed land claims with the surveyor-general, laid out two new townships to be settled by immigrants working on the canal, and "satisfied many very anxious petitioners."

Then on September 29, at 3 p.m., Lord Dalhousie and party met at Colonel By's house and proceeded downhill to the canal works, where Mackay's masons had erected a giant wooden tripod with a

Figure 6.8. Lady Dalhousie on the rope bridge, 1827.
Source: R. M. Bouchette, 1827, Library and Archives Canada.

block and tackle system, from which was suspended a massive block of stone weighing nearly two tons.

At exactly 3:10 p.m., the age-old Masonic ceremony was ready. At a nod from Dalhousie, Thomas Mackay struck the stone with "three mystic blows of the hammer." Dalhousie then proceeded to lay the true cornerstone of the first canal lock, under the level of the river on the east side.

As the stone was gently lowered, baptizing the Rideau Canal, the masons set off a volley of explosives on the surrounding heights, in lieu of artillery. Mackay's foreman, John Robertson, then broached a puncheon of rum grog to be enjoyed by all.

That evening, the Dalhousies were feted on Barrack Hill with bonfires and general merriment. It was a memorable occasion for the viceregal couple:

> We went to dinner at Colonel By's, and at dark were agreeably surprised in seeing prodigious bonfires lighted on all the prominent points and headlands up to the Chaudière Falls. When we took leave we were marched through a double line of the people each holding a Cedar torch with bark of birch giving a blazing light, and as we passed all followed on. We heard by some, muttered loud enough to be heard "Long life to your Honour, and good luck wid you" another had a bad fiddle and played the "God Save the King" as if he were going to sleep on it—and another had a fife on which he made also a very lame attempt; but when we put off in our Batteaux, all gave three Glorious cheers, and made a general fire of the torches—there was no drunken man there, all admirably contrived and well behaved.
>
> The scene was quite magnificent, and as we passed up the river it became still more spirited, by the shouting hurrahs on every point & fire, returned to them by the loud mixture of the Canadian Boat Song from Finlay and my 14 rowers. The whole river was illuminated so as to have easily read a book and a bright full moon in all her splendour stood high in Heaven over the Grand Cataract without any exaggeration so finely that it might have been imagined Col. By had chosen the moment a month before.

After receiving congratulatory addresses the following morning, the glamorous Dalhousies returned downriver to Montréal on their viceregal barge, and the masons returned to work.

Tots of rum and twists of tobacco served as fuel for the hard-working craftsmen, particularly during the winter months, when work continued on sites operated by Thomas Mackay at Bytown, John Redpath at Jones Falls, and Robert Drummond at Kingston Mills.

Mackay treated his masons well. John Mactaggart, Colonel By's clerk of works, noted that Mackay,

> the master mason, was the only person whose ideas were valued. He was not only the best mason in the colony, but one of the most sensible and worthy of men. Very active among the quarriers and at the bridge, he saw every block cut to its proper mould. The artisans were well looked after; their master found them the best food and lodging the dismal place could afford, and grog was served round once, and sometimes twice a day. Food supplies included fresh beef, salt pork, flour, salt and tea, as well as plugs of tobacco.[7]

The men responded in kind. Mackay wrote in 1837 that during the first five years he spent canal building, he employed from a hundred to three hundred men. Two thirds were from Ireland, and he never experienced any difficulty in "keeping them quiet." During the second five-year period, he employed from forty to fifty men and "never saw or heard of a quarrel among them."[8]

Mackay was a big man, and hard to cross. John Mactaggart describes an incident coming up the Ottawa River past a village called the Grand Brulé, when one of the voyageur porters got into an argument with Mackay about carrying some luggage. When voices were raised, "the whole village turned out, as if they would devour us at once; but Mac, knowing their nature, lifted up the porter, and gave him a *shake* or two before them, when the whole crowd quietly retired."

"Mac" was a hands-on chief. At the ceremony marking the completion of the Sappers' Bridge in 1827, the Royal Sappers and Miners were having trouble inserting the final keystone of the Bridge. Mackay immediately shouted out, "Stop a little, and I'll fit it in its place."

---

[7] John Mactaggart, *Three Years in Canada*, vol. 1, 338–341.
[8] Brault, *Ottawa Old and New*.

1827: Canal Cornerstones 105

Figure 6.9. Sappers' Bridge, Lower Bytown from Barrack Hill, 1845.
Source: Thomas Burrowes fonds, Archives of Ontario, C 1-0-0-0-11.

He came forward and placed the stone with the greatest apparent ease. Apparently, Colonel By, who had a tendency to look down his nose at mere "civil engineers," was mightily impressed.[9]

---

[9] The first recorded child of European descent born in Bytown, on July 5, 1827, was Thomas Mackay Robertson, the son of Mackay's foreman.

CHAPTER 7

How to Build a Canal

King Solomon drafted labour out of all Israel—80,000 men to work in the hill country cutting stone, also 70,000 men to carry the stones. There were 3300 men to supervise the workers. Solomon commanded them to quarry large blocks of the finest stone for the foundation of the Temple. Then the craftsmen of Solomon and Hiram and workers from Byblos cut and prepared the timber and stone for the building of the temple.

—1 Kings 5:15—18

The Ottawa Locks have been described as "a sculpture in stone." Or, as UNESCO says, "a masterpiece of creative human genius." They were also a fine example of masonry that was state-of-the-art for its time.

The Rideau Canal locks we see today are a shrine to the goddess of progress, and in some ways celebrate the dawn of the Industrial Revolution and the coming of the age of steam.

As "form ever follows function," the locks were plain, practical, and useful. But they were also beautiful, with bragging rights. The graceful curves of the entry lock on the Ottawa River were carefully carved from limestone for an aesthetic purpose—to show off the skills of Thomas Mackay's masons.

Mackay's craftsmen used simple, time-honoured methods of masonry construction, adapted to the Ottawa Valley climate. As winter approached, they drilled the stones laboriously by hand, then at freeze-up they poured water into the holes. The expanding ice naturally split the rock. In the late winter and early spring, the masons then chiselled the stones to the desired shape and size.

The Ottawa lock site became a cacophony of noise—the thump of wooden mallets and the clang of iron on stone, the rasp of the stone drills, and the rattle of wheelbarrows, as men moved the rubble to the side, all punctuated by the growl of foreman Robertson.

At that point, workers started hoisting the huge finished stones onto skids and dragging them to the lock pits, where they were hauled up planks using block and tackle. Then they manhandled the stones into their proper positions using crowbars and wooden mallets. As the locks grew higher, they had to use hand-operated winches and derricks that squealed like stuck pigs as they raised the finished stone.

With the help of the Royal Engineers, Mackay's carpenters then built wooden lock gates and inserted them into channels in the stone walls, angled into the current, which forced the gates of the chamber tightly closed, to keep water usage to a minimum. They also built sluices and valves into the gates and walls to let water in and out of the chamber.

This type of angled and mitred lock gate may have been invented by Leonardo da Vinci in 1497, when he was engaged by the Duke of Milan to build six locks on the Naviglio Grande, a canal built to bring

Figure 7.1. An overdressed Mackay and Colonel By, 1826.
Source: C. W. Jefferys, Library and Archives Canada, C-073703.

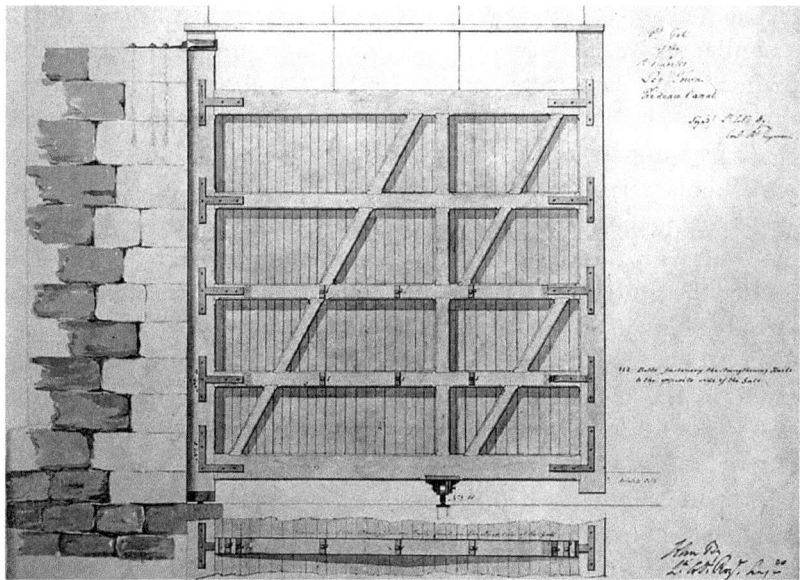

Figure 7.2. Colonel By's drawing of a lock gate.
Source: Library and Archives Canada.

marble to the city to build the Duomo cathedral. The locks are still in use today.

Scottish Technology

Some of the technologies used by the Rideau Canal contractors were radical innovations brought into being by the Scots—the steam engine being the prime example. Inventor James Watt had worked on the Clyde and Tay canal as a civil engineer to raise capital to perfect and patent his more efficient steam engine. In 1769, he was awarded a patent for the first practical device—a ten-horsepower machine that produced continuous rotary motion without overheating. This was the major invention that ushered in the Industrial Revolution.

A generation later, in 1802, William Symington used Watt's engine to power the world's first practical steamboat, the *Charlotte Dundas*, towing barges on the canal between Glasgow and Edinburgh. By 1823, there were seventy-two steamers on the Clyde.

In 1809, steam transport came to Canada, as John Molson of Montréal launched his *Accommodation*, the first steamboat on the

St. Lawrence, to ease the voyage to Québec. In 1813, his *Swiftsure* began a regular service between the two towns, and proved useful in supplying the army in the War of 1812. In 1816, Loyalist John Ward started the first steamer service on the Saint John River with the *General Smith*, a sixty-passenger "floating palace" that could travel at a speed of six knots upriver to Fredericton.

During the Canal's planning stages, Colonel By had insisted that the waterway must be wide enough to accommodate steamboats. To service the growing army of workers on the canal, steamboats were already being used to take supplies up the Ottawa River to the Long Sault rapids, site of the construction of the Carillon and Grenville canals by the Royal Staff Corps, where they were portaged above the rapids and loaded onto Philemon Wright's steamboat, the *Union of the Ottawa*, bound for Bytown.

At the southern end of the canal, near Kingston, Robert Drummond would later build a small twelve-horsepower paddle-wheeler called *Pumper*, fitted with a steam pump to speed up excavation of the locks. With the completion of the canal in 1832, *The Pumper*, renamed the *Rideau* for the occasion, would take Colonel By, along with some friends and family, on an inaugural seven-day cruise to Bytown. Two years later, with the opening of the Grenville Canal, the entire Ottawa River system up to Bytown was navigable by steamboat from Montréal.

The other advanced technologies used by Thomas Mackay were more mundane. To build his frost-resistant lock basins in the Lachine and Rideau Canals, he employed the latest advances in limestone mortar and masonry, taking full advantage of local materials found on or near the site.

The Concrete Revolution

The Egyptians used lime mortar as a plastering material on the pyramids six thousand years ago, although there is evidence such mortar was used at Göbekli Tepe twelve thousand years ago.

The true Concrete Revolution began over two thousand years ago, when the Romans discovered that limestone, when roasted to a powder and then reconstituted with water, produced a material that would harden with age. They used lime-based mortar extensively to revolutionize architecture, and they knew the difference between use under water and with dry stone. Roman architect Vitruvius gave these basic guidelines for lime mortar mixes:

> When the lime is slaked, let it be mingled with the sand in such a way that if it is pit sand, three of sand and one of lime is poured in; but if the same is from the river or sea, two of sand and one of lime is thrown together. For in this way there will be the right proportion of the mixture and blending.[1]

Regular mortars made with only lime and sand draw carbon dioxide from the air to harden, and can absorb or leak water. To use mortars in or under water (hydraulic mortars) for cisterns, fish-ponds, aqueducts, and canals, the Romans added a fine "pozzolan," such as brick dust or volcanic ash. Mackay used dried clay powder for his "water cement."

In 1756, Leeds engineer John Smeaton rediscovered this technology and developed perhaps the first hydraulic lime product containing clay as a pozzolan. He used this clay-lime mortar mixture to rebuild the famous Eddystone Lighthouse in Cornwall. In 1771, he also constructed a bridge over the Tay in Thomas Mackay's home town of Perth. The bridge is still standing, solid proof against flood and frost and ice.

Smeaton's technology was well known to civil engineers in the US as well. Erie Canal engineer Canvass White was using locally produced "natural hydraulic cement" as early as 1818.

Before beginning the construction of the Ottawa Locks, Mackay the perfectionist made plain to Colonel By his need for fine limestone and clay to make hydraulic cement. Local limestone would do. Philemon Wright's son Ruggles was engaged to build a lime kiln in the Wrightstown quarry in today's Lac Leamy.[2] To create calcium oxide, or quicklime, Wright's kiln roasted limestone dust to above 825 °C (1,517 °F), to drive off the carbon dioxide (CO_2). Mackay also got his fine clay and sand nearby, from the mouth of the Gatineau River.

Mackay was delighted with the product, and so was the Ordnance. According to Lieutenant Frome of the Royal Engineers,

---

[1] Vitruvius, *De Architectura*, trans. Frank Granger (London: Heinemann, 1931), Book II, V.

[2] Beginning in 1889, the quarry was operated by the Canada Cement Company, Canada's first producer of portland cement. Before that time portland cement was imported from England in wooden barrels.

Hull cement was made from a stone quarried on the opposite side of the Ottawa, which, being burnt and ground very fine, proved a better water-cement than some obtained from the States, and far superior to the Harwich (English) cement, which was nearly spoilt before it reached the Canal.

According to his friend John Mactaggart, Colonel By's clerk of works, Mackay was a perfectionist—a "good practical mason" who scorned "to slim any work." His reluctance to cut corners can also be seen in the underlying design of the Ottawa Locks.

Colonel By's specifications were similar to those of the Lachine Canal. The walls were to be made of a cut stone facing of coursed masonry backed by a wall of rubble masonry. A 3-foot-thick [1-metre-thick] clay puddle wall was then placed against the rubble to form a barrier impervious to water. The masonry of the walls was to be 8 feet [2.4 metres] thick at the base, narrowing to a 5-foot-thick [1.5-metre-thick] masonry wall at the top.

Due to the wet nature of the ground, and the constant draining from the creek down the valley, Mackay's masons started their work by building at bedrock a foundation of macadamized stone bonded with hot lime mortar. They then constructed round masonry arches—the same as those used in Roman aqueducts and Romanesque cathedrals—to support the gently sloping floor of each lock basin, with its weight of water.

The masons sealed the arches, the lock floor, and the side walls with concrete grout. They did this by first boring holes in the lock stone at regular intervals. They then "pressure fed" the grouting, taking advantage of gravity, pouring hydraulic cement slurry into a funnel and down a tube stretching about 4 metres from the top of the lock. This gave them a solid mass of virtually waterproof and frost-resistant masonry. (Not completely frost-proof. As late as 1840, Colonel By recommended annual spring and summer regrouting of the Canal locks with Ruggles Wright's cement.)

Local materials, including clean quartz sand from the mouth of the Gatineau River, also enabled Mackay to use a state-of-the-art road-building technology invented by Scottish engineer John Loudon McAdam around 1820—macadamizing. Before the advent of asphalt paving, macadamizing created very serviceable roads that could be easily repaired.

One of Mackay's invoices to the Ordnance shows a £356 bill for "macadamizing" the paths along each side of the lock walls to drain water away from the masonry.

To macadamize the paths, the masons used single-sized crushed stone layers of small angular pieces compacted thoroughly, covered by binding layers of sand and fine stone dust. They raised the path slightly in the centre so water drained off both sides.

Mackay's iron hardware was also state-of-the-art, some of it custom-made in his own smithy under the Sappers' Bridge, using iron bars from Bell's Foundry (Les Forges du Saint-Maurice), near Three Rivers, Lower Canada. As Colonel By wrote to his superior, Colonel Elias Durnford, "The Iron of this Country is much superior to the English ... my preference arises from the Metal in this Country being melted with Charcoal, and absorbing a portion of the Carbon, renders it tough and more malleable than the English Iron which is melted with Sea Coal."

Figure 7.3. Rideau Canal crab.[3]
Source: Friends of the Rideau Canada. Courtesy Ken Watson.

---

[3] These are the lock openers still in use today, along with the swing bar crab system, the push bar crab system, and the electric-hydraulic system.

Iron chains were procured from the Kingston Dockyard. For the rest of the lock hardware, such as hinges for the lock gates, as well as the endless chain and crab system with hand winches, Colonel By's new clerk of works—Mactaggart's replacement, Nicol Hugh Baird—made sketches that the carpentry shop of the Royal Engineers made into full-scale wooden patterns. These were then forwarded to the Bell foundry in Three Rivers for casting.

Baird, who had worked on Thomas Telford's Union Canal in Scotland, also kept an eagle eye on the work performed by Mackay's masons, and in some cases, recommended the work be redone, for example, in the case of a pier that was a half-inch [12.7 millimetres] off true. Mackay had the stone redressed.

Finally, when testing the great stone stairway of eight locks, Mackay found that when the sluices were opened, the water came through with such force that it pushed some large stones out of place from the sill. After consulting with Redpath and Colonel By, he remedied the problem by using heavier sills and bolting the stones together with heavy iron straps.

Once repairs were done in September 1831, Philemon Wright's steamboat *Union* had the honour of being the first vessel to pass through the Ottawa Locks.

With Mackay's completion of the Ottawa Locks, the total expenditure had risen from the estimated £58,889 to a total of £70,643—money well spent. In his 1832 report to His Majesty's Board of Ordnance, Joseph Hagerman stated:

> The excellence of the workmanship and the superior construction of the locks and dams require no praise. They speak for themselves, and are the subject of much admiration, and in the opinion of those most competent to just such works, exceed anything of this kind in any parts of the world.

By way of comparison, Thomas Mackay's eight Ottawa locks were narrower and steeper than Thomas Telford's Neptune's Staircase, a flight of eight locks built on the Caledonian Canal in Scotland in 1811:

Neptune's Staircase
Length   180 feet [55 metres]
Width   40 feet [12 metres]
Fall   64 feet [20 metres]

Ottawa Locks
Length   134 feet [40.8 metres]
Width   33 feet [10.1 metres]
Fall   80 feet [24.4 metres]

The Caledonian Canal finally opened in 1822, having taken an extra twelve years to complete, and cost £910,000.

The Duke of Wellington Takes Charge

On January 22, 1828, the Duke of Wellington resigned as commander-in-chief of the British Army to take the reins of power as prime minister.

Wellington's term was marked by the granting of greater civil rights to Catholics. In 1811, Catholic soldiers were given freedom of worship and his 1829 *Catholic Relief Act* passed with a majority of 105. Many Tories voted against the *Act*, and it passed only with the help of the Whigs and under Wellington's threat to resign if the King did not give Royal Assent.

The nickname "Iron Duke" originates from his term of office. It refers to his resolute political will, and his hard Old Tory sentiments against political reform.

Wellington would serve for almost three years, until November 16, 1830, not coincidentally during the Rideau Canal's most active construction period, when he was determined to spend what it would take to preserve Canada. Included in these plans were building a fortress to guard the north end of the canal. In October 1830, Lt.-Col. By put together a detailed plan for surrounding the existing barracks with bombproof casements, massive storage facilities, and ramparts in case of land attack. He projected a cost of £205,450.

At the same time, Colonel By's revised estimate for the canal work rose to £576,578—a colossal sum, but it was accepted without question. The Ottawa fortress would have to wait until the completion of the Canal, and Fort Henry at Kingston.

At Bytown, the military settlement was beginning to take shape. As Joseph Bouchette, Surveyor-General of Lower Canada, remarked in the summer of 1828,

> The streets are laid out with much regularity, and of a liberal width that will hereafter contribute to the convenience, salubrity and elegance of the place. The number of houses now built is about 150, most of which are constructed of wood; frequently in a style of neatness and taste that reflects great credit upon the Inhabitants. On the elevated banks of the Bay, the Hospital, an extensive stone building, and three barracks stand conspicuous; nearly on a level with them, and on the eastern side of the Bay, is the residence of Colonel By, Commanding Royal Engineer at that Station.

While visiting Colonel By, Bouchette remarked that:

> From the verandah the most splendid view is beheld that the magnificent scenery of the Canadas affords. That bold eminence that embosoms Entrance Bay, the broken and wild the verdant and picturesque island between both banks and the occasional canoes, barges and rafts plying the broad surface of the Grand River, or descending its tumultuous stream, are the immediate objects that command the notice of the beholder.[4]

Meanwhile, a hundred kilometres due south, work was well under way at the Jones Falls dam site, where Redpath and his crew had to prevail not just against powerful river rapids, but against the scourge of malaria.

---

[4] Joseph Bouchette, *General Report of an Official Tour Through the New Settlements of the Province of Lower Canada.*

CHAPTER 8

Jones Falls, Malaria, and Black Powder

At Kingston Mills, 100 men ill and 12 dead. Brewers Mills, work at a stand still. Chaffey's Mills, contractor and many men ill. Davis Mills, many men ill. Jones Falls, work stopped because of illness, except at quarry six miles [9.6 kilometres] from site. Isthmus, one of contractors very sick, several deaths, only four men on the job. Ottawa River side, Rideau Lake, epidemic less severe, but many sick.

—Captain Savage, September 6, 1827

Redpath's Magnificent Dam

On November 27, 1827, Mackay & Redpath signed a contract, then consulted with Colonel By's staff in planning the most extensive single engineering feat along the Canal—the locks and massive cut stone arch dam at Jones Rapids. Redpath competed the work in 1831.

Regular gravity dams rely on their massive size and weight to withstand the water pressure behind them. The Hog's Back Dam in Ottawa is a good example. The Great Stone Arch Dam was relatively thinner and lighter, resisting the load by horizontally transferring it to the bedrock of the ravine walls.

The technology is ancient. The Romans built arch dams, and examples still exist from the fourteenth century in Iran.[1]

---

[1] Hydro Québec's Daniel-Johnson dam, formerly known as Manic-5, is a thirteen-arch dam.

Figure 8.1. Dam at Jones Falls from the west end.
Source: Thomas Burrowes fonds, Archives of Ontario, C 1-0-0-0-52.

Mackey initially helped Redpath set up the works at Jones Falls, including the building of a smithy and housing for two hundred workers. He then returned to Bytown.[2]

During peak construction at Jones Falls, Redpath had two construction camps, one for the locks and one for the dam. The dam today is about 18 metres [60 feet] high and 106 metres [350 feet] in length. The locks were primarily built up a dry gully to the west, above the pre-canal water level, by 220 French-Canadian stonemasons and labourers.

A workforce of forty Scottish stone workers, managed by Redpath's foreman—his brother-in-law Thomas Fairbairn—quarried rough sandstone blocks for the locks and dam. Wagon teams then hauled them over a 10-kilometre-long road from Halliday's Quarry, near present-day Elgin. At the dam site, Redpath's masons did the finishing work on the stones, bevelling them at an angle to key the arch.

---

[2] Ken Watson, *Engineered Landscapes: The Rideau Canal's Transformation of a Wilderness Waterway* (Elgin, 2006).

Redpath's workers dug the stone arch dam foundation 2.4 metres [8 feet] deep into the canyon bed, locking each end into the granite walls of the gorge. Upstream they added a 39-metre-long [127-foot-long] long underwater rubble and mud slope to reduce water pressure against the dam. They also built an adjustable wastewater weir through bedrock to control the level of the lake between the upper lock. This weir is today regarded as Jones Falls. As the arch dam neared completion, a temporary cofferdam was used to block the flow from Sand Lake, and the gap in the stone quickly filled in to raise the dam to its full height.

When it was completed in 1831, the dam flooded the entire rapids back to Sand Lake, raising its level by almost 8 feet [2.4 metres]. The canal dam at Upper Brewers provided additional flooding of the Drowned Lands, creating today's Whitefish Lake.

At the time the Jones Falls dam was built, newspapers hailed it as the tallest in the British Empire, and "one of the most significant engineering works of the nineteenth century in North America." Other pundits compared it favourably to the masonry arched (curved) dam built by the Romans at Aix-en-Provence in France.

The Malaria Epidemics

In the summer of 1828, Colonel By had as many as two thousand men working on the canal between Bytown and Kingston. Following a warm spring, an outbreak of malaria or "swamp fever" spread along the canal that summer, thriving in the work camps where men lived under canvas beside swamps where the Anopheles mosquitoes bred.

Some suggest that the strain may have been brought to Canada by soldiers who had recently served in Africa or India. But there is a milder, less virulent temperate variety, Plasmodium Vivax, which survives in colder climates by staying dormant in the human liver until the mosquitoes start biting. It also emerged and reached critical mass in urban areas—P. Vivax was already well established in Kingston, Perth, and York by the time canal construction started. And in the US, a decade earlier, close to a thousand Erie Canal workers died of malaria in the Montezuma Swamp between Rochester and Syracuse, New York.

About 60 percent of the Rideau workforce caught malaria each year and about 2 percent of the victims died. But many more were debilitated and unable to work for months at a time. Mackay's friend

John Mactaggart, appointed as clerk of the works under Colonel By in 1826, experienced the sickness firsthand, describing it as

> an attack of bilious fever, dreadful vomiting, pains in the back and loins, general debility, loss of appetite, so that one cannot even take tea. After being in this state for eight or ten days, the yellow jaundice is likely to ensue, and then fits of trembling—we feel so cold that nothing will warm us; the greatest heat that can be applied is perfectly unfelt; the skin gets dry, and then the shaking begins. Our very bones ache, teeth chatter, and the ribs are sore, continuing thus in great agony for about an hour and a half; we then commonly have a vomit, the trembling ends, and a profuse sweat ensues, which last[s] for two hours longer. This over, we find the malady has run one of its rounds, and start out of the bed in a feeble state, sometime unable to stand and entirely dependent on our friends (if we have any) to lift us on to some seat or other.[3]

Colonel By also succumbed to the disease—he had already survived an attack of typhus (army fever). But he was able to recover and resume work with the aid of quinine, an expensive extract of cinchona bark recently developed by French scientists.

Thomas Mackay escaped infection, but John Redpath was hit hard. In December 1831, he wrote that

> the exceeding unhealthiness of the place from which cause all engaged in it suffered much from lake fever and fever & ague, and it has also retarded the work for about three months each year. I caught the disease both the first [1828] and second year missed the third but this year had a severe attack of Lake Fever—which kept me to bed for two months and nearly two months more before I was fit for active service.

If he had known what he was getting into, said Redpath, he would have refused the Jones Falls work—"Nothing can compensate for the worse of health so no inducement whatever would stimulate one to a similar undertaking."[4]

---

[3] Mactaggart, *Three Years in Canada*, vol. 2, 16–17.
[4] Ken Watson, *Malaria: The Secret Immigrant*.

Dysentery, smallpox, tuberculosis, and influenza also hit the workforce during the four years of construction. In Bytown and along the canal, almost a thousand workers and citizens perished from these diseases, from accidents, and from the cold.

Epidemics of cholera and typhoid came later, after the completion of the canal. In 1832, cholera raged up the Ottawa and St. Lawrence rivers, and Janet McPhee, Redpath's wife, succumbed, as did John Drummond at Kingston.

John Mactaggart Dismissed

John Mactaggart had nearly recovered from malaria in October 1828, at which point he was dismissed from his post on the orders of new governor Sir James Kempt—who had commanded a brigade at Waterloo—for "being drunk on duty."

That summer, Kempt had been temporarily engaged in what he regarded as a pointless military assignment, the presidency of a commission of inquiry into the building of the Rideau Canal. He was obliged to make a cursory inspection of the canal site, spending as long as seventeen hours a day traversing rough terrain between Bytown and Kingston in sweltering temperatures. "*Thank God,*" he exclaimed on reaching Kingston, "I am at last again in a Christian Country and out of the land of Swamps and Mosquitoes." His cranky report had no effect in stopping escalating costs.[5]

Mactaggart's friends came to his defence. The Roman Catholic Bishop of Kingston, Alexander McDonell, wrote to the Colonial Office that Mactaggart was "perhaps the ablest practical engineer and geologist, and the properest person that has ever been in these Provinces for exploring the natural productions and latent resources of the country."

Colonel By wrote to General Mann that Mactaggart was "a man of strong natural abilities, well grounded in the practical part of his profession, and a zealous, hard-working man in the field."

But Mactaggart was also a fearless and opinionated Scot, and may have targeted Kempt while in his cups. The Governor did not waver, and Mactaggart was forced to return to England in late 1828. One suspects he was able to take with him some bottles of his

---

[5] Peter Burroughs, "KEMPT, Sir JAMES," in *Dictionary of Canadian Biography*, vol. 8 (University of Toronto/Université Laval, 2003).

favourite Upper Canada whisky: "Craigdarroch—made after the Glenlivet mode" in Perth, and "by far the most excellent spirit distilled in the country."[6]

Within a year of his exile, Mactaggart published *Three Years in Canada*, a two-volume record of social and scientific observations. He adored the natural beauties of the Canadas, which were "not to be matched in the world." The potential wealth of the country gave a "consequence to Britain not to be sneered at." And finally, he speculated on a canal system up the Ottawa to the Great Lakes and beyond to the far Pacific Coast.

Regarding the settlers in Canada, he picked on the "gentry," the legal profession, the Irish, and particularly the "Yankees" of Upper Canada, whom he found lacking in warmth and colour. Only the vitality of the French-Canadians and Indigenous people he found worthy of particular praise.

Black Powder Explosions

Malaria was a serious risk to the workers, but just as dangerous was the black "merchant powder" used by the contractors to blow up any rock harder than limestone. This substance—made of three parts nitre to one part of a mixture of sulphur and charcoal—was far less stable than the dynamite yet to be invented by Alfred Nobel.

During the summer of 1829, work began at the isthmus on the height of land between the Rideau River watershed, flowing north, and the Gananoque/Cataraqui watersheds, flowing south. The contractors and engineers began excavating a 1,500-metre [4,800-foot] artificial waterway to connect Rideau Lake and Mud Lake with a series of locks (now the Newboro Locks). They soon found they were not dealing with the mud, gravel, and limestone they expected but a ridge of hard Precambrian granite bedrock.

Two sets of local contractors quickly bailed out of the project, so Colonel By ordered to the worksite two Royal Engineers, and a fifty-nine-man crew from the 7th Company of the Royal Sappers and Miners from Bytown, along with 250 civilian labourers.

Half of the Sappers and Miners were married, and the lock site had family quarters, for the twenty-seven women and forty-six children

---

[6] Victoria Spirits currently distils a whisky they call Craigdarroch in Sydney, B.C.

who arrived with the company of soldiers. They called their settlement Newboro. By the fall of 1830, the village had sixty log buildings.

The work went slowly. The three-man blasting crews began by hammering and hand-drilling holes into rocks, then packing them with black powder. They then lit a wick to ignite the powder and ran for safety. After setting off the blast, the workers broke up the debris with sledgehammers and carted it away in wheelbarrows.

The exploding rock killed many workers—five of the Sappers and Miners would die from blasting accidents, some due to ignorance. Mactaggart saw one man "blow a red stick and hold it deliberately to the priming of a large shot he had just charged—off went the blast and took away his arm, and half of his head: he was killed in a moment."

Colonel By finally resolved the Newboro bedrock problem by simply adding height to the canal. He ordered the building of an extra dam and lock station across the Upper Narrows of Rideau Lake, today's Narrows lock station, in the south-west corner of Rideau Lake. This neat solution raised the water level of what is now Upper Rideau Lake by almost 1.5 metres [4 feet, 10 inches]. This dramatically reduced the amount of hard granite excavation needed.

To the south, in Robert Drummond's Kingston Mills sector, blasting operations also killed several workmen. Drummond himself narrowly escaped death in February 1831—a 300-pound rock came smashing through the side of his house as he was dining with a group of friends, missing him by 6 feet [2 metres].

CHAPTER 9

The Hog's Back Dam Disasters

The failure was due in part to inexperience with cold weather engineering.

—Ken W. Watson

Back in Bytown, Colonel By was fortunate in that his canal excavators found no granite bedrock while digging 2.4 kilometres [1.5 miles] between the Ottawa Locks and the small Three Rocks Rapids on the Rideau River. The water dropped about 2 metres over a distance of 600 metres through a limestone ridge called Hog's Back.

Hog's Back was where the Rideau Canal had to branch off from the Rideau River and make its way to the Ottawa River purely as an 8.4-kilometre [5.2-mile] excavated and flooded canal.

Colonel By's first instinct was to build a simple European-style spillway or overflow dam to back up enough water to feed the remaining locks of the canal system. Too much would flood the system, destroying the locks; too little would render the canal useless. Any waste water would be allowed to spill into the Rideau River. But after seeing the river in flood, he realized that the spring overflow would quickly erode the bedrock foundation at the base of any dam.

So the Colonel quickly changed plans, deciding to scrap the overflow dam idea and build a very large fixed structure, 45 feet [13.7 metres] high and 170 feet [52 metres] wide, to store enough water to feed the three planned locks at Hog's Back, as well as the eight Ottawa Locks being built by Thomas Mackay. It also had to flood the Rideau River all the way upstream to his planned Black Rapids lock.

For the Black Rapids to the Long Island segment of the Canal, the Colonel signed a contract with Mackay & Redpath, partnering with Thomas Phillips and Andrew White, who had worked with them on the Lachine Canal. Phillips opened a quarry at the foot of the Black Rapids, and built a dam across the Rideau River 280 feet [86 metres] wide and 10 feet [3 metres] high, with a lock of 10 feet [3 metres] lift, which formed a sheet of still water 5 miles [8 kilometres] long, reaching to the foot of the Long Island Rapids. At Long Island, White took over, building locks of 8 feet [2.4 metres] lift each, and a cut stone dam across the Rideau that was 158 feet [48 metres] wide and 24 feet [7.3 metres] high, to add another 3 miles [5 kilometres] of still water, taking the Canal about 37 miles [60 kilometres] from the Ottawa Locks.

Hog's Back One

The work at Hog's Back began in June 1827, under Colonel By's overseer, Captain J.C. Victor of the Royal Engineers. The Colonel awarded the contract for the work to Walter Fenlon, earlier dismissed by Mackay as a mere "excavator." It was a gently curved dam, unlike Redpath's 60-foot [18-metre] arch dam at Jones Falls.

Fenlon started to construct the dam on the east bank of the river, with Philemon Wright & Sons building a cofferdam upstream to divert the river to the west side. Like most mill dams, it was made of stones, earth, and rubble, with a sloping crib of large timbers facing upstream, locked in place by water pressure.

Under Colonel By's direction, the Royal Engineers also built a tramway—possibly the first railway in Canada—to bring stone from a quarry that they opened on the east bank.

Fenlon started to build his stone dam by excavating a wastewater "by wash" in the east bank, about 27 feet [8 metres] above the bed of the river. But in February 1828, once he had raised the main portion of the dam to 37 feet [11 metres], it started to drain through the bywash. A winter thaw had caused the river to rise higher than normal, and the west side washed completely away, killing two men, smothered under a bank of clay. Another man died in a fall from the dam, due to "intoxication by Ardent Spirits."

Hog's Back Two

Poor Fenlon then tried a slightly modified plan, excavating the bywash 4 feet [1.2 metres] deeper and 40 feet [12 metres] wide. Huge logs of hemlock and pine were then laid in the cofferdam. But it was all in vain; on April 1, 1828, the spring floods reached over the cofferdam, eroded the banks, and severely damaged the stone dam.

Hog's Back Three

By June, the hapless Fenlon was pretty much bankrupt and wrote Colonel By:

> I cannot possibly continue the Work at the prices that I am at present getting according to my Contract and I am the loser to a great amount on what I have already done. My humble prayer at this time, is, that Government would take the job and release me from all claims on the Contract. I trust I shall be allowed an estimate on what I have done in preparation for carrying on the work, and my losses I submit to the Consideration and discretion of the Commanding Officer.

On November 1, Philemon Wright & Sons took over part of Fenlon's contract, working alongside the Royal Sappers and Miners to repair the cofferdam and build the keywork of the dam. By March of 1829, with the help of over three hundred labourers, they had widened the bywash channel to 60 feet [18 metres], and raised the dam 15 feet [4.5 metres] above the required height of 45 feet [13.7 metres].

Yet Colonel By was worried, because he knew the power of the spring floods. On the late afternoon of April 2, he was on top of the dam with a work party when he spied grey water leaking just above the first course of stones, under the enormous water pressure of the rapidly rising Rideau.

Alarmed, he gave orders to the men to throw everything they could into the leak—brush and timber, clay and earth—but the centre section of the dam started to slump the following day. Yet the upper material, frozen hard by winter frost, still held, forming an arch. But suddenly the arch started to crumble and give way—Colonel By and the workers raced to the safety of the shore as the stones literally fell away beneath their feet.

As he reported to Sir James Kempt, the new governor,

> The arch key-work, 26 feet [8 metres] thick at the base, gave way about 15 feet [4.5 metres] above the foundation, and near the centre of the dam, with a noise resembling thunder. I was standing on top of it with forty men, employed in trying to stop the leak, when I felt a motion like an earthquake, and instantly ordered the men to run... The force of the water was such that stones of 2 and 3 tons of weight were tossed about as if they had been blocks of wood; and the frozen earth was carried over the Rideau Falls, a distance of between 5 and 6 miles [8 and 9.6 kilometres].

Hog's Back Four

According to Ottawa city clerk William Pittman Lett:

Figure 9.1. Hog's Back Dam showing the 1830 breach and stonework.
Source: Thomas Burrowes fonds [1845], Archives of Ontario, C 1-0-0-0-15.

Colonel By was a man of great energy and determination, so much so, that when the Hog's Back Dam at one time, when just completed, owing to some defect in position, was swept away by the spring flood, he said he would rebuild it again and again until it would stand, if he had to build it solid with half-dollar pieces.

After his near-death experience, Colonel By looked to Thomas Mackay and the Engineers for causes and solutions. Mackay and his foreman, John Robertson, suggested that the dam had been lost because the puddled clay placed as fill during the winter had frozen before it was fully compacted. This allowed fractures to form, which were opened up by heavy hydraulic pressure, washing away the clay. Indeed, that same thing happened three weeks later at the Smiths Falls dam, which was saved only by quick action on the part of Lieutenant Pooley of the Royal Engineers.

The solution they came up with was to rebuild the dam with stone-filled wooden cribs, and avoid using clay as a filler. Philemon Wright's crew and the Sappers and Miners would enlarge the waste weir, to let spring flood waters escape into the man-made waterfall and rapids on the east—today's Prince of Wales Falls—without damaging the main dam or canal locks.

According to Ken Watson,

> The new timber dam construction was a model of simplicity. Timber cribs were laid on the bedrock of the river. As the first course of timber was laid, it was filled with large broken stones to resist the flow of the river. Once this base was secure, they laid courses of timber on top, creating an open timber framework

Figure 9.2. Hog's Back [Prince of Wales] Falls and completed locks, 1832.
Source: Library and Archives Canada.

through which the river flowed. The timber crib work was raised to the required height of the dam.

A roadway was built on top of the timber cribs and the cribs were filled with stone, starting from the flanks and working towards the centre. At the same time, earth, stone and rubbish was used to build out an apron in front of the cribs. This apron was huge, extending out almost 300 feet [91 metres]. Great quantities of large broken stone [still visible today] were piled onto the back (downstream) side of the timber cribs to help stabilize them.[1]

Back to the canal works—instead of constructing three locks at Hog's Back, Mackay built a single lock with two sections—first a "guard lock" facing the river that could be shut to hold off rising floodwaters and floating debris, and then the canal lock itself. Then he added two new locks down water at Hartwells, halfway to Dow's Great Swamp.

Philemon Wright's crew excavated the trench for the locks, finding it was largely unstable clay filled with boulders. Mackay then used the same technique as with the Ottawa Locks, installing inverted masonry arches to support the floor of each lock, and hydraulic cement under pressure to seal the arches, the lock walls, and the basin.

Then, just above the new Hartwell locks, Mackay and the Engineers built a masonry wastewater weir to carry the spring overflow east to the Rideau River, running through the land today occupied by Carleton University. This outlet channel still exists, going under the University through a culvert.

Colonel By's experience at Hog's Back made him additionally pleased and relieved with the quality of the work done by Mackay and his masons, the Royal Sappers and Miners, and Philemon Wright's crew. In March of 1830, he celebrated the completion of the Rideau Canal to Hog's Back with a gala banquet, where "an ox, properly prepared and roasted whole, was fixed in a standing position. The guests then proceeded to study its anatomy in a very practical manner, after which singing and dancing completed the celebration."

---

[1] Ken W. Watson, *Washed Away: The Story of the Building of the Hog's Back Dam*.

Figure 9.3. Hog's Back in 1845.
Source: Thomas Burrowes Fonds, Archives of Ontario.

CHAPTER 10

1829: Handsome Profits

The British wisely hoarded a good deal of this Mexican silver, and a fortune in Mexican coinage, shipped to Quebec in chests and barrels, was used judiciously and wisely, to protect the Canadas from American invasion. It was these dollars that saved British North America.

—David Gates, *The Napoleonic Wars, 1803–1815*

A Silver Bonanza

By the end of 1829, Thomas Mackay's labour on the Ottawa Locks was essentially complete, while the work at Hog's Back and Hartwells was not finished until the summer of 1831. He and most of his masons had already made the decision to stay in Bytown, while John Redpath and partners Philips & White returned to their Montréal businesses the following year. Mackay and Redpath still continued their joint shipping business in the Ottawa and Rideau Forwarding Company with the help of Redpath's wife, Janet. In 1832, Bank of Montreal directors John Molson Jr. and Peter McGill joined the company as investors.

How wealthy was Thomas Mackay at this time?

His friend, Perth lawyer and later judge John Malloch—also born in Perth, Scotland—estimated that Mackay emerged from the Rideau Canal contracts about £32,000 richer.[1] In an accounting made on March 17, 1831, Mackay shows a handsome profit of £28,205 for the Bytown canal work, and Redpath £20,847 from the Jones Falls dam

---

[1] J. G. Malloch, *Diary (OA)*.

and locks. Philips and White were also paid £7,600 for work at Black Rapids, Long Island, and for completing the Jones Falls work.[2]

How were they paid?

According to the Reverend J.L. Gourlay, in his history of the Ottawa Valley, "Redpath and Mackay had to cart home, in Mexican silver half dollars, etc., their part of the profits of the contract."[3]

This coinage, packed in barrels, was likely forwarded by the Ordnance from Québec, and stored at the fortress on St. Helen's Island opposite Montréal. The funds were then delivered by wagon and wheelbarrow into the vaults of the Bank of Montreal, and credited to the accounts of the partners. Of course the bank immediately put this capital to good use.

Why were Mackay and Redpath paid in Spanish silver coinage? For one main reason—the War Office was flush with booty from Spanish treasure ships captured by the Royal Navy.

Napoleon's Need for Cash

> *"Bonaparte does not understand anything and thinks that we conduct finances as we do with armies."*
>
> —Napoleon's Financier Gabriel Ouvrard

The silver bonanza also originated in Bonaparte's desperate desire for money.

On February 16, 1808, under the pretext of sending reinforcements to the French army occupying Portugal, Emperor Napoleon invaded Spain and installed his brother Joseph on the throne. So began the Peninsular War, a conflict that lasted for seven years.

The Bonaparte brothers were now owners of the gold and silver of Spanish America, with no way to get at their spoils because the Royal Navy was dominant on the high seas, ruling the waves since Nelson's victory at Trafalgar.

In 1808, during a truce, Napoleon's banker, Gabriel Ouvrard, suggested to his British counterpart Sir Francis Baring that, if the Royal Navy sent a fleet to Mexico and shipped a large consignment

---

[2] McCord Museum, Redpath fonds.
[3] J. L. Gourlay, *History of the Ottawa Valley*.

of Spanish dollars to its owner, the King of Spain, in return, would allow the British Admiralty to keep half of the Spanish-American booty.

The deal was satisfactory to the British and the Royal Navy happily complied.

In the spring of 1808, the admiralty ordered a fleet of twenty-six British frigates and transports to sail to Havana and to the Mexican mint at Vera Cruz. The ships loaded hundreds of tons of silver coinage into their holds. As agreed, they delivered half the cargo to Cadiz, where it soon went to pay Spain's debt to Napoleon. The other half remained in the hands of the British Admiralty and army—off the books and most decidedly offshore.

Under the ancient *Cruizers and Convoys Act* of 1708, the Admiralty was now in sole possession of a substantial offshore fortune. But, mindful of how Spanish bullion had debauched the economy of Spain, the Lords of the Treasury approved keeping the bullion offshore, and in 1825, Lord Liverpool passed the *Sterling Silver Money Act*, which made British coins the only recognized form of currency in the British Isles, and ended any legitimate onshore use of the Spanish dollar.

During the very expensive War of 1812, the cash-flush British military used these Spanish dollars to erect fortifications and move supplies unto Lake Ontario, where they easily outspent the Americans. Indeed, the colossal HMS *St. Lawrence,* entirely constructed at the Kingston dockyards, was a warship bigger than Nelson's *Victory.*

Some was paid out to six-hundred-odd New England ship captains, who had been ruined by the Jeffersonian embargoes, and who spent the War of 1812 in the Baltic, hauling Russian hemp and Swedish timber for the Royal Navy—which took payment in gold and silver bullion.[4]

After the war, on the recommendation of the Duke of Richmond, the Spanish silver booty helped pay for building a more secure armoury on Île Notre-Dame and constructing Fort Lennox on Île-aux-Noix. Some was used to subsidize the Lachine Canal, to build a new Fort Henry and to construct the Rideau Canal. However it was used, we know that profits amounting to at least £50,000 worth of Spanish silver made their way into each of Mackay and Redpath's accounts in the Montréal banks. This was an extraordinary amount of cash.

---

[4] Alastair Sweeny, *Fire Along the Frontier,* 178.

The British could afford to reward its canal builders lavishly. To put things in perspective, the hold of one particular galleon taken in 1805 contained silver worth over £800,000. That is almost exactly what the Ordnance would pay out to build the Rideau Canal.

The final cost of the Rideau Canal, tallied up in January 1834, was £822,804, which included land acquisition. In 2007, Parks Canada estimated the cost in current Canadian dollars at over $1 billion.

Thomas Mackay received about £32,000 or 1/25th of the total—in today's dollars over $40 million. Redpath received a lesser amount, as he had to bow out of the project due to bouts of malaria. But they were handsome profits, indeed, added to the £10,000 apiece they earned on the Lachine Canal, and more on Fort Lennox and Île Ste-Hélène. Lord Dalhousie and Colonel By needed high-quality work, carried out by trusted contractors, and they got it.[5]

Dalhousie and the Ordnance also knew that depositing the silver dollars in British North American banks would boost the economy and help drive out Yankee coin—John Mactaggart, clerk of the works for the Rideau Canal, complained that American half dollars were helping to make "Yankees of the colonists."

The British also paid canal workers in copper pennies. The required money to cover the Sappers and Miners' salaries were in silver half crowns—each coin amounting to two shillings and sixpence—brought from England to Montréal in small barrels and then to Bytown in birchbark canoes or flat-bottomed batteaux. This cash stimulated the local economy with a trusted medium of exchange.

By paying handsome profits to the Rideau Canal contractors—Thomas Mackay, John Redpath, and Robert Drummond—the British had influence over three solid citizens—builders—who accepted their growing responsibilities, and who would invest their capital in the Canadas and work to keep Canada British. This capital ensured that the settlement of Bytown had the wherewithal to grow and thrive, with help from Thomas Mackay's investments in lumbering, milling, shipping, and railways. Inspired by Dalhousie, and flush with capital,

---

[5] By way of comparison, Thomas Telford's Caledonian Canal in northwest Scotland, which finally opened in 1822, took 19 years to complete, at a cost of £910,000. Over 3,000 local people were employed in its construction. To save costs, the draft of the canal was reduced from 20 feet (6.1 m) to 15 feet (4.6 m). To put things further in perspective, an American Gerald Ford class aircraft carrier costs a whopping $13 billion.

1829: Handsome Profits 137

Figure 10.1. Spanish four-real coin from the Nueva Granada Mint.

Thomas Mackay's duty became clear—to help the young military settlement of Bytown grow and prosper, turning it into a city worthy of becoming the capital of a new nation.[6]

---

[6] How Spanish-American silver was used to reward the contractors of the Rideau Canal, and establish what is now the City of Ottawa, is one of the most astonishing and amusing stories of the Napoleonic Wars. For a more detailed account, see Appendix 1: Pieces of Eight.

CHAPTER 11

1831: Finishing the Work

However expensive the works upon the Rideau, nobody now doubts the wisdom of the plan, its efficacy, and above all, its economy.

—Duke of Wellington,
1841 reappraisal of the Canadian defence plan

The Royal Engineers' design for the Rideau Canal was not without its faults. By 1831–1832, maintenance had already proved necessary. Many of the original gates had threatened to buckle under the pressure of the water they were meant to control.

Mackay and the engineers solved the problem by bolting reinforcing rails across the face of each gate. In 1839, the engineers installed an endless crab and sluice valve system in smaller locks to replace the original in-culvert sluice valve mechanism. Ongoing maintenance efforts in the 1920s led to the replacement of much of the original stone facing with concrete.

Military Considerations

The canal, designed as a military supply line, was itself vulnerable to attack. In March of 1830, Colonel By proposed to purchase additional land and build several defensive blockhouses, and "works of defence not sanctioned" at a cost of £69,230 (about $2.6 million today). The Ordnance decided that due to the high cost of the canal, any defensive works would have to be postponed. However, they neglected to inform the Colonel of this decision until the spring of 1832, when he was preparing to leave.

Hearing no word from the Ordnance, and knowing that the defence of the canal was crucial, Colonel By started to build several blockhouses to defend against raiding parties intent on opening the heavy lock gates and flooding the canal system. So today we are blessed with four blockhouses and stone lockmasters' houses: at Kingston Mills, the Isthmus (Newboro) at the summit of the Canal, the Narrows on Rideau Lake, and Merrickville.

The blockhouse at Merrickville was extremely important to the defence of the canal. The original defence strategy had been to maintain a wilderness buffer around the Canal. This would prevent easy access by enemy troops to the canal works. However, in 1832, the provincial government began to upgrade the Prescott Road, providing easy access between the St. Lawrence and the Rideau. In the event of hostilities, the blockhouse at Merrickville would become a key defence point.[1]

Figure 11.1. *Blockhouse at Merrickville, 1839.*
Source: Henry Francis Ainslie, Library and Archives Canada.

---

[1] Parks Canada has erected a plaque near the Merrickville blockhouse to mark the twinning of the Rideau Canal and the Caledonian Canal in Scotland. A similar plaque marks the Caledonian/Rideau twinning at Corpach Lock near Fort William, where the Canadian flag is flown along with the Cross of St. Andrew by its Scottish keepers.

Figure 11.2. Troops entering the Ottawa Locks in Durham boats, 1838.
Source: Philip John Bainbrigge fonds, Library and Archives Canada, C-011864.

These defensive works proved their worth during the Rebellion of 1837–1838, standing against potential raiding parties who threatened to sabotage the canal. However, the Rideau Canal never saw military activity except in 1838—when troops were taken from Montréal to Kingston on barges pulled by steamboats. And in September 1839, the army gathered rebel prisoners at Kingston and safely sent them to Québec via the Rideau Canal.

Following the Upper Canada rebellion of 1837–1838, wooden guardhouses were built at Jones Falls and Morton, and defensible stone lockmasters' houses were built at several locks along the canal. No new blockhouses were constructed.

Robert Drummond and Kingston Mills

Engaged by Colonel By to build the southern portion of the canal, Robert Drummond and his family had left Bytown in January 1828, travelling in sleighs to Kingston. His works at Kingston Mills were the third largest of the waterway. The lock sites on the Cataraqui River were hit hard by the malaria epidemics, which killed almost five hundred men, mostly Irish immigrants.

Figure 11.3. Troops leaving the Jones Falls Locks in Durham boats, 1838.
Source: Philip John Bainbrigge fonds, Library and Archives, Canada C-011835.

With his share of the canal profits, Drummond invested in a line of steamers in the Montréal, Bytown, and Kingston service. On June 6, 1829, he launched the first steamer to serve on the canal. The *Rideau*, 80 feet [24 metres] in length, was later renamed *Pumper* because Drummond used its twelve-horsepower steam engine to pump water from behind the cofferdam protecting the lower Kingston Mills lock during construction.

In August 1831, Colonel By presented him with an engraved and handcrafted silver cup, with an inscription praising "the zeal displayed by him in the performance of his contracts" and the Colonel's "complete satisfaction" with his work.

Drummond's second boat was the *John By*, a 110-foot [33-metre] sternwheeler of 200 tons, launched at Kingston in November 1831 with the band of the 66th (Berkshire) Regiment of Foot in attendance. Unfortunately, it drew more water than planned, and couldn't be used on the Rideau Canal. He also operated the steamer *Margaret*, the schooner *Lady of the Lake*, and a fleet of barges.

A Triumphal Cruise

In May 1832, at the Kingston Mills lock station, Robert Drummond's *Rideau* took on board Colonel By, his wife Esther, and their daughters, 13-year-old Esther March By and 11-year-old Harriet Martha By, as well as Royal Engineer Captain Briscoe, and (possibly) contractors Mackay and Redpath, for an inaugural five-day cruise to Bytown.[2]

At noon on May 24, 1832, the great journey got under way. The *Rideau* had a forward escort in the Kingston naval dockyard cutter *Rattlesnake*, and towed a rear escort of two barges as far as Jones Falls.

The *Rideau* reached Smiths Falls at six in the morning the following day, and woke the town with a cannon shot. Then, on May 29, the little paddle-wheel steamboat finally docked at the Bytown Wharf, after a 200-kilometre five-day cruise through the 47 masonry locks of the Rideau Canal, to mark its official opening.

On his return to Kingston, Drummond put the *Rideau* into commercial service, and six weeks later, the little steamer reached Bytown

Figure 11.4. Paddlewheel steamer *Pilot* on the Rideau Canal, August 3, 1844.
Source: George Seton, Library and Archives Canada, C-001072.

---

[2] Robert Legget, *Rideau Waterway*; other accounts do not have the contractors on board during the trip.

on its first cruise, with several passengers and a cargo of two hundred barrels of flour and sixty barrels of pork.

The Rideau Canal was now a working success. Where water had once roared through rapids and deep gorges, there were now forty-seven masonry locks, fifty-two dams and long stretches of calm water. In less than six years, Colonel By's contractors, labourers, excavators, masons, and engineers had created a navigable 125-mile-long [202-kilometre-long] waterway suitable for steamboats.

When the Ottawa River Canals opened two years later, the first St. Lawrence Seaway became a reality—when steamboats could at last sail up the St. Lawrence to Montréal, through the Lachine and Ottawa canals and on through the Rideau to Kingston on Lake Ontario, and even onward through the Welland Canal to Lakes Erie and Huron, and through the Sault Canal to Lake Superior, extending Montréal's reach as far as Fort William.

The Rideau Canal was officially opened for general transportation that August. The population of the future capital of Canada was then about a thousand people.

Later that year, Drummond left Kingston to reconnect with his relatives in Edinburgh. In January 1833, he visited a retired Colonel By at his country seat in Sussex. The Colonel presented him with a silhouette portrait, and also offered his support for a contract to widen the Grenville Canal locks. Drummond demurred, wanting to leave canal building behind. On his return to Kingston, on August 20, he tragically succumbed to the virulent cholera epidemic then raging in the Canadas. He was only 43 years old, and was survived by his wife and his five children, ranging in age from 1 to 13.

Redpath Returns to Montréal

Thomas Mackay and his wife opted to stay in Bytown—he had completed his major projects and he and his masons were well into building a Rideau Falls sawmill and grist mill complex that could keep his crew, now barely employed, together. A woollen mill, cooperage, and distillery would soon follow.[3]

---

[3] Grist is grain separated from its chaff before grinding into meal or flour, depending on how coarsely it is ground.

John Redpath, on the other hand, was totally focused on returning to his family in Montréal, and after two bouts of malaria, had no desire to return to Jones Falls.

Redpath was also tired of travelling back and forth to Montréal during canal construction—he had other irons in the fire, and his wife, Janet McPhee, whom he had married in 1818, had stayed in Montréal with their ten children while he was in the field.

Finally, John Redpath was more animated by the profit motive than Thomas Mackay, and during Rideau Canal construction, had always maintained a foothold in the booming metropolis of Montréal.

Redpath's departure left some of the canal work unfinished. A solution had to be found, and it was close at hand. From March 1827 until 1831, Redpath and Mackay had maintained a co-partnership with their former Lachine Canal excavators, Thomas Phillips and Andrew White, and had brought them into the Rideau Canal works. Philips and White had shown themselves capable of not just excavation but lock construction (at Black Rapids and Long Island).

On March 17, 1831, the four men met in Montréal and signed a document winding up their "co-partnership." Philips and White agreed to finish up the remaining central Rideau Canal work in return for taking part of Redpath's profit.

The agreement was transparent and fair to all parties—with open books, and clauses whereby they agreed to complete the work in case of sickness, etc. They knew that they had to rely on each other to complete the work. In the case of Redpath, the Jones Falls dam was nearly complete, but there was other lock work needed on the site, which they knew Philips and White were quite capable of completing.

Tragedy followed Redpath three years after his exit from the Rideau contracts. In 1834, his wife Janet was struck down during a new cholera outbreak in Montréal. He and his children were forced to remain with her body until it was determined they were not carriers. So widower Redpath visited Jones Falls for a final time that year, bringing his children to live at brother-in-law Thomas Fairbairn's house, to escape the epidemic.

Several years later, Redpath would marry Jane Drummond, the daughter of his old masonry mentor George Drummond of Edinburgh. She was a young woman almost half his age, and they would have seven children.

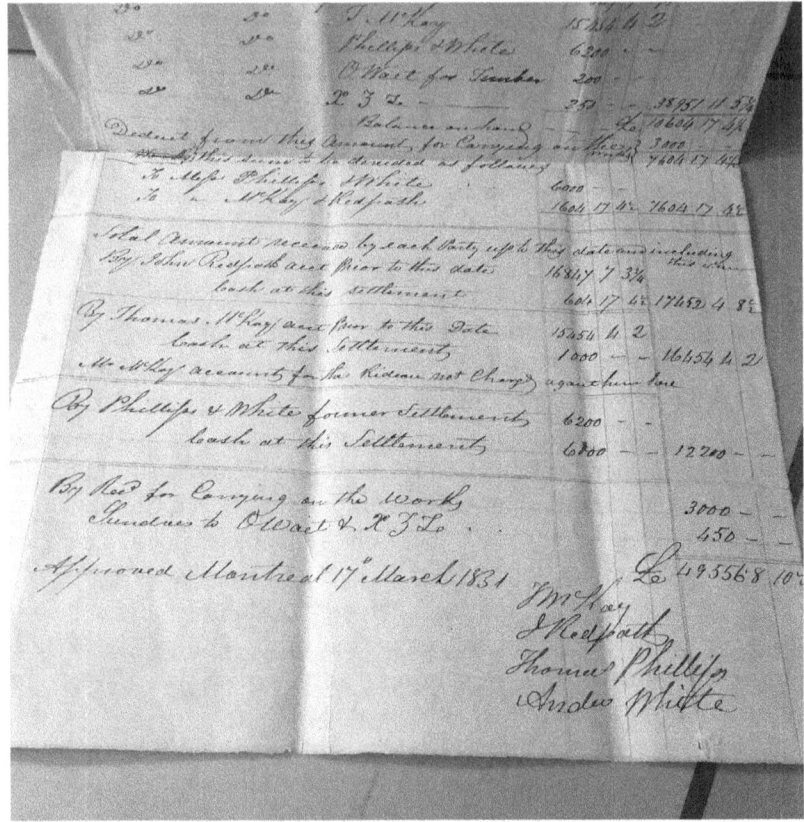

Figure 11.5. March 17, 1831, partners' agreement.
Source: McCord Museum.

Redpath's Montréal Investments

Settled back in Montréal, Redpath was comfortably well off with his silver booty in the Bank of Montreal. He was elected to the board of the bank in 1833, and until his death he was a director, after 1860 a vice-president, and always a large shareholder.

Redpath continued his masonry work. He helped complete Notre-Dame Basilica and erected some of the first buildings at McGill University. But in the 1840s he began to diversify his holdings with his Rideau Canal capital. Spread wisely, it would greatly benefit the city of Montréal, and help grow several enterprises in Montréal's burgeoning economy of the 1840s, '50s and '60s.

Figure 11.6. John Redpath, 1836.
Source: Antoine Plamondon, McCord Museum, M994.35.1.

Redpath was an early investor in the Montreal Telegraph Company, founded in 1847. The company rapidly established telegraph lines to Toronto and Québec City from Montréal, and then New York by August 1847. Ottawa joined the network in 1849.

By the end of 1847, the company had installed 870 kilometres of wire and transmitted 33,000 telegrams.

Figure 11.7. Montreal Telegraph Company logo.
Source: John Henry Walker, McCord Museum, M930.50.1.536.

The world was getting smaller. On November 15, 1849, the first steamer to arrive in Halifax from Europe had news and commodity prices telegraphed directly to Montréal and New York.

In 1851, steamship owner Hugh Allan took over the Montreal Telegraph Company, and a year later acquired the Toronto, Hamilton, Niagara, and St. Catharines Electrical Magnetic Telegraph Company, founded in 1846, which let Toronto newspapers receive dispatches from the New York press, which was receiving dispatches from Europe.

Redpath also invested substantial sums in Canadian mining ventures—some in the Eastern Townships—including the Belvedere Mining and Smelting, Bear Creek Coal, Rockland Slate, Melbourne Slate, and Capel Copper companies. In addition, he owned a large share of the Montreal Investment Association, and held shares in shipping companies such as the Montreal Towboat Company and the Richelieu Company. He was also a promoter of the Canada Marine Insurance Company, the Metropolitan Fire Insurance Company, and the Canada Peat Fuel Company.

Redpath had started several years earlier to purchase land along the Lachine Canal from the Sulpicians. In 1854, he decided to begin construction of the Canada Sugar Refining Company—the first sugar refinery in the Province of Canada. One of his first hires was his wife's brother, George Drummond Jr., who would marry Redpath's eldest daughter, Helen.

Redpath put £40,000 into land, buildings, and machinery. Within a year, he had more than a hundred employees and was producing three thousand barrels of refined sugar per month for the Canadian market. His plant depended entirely on supplies of cane sugar imported from the West Indies, much of it in his own ships, the *Helen Drummond* and the *Grace Redpath*, named after his daughters.

According to Redpath biographer and former Redpath Sugar Museum curator Richard Feltoe:

> The fact is that the sugar industry as a whole is tied to slavery, it's there, you can't hide it… Once John Redpath actually started his sugar company we actually have a list of the companies he bought his sugar from. Every single one of them is a nonslave source. We are talking ethical sourcing in 1854.[4]

Canada Sugar was one of the largest establishments among more than twenty new plants in the booming industrial quarter after the government decided to allow the use of the canal's water to drive machinery. His seven-storey factory's towering boiler stack became one of the city's landmarks. The refinery proved to be a major Montréal employer, within a few years annually processing approximately 7,000 tons of raw sugar.[5]

---

[4] Emily Mathieu, "Redpath Sugar Museum Curator Is Saying Goodbye to the Sweet Life after 43 Years," *Toronto Star*, December 28, 2019, https://www.thestar.com/news/gta/2019/12/28/redpath-sugar-museum-curator-is-saying-goodbye-to-the-sweet-life-after-43-years.html.

[5] Unable to compete with giant low-cost producers in the US, the company ceased operations between 1876 and 1878. It reopened in 1879 under the tariff protection of the National Policy.

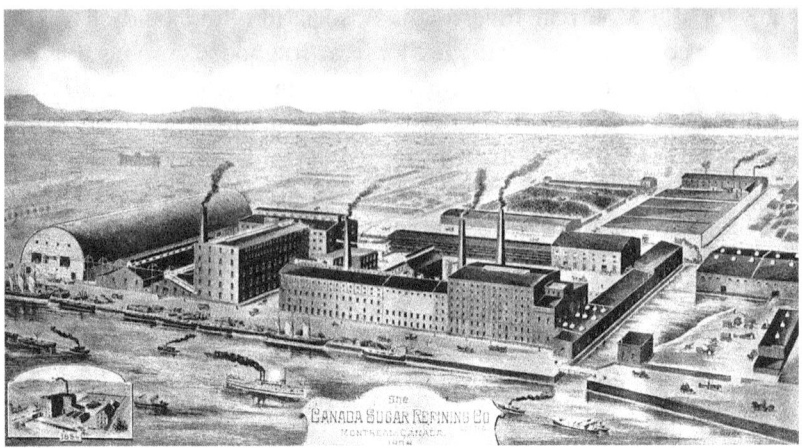

Figure 11.8. Redpath Sugar, Montréal.
Source: Redpath Sugar Museum Archives.

Before his death in 1869, Redpath acquired much of the most desirable mountainside property in the city, where he built a magnificent mansion, and helped put McGill University on a sound financial footing. His son and business successor, Peter, was a member of the McGill University Board of Governors from 1864 until his death. He established the Redpath Museum and Redpath Library, endowing about half a million dollars in money and books to McGill University.

CHAPTER 12

1832: Colonel By's Recall

The Rideau Canal was so well built that maintenance costs in subsequent years were considerably lower than other canals built during the period ... although chastised by the government for cost overruns, Colonel By had created the finest navigable waterway in North America ... one of the greatest engineering feats of the 19th century. The exquisite stonemasonry of the control dams and locks are admired by waterway travellers to this day.

—Ken W. Watson, *Engineered Landscapes*

Colonel By to England

On August 11, 1832, Colonel John By received an official Ordnance notice of his recall to discuss the final estimates—totalling £803,774—he had submitted on February 23. After winding up his work and collecting his papers, he handed over superintendence of the Rideau Canal to Captain Daniel Bolton, and left with his family on a steamer for Montréal, never to return to Bytown.

A year earlier, he had commissioned a London goldsmith, John Bridge, to make four sterling silver presentation cups, 12 inches [30 centimetres] high and 9 inches [22 centimetres] in diameter, for his four major contractors who were building the Rideau Canal. Colonel By had expected that the Canal would be finished by August 21, 1831, and had had that date, as well as the name of the recipient, inscribed on the cups.

In Montréal, on September 1, 1832, the Colonel presented Mackay, Redpath, and Drummond with an engraved silver cup each, and another to the partnership of Philips & White, in recognition of their services.

Figure 12.1. Silver cup given to Mackay and Redpath.

On October 21, he and his family sailed from Québec on the troopship *Brothers*, arriving at Chatham Naval Dockyard on November 25.

Colonel By soon found out to his dismay that his last estimate to the Ordnance in the spring had been submitted directly to the Lords of the Treasury without comment. The Treasury had then issued a minute to the Ordnance on May 25, who censured Colonel By for overspending and demanded his return to answer questions about his accounts.

However, by that point, discussion in Parliament about the Rideau Canal had just about petered out. Earl Grey's new Reform government, now back in power, had already studied how Ordnance capital was spent on the Rideau Canal, by relying on Colonel By's spring estimate. On June 15, a Treasury committee had interviewed Colonel By's Montréal superior, Colonel Durnford, Commander of the Royal Engineers in Canada, and that was the end of the matter.

Buffeted by political turmoil, for political and practical reasons, the Lords of the Treasury focused on a single goal—to avoid payment to the Ordnance for the cost of the Rideau Canal.

Suspicion of overspending on the Rideau Canal was not at all an excuse for the recall of Colonel By. It was an Ordnance problem, not his. And yet he made a handy symbol of uncontrolled excess, during the Whig attempt to rein in the Ordnance.

Colonel By found that he still had to appear before the Board of Ordnance, to submit his final budget, but also to answer serious charges made by Henry Burgess, a disgruntled former Rideau Canal clerk, that Colonel By had misappropriated public funds.

Colonel By had hired Burgess in 1829 to oversee certain financial aspects of the canal project. In March of 1830 the Colonel dismissed Burgess on the grounds of "insubordination, drunkenness, sub-par work habits and missing duty." The man, clearly a denizen of Lower Town, arrived at By's office eight months later, demanding to be paid the entire sum of his expected contract. By refused.

Burgess then stormed off to England, where he loudly claimed to be the "only person living who is able to explain the accounts for the construction of the canal." When he took his charges to the Board of Ordnance, they were required to investigate further and ordered Colonel By to produce official documents, account information, and correspondence.

Of course, his Ordnance colleagues knew perfectly well that Colonel By was innocent of all charges of overspending. The Duke had trusted Colonel By enough to give him carte blanche to build the Rideau Canal to the best of his judgment and abilities. The matter was urgent. Wellington had ordered Colonel By in a letter "not to wait for Parliamentary Grants, but to proceed with all despatch consistent with economy."

In the end, the Ordnance investigation of the Burgess claims was a minor act in an elaborate Kabuki theatre designed to close the curtain on an annoying problem for both the Whig ministry and the Duke of Wellington. Colonel By had to play his part, to appear on stage, deliver his lines and disappear.

In the end, Colonel By, a diligent and dutiful servant of the Crown, felt he was being hung out to dry by politicians and functionaries. In 1833, he wrote Colonel Durnford that "the present government appears to throw blame on me for not waiting for Parliamentary grants; forgetting that it was ordered by his grace the Master-General"—the Duke of Wellington himself.

Colonel By's complaints that he had been treated badly went nowhere, although Lord Dalhousie, in far-off Edinburgh, expressed his sympathies.

By's health deteriorated, perhaps due to the stress of the Burgess investigation. He was a portly man, a lover of fine food and wine. Whether or not this was a contributing factor, Royal Engineer John By died peacefully on February 1, 1836, at age 53, at his home in Frant, East Sussex, shortly after the Burgess investigation ended.

Was Colonel By a Profligate Spender?

Colonel By's 1832 estimate of £777,146 held up very well. It was above the Kempt Committee's numbers. His final figure of £822,804 was largely due to land acquisition settlements made under the *Rideau Canal Act* of 1827, which stated that settlements for expropriated land—including land needed to create slack water lakes—were to be made by arbitration or by jury.

The Rideau Canal was in fact a model project, built in only five years and costing less than 43 percent over the 1828 estimate. The Welland Canal took a decade to complete and went 55 percent over budget. Indeed, the final Rideau Canal cost was only 19 percent over Colonel By's March 1830 supplementary budget, which was accepted by the Duke of Wellington's ministry.

Figure 12.2. *First Eight Locks of the Rideau Canal, 1834.*
Source: Thomas Burrowes fonds, Archives of Ontario, C 1-0-0-0-13.

In a report to His Majesty, Joseph Hagerman stated:

> The excellence of the workmanship and the superior construction of the locks and dams require no praise. They speak for themselves, and are the subject of much admiration, and in the opinion of those most competent to just such works, exceed anything of this kind in any parts of the world.

Before Colonel By left the Canadas in 1832, the Montreal Committee of Trade held a banquet in his honour, and presented the chief engineer of the Rideau Canal with a moving, though wordy, address:

> An undertaking of great magnitude and importance, the successful accomplishment of which, in so comparatively short a period, notwithstanding the unheard of inestimable difficulties and impediments which had to be encountered and surmounted, in an almost unexplored and uninhabited wilderness, evinced on your part a moral courage and an undaunted spirit and combination of science and management equally exciting our admiration and deserving our praise.[1]

Colonel By's Legacy

After Colonel By left for England, his military successors focused on a potential fortress on Barrack Hill, and on the Canal as a defence route. They did not share Colonel By's vision of the Canal as an industrial artery.

The Colonel had envisioned the twenty dam sites along the route being used for milling, and predicted that millers would export up to a hundred thousand barrels of flour a year. But only five mills were ever fully developed. Some mills were in place before the canal was built, but several of those had to be torn down before being flooded during lock building.

Despite Colonel By's prediction, no more than twelve thousand barrels were ever shipped annually, mostly from Thomas Mackay's Rideau Falls mills, the construction of which was backed and enabled by Colonel By.

---

[1] Ken W. Watson, *Bye By: The Story of Lieutenant-Colonel John By, R.E. and his fall from grace.*

Figure 12.3. Reputed image of Lieutenant Colonel John By.
Source: Parks Canada.

Instead, the canal hosted an unexpected lumber boom, opening up tracts of rich virgin forest that were quickly leased and cut. Soon the Rideau was choked with floating log booms heading for Bytown and Kingston. Thomas Burrowes recorded that from 1834 to 1850, the locks at Kingston Narrows collected tolls on 382 barrels of flour, 22,000 bushels of wheat, 1.5 million feet [457,200 metres] of oak, and 10,000 sawlogs.

Colonel By also estimated that the Canal could become self-financing by charging tolls and collecting rent from government-leased land. In the year he left, the Ordnance started taxing all the items the steamers and barges carried—passengers, grain and flour, butter and lard, and tobacco and whisky. But when they started charging tolls on timber rafts, all involved in the industry raised a stink and the tolls were dropped.

The canal broke even only in the years 1844–1845, but it did profit the country in other, less tangible, ways. Before adequate roads and railway tracks were cut out of the forest, Rideau steamboats and barges helped Kingston, Ottawa, and the settlements in between, to survive, thrive, and prosper. Today, the Rideau Canal is a world heritage treasure, and a gift to the people of Canada, not from the British taxpayer, but from the Royal Ordnance and its master, the Duke of Wellington.

The Rise of the Whig Reformers

Meanwhile, on May 25, 1832, the day that Colonel By and his party were passing through Smiths Falls on the steamboat *Rideau*, Earl Grey's Reform government recommended to the Board of Ordnance that the Colonel make himself available in England to explain cost overruns in the building of the waterway.

The real reasons for Colonel By's recall and the whole issue of the financing of the Rideau Canal have been lost in the fog of the political turmoil of the time.

For two years, riots had swept England—the result of poor harvests and a labour market swamped by demobilized servicemen. Desperate workers demanded poor relief, and turned to poaching, arson, and the breaking of machines such as steam threshers.

The Duke of Wellington's absolutist views were proving to be extremely unpopular, even within his own Tory party. He barricaded himself in his London mansion, Apsley House, as it came under attack by an angry mob.

At the same time, the Reform faction of the Whig Party began to make its power felt.

The Whig political program backed free trade, Catholic emancipation, abolishing slavery, expanding the electorate, and improving the state of the public finances.

Regarding the military defence of British North America, and Rideau Canal funding, the Whig reformers seemed not so much upset at Colonel By's apparent cost overruns as they were at the Board of Ordnance's seeming defiance of parliamentary authority, by paying for the project on its own terms—with pieces of eight—regardless of the actual amount of the parliamentary grants. But it was clearly time to shift spending from military to civilian purposes, and tighten peacetime control over the Ordnance.

As Robert Legget has suggested, many reformers were mystified by the fact that the Rideau Canal was completed "with no real authority from the British Parliament, the only authorization being for a preliminary expenditure of £5,000."

The truth of the matter is more complex, and here we must turn to the proceedings of the House of Commons, and its cast of characters, to clarify how the Rideau Canal was financed and why.

Much turned around the growing desire of the Whig reformers to do more to ease the crisis of the poor. At the same time, many Reform MPs wanted the military to back away from asking Parliament to reimburse the Ordnance for money spent on the Rideau Canal—a military project which the Ordnance had already funded with Spanish silver.

Three of the leading Whigs were fully aware that the Ordnance was rich enough to bend to this desire. It was a family affair. Grey himself and two members of his ministry were intimately related to Baring Brothers, the bankers who originally arranged the pieces of eight caper with their opposite number in Paris, Napoleon's banker Gabriel Ouvrard. Henry Labouchere, a Whig Treasury Lord, was the grandson of Sir Francis Baring, another Treasury Lord and a cousin of Earl Grey.

An Annoying Problem Solved?

The evidence strongly suggests—see Appendix 2: The Rideau Canal Debates—that the new Whig government, dealing with rioting and distress around the country, passage of the great *Reform Bill*, and poor law reform, and facing a £700,000 deficit, moved to save tax money by having the [War and] Colonial Office swallow most of the cost of the Rideau Canal, and not ask for funds to reimburse the Ordnance for the work.

Indeed, the use of Spanish silver instead of British Sterling was a salutary solution for all sides. For the reformers, they were able, at no cost, to both embarrass the opposition and balance the books. For the Ordnance, it was a chance to escape further scrutiny of its finances.

When Earl Grey's government fell in 1832, over the *Reform Bill*, Wellington was unable to form a Tory government, partly because of a run on the Bank of England. King William IV restored Grey to the premiership. Eventually the *Reform Bill* passed the House of Lords, after the King threatened to flood that House with newly created Whig peers.

From the perspective of the politics of the time, the Rideau Canal question was very near the bottom of the Grey government's list of priorities, except as a way to squeeze the military to cut spending. It seems likely that internal disagreement among the Whigs in the Commons over the issue finally convinced the Grey ministry that probing any more deeply into Rideau Canal finances would be a fruitless and even damaging endeavour.

We may never be able to prove beyond a doubt what happened exactly, because on October 16, 1834, a catastrophic fire destroyed much of the old Palace of Westminster. The flames devoured countless priceless and important records, along with the building itself, parts of which dated from shortly after the Norman Conquest.

Figure 12.4. Palace of Westminster destroyed by fire, 1834.
Source: Unknown artist.

The blaze was caused by employees of the Exchequer burning the small wooden tally sticks that were used as part of their ancient accounting system. Overloaded into two coal furnaces, they caused a chimney fire that spread under the floor of the House of Lords. Only medieval Westminster Hall was saved from the fire. The ruin on the north bank of the River Thames was eventually cleared to build the current Victorian-era Houses of Parliament.

PART TWO

New Edinburgh and Rideau Hall

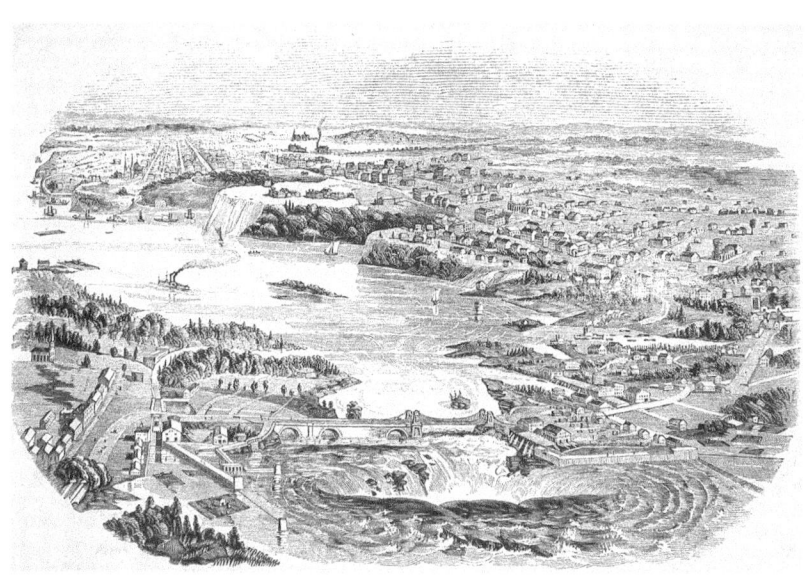

Figure 13.1. Bytown waterscape, 1851, showing Mackay's stone arches and Keefer's suspension bridge.
Source: John Henry Walker, McCord Museum, M930.50.7.4.

CHAPTER 13

Militia, Politics, and Civics, 1830–1838

Ottawa in 1833 was a "local habitation" with the ungainly name of Bytown, comprising thirty or forty houses, nine-tenths of which were wooden. The devastation effected by the second cholera epidemic in 1834 and the abscondings and removals resulting from the stagnation of business, reduced the centre literally and virtually to a "By Town," an out-of-the way place. A solitary steamer, in helpless inactivity, might remain moored to the wharf for three whole days; Royal Mail was only delivered and dismissed every alternate day; a plain two-storey house was pronounced to be a splendid hotel; there was neither printing press, foundry, tannery nor even a butcher's stall in the whole town and no fire engine to quench the not-infrequent conflagrations. Today, in less than a quarter of a century, the city has five printing presses, large, commodious hotels, various foundries, tanneries and markets and half a dozen fire engines. Well may her citizens evince pride and wonder at her astonishing advancement.

—Gertrude Van Cortlandt,
"Records of the Rise and Progress of the City
of Ottawa from the Foundation of the Rideau
Canal to the Present Time," *Ottawa Citizen*, 1858

Mackay the Operative Mason

Philemon Wright of Hull and Thomas Mackay of New Edinburgh shared similar political principles. Wright was elected to the assembly of Lower Canada to represent Ottawa County in 1830. He voted against Papineau's 92 Resolutions demanding an elected council. He was also the leader of freemasonry in the area for many of the villagers and surrounding communities.

On the south shore of the Ottawa River, it was a different matter. Freemasonry—symbolic instead of craft masonry—had evolved by the late eighteenth century into a kind of social and charitable organization. It was also influenced by the principles of early Masonic guilds that a man became a mason with the help of elder operatives, as if he were a rough stone that had to be shaped to become useful and good, in building the edifice of civilization.

The guild idea originally evolved into freemasonry to promote free thinking and the ideas and goals of the enlightenment.

Freemasonry also became popular, if not mandatory, in the British army, and each regiment had its own lodge. The Duke of Wellington was a member of his family lodge in Trim, Ireland, and his brother later served as grand master of Ireland. The King was a Freemason.

Governor General Lord Dalhousie was also grand master of the Grand Lodge of Scotland from 1804–1806, as well as head of the Scottish rite of Freemasonry, as were his father and his son. Thomas Mackay was one of the founders of the first Ottawa lodge, named in Dalhousie's honour.[1]

Freemasonry was also a useful philosophy to adopt if the aim was to create disciplined and responsible soldiers.

The Duke of Wellington valued Freemasonry as an agent of discipline and morale. In 1813, he spoke fondly about volunteer soldiers in the British army:

> A French army is composed very differently from ours. The conscription calls out a share of every class—no matter whether your son or my son—all must march; but our friends—I may say it in this room—are the very scum of the earth. People talk of their enlisting from their fine military feeling—all stuff—no such thing. Some of our men enlist from having got bastard children—some for minor offences—many more for drink; but you can hardly conceive such a set brought together, and it really is wonderful that we should have made them the fine fellows they are.

---

[1] By-Laws of the Dalhousie Lodge, of Ancient, Free and Accepted Masons, 1868.

Figure 13.2. Dalhousie Lodge by-laws. Mackay was a founding member of the Dalhousie Lodge of Freemasons.
Source: John Henry Walker, McCord Museum, M930.50.1.560.

Freemasonry had a lot to do with making "fine fellows."

In 1815, the English lodge bowed to Wellington's pressure by adopting new rules disallowing military lodges from bringing in civilians. However, in a military settlement like Bytown, this caused few difficulties. Thomas Mackay was a mason—a real "operative" mason—and was initially not eligible to join a military lodge until he joined the militia. But in Upper Canada, every man of military age— 19 to 39—was subject to service in his local colonial regiment of militia. Every year on the King's birthday, every militiaman had to report to the nearest permanent military outpost, where he registered, declared that he owned a musket in good working order, and was trained in basic military drill.

Overall, freemasonry exerted a unifying influence in the Ottawa Valley, in some cases moderating religious prejudices brought from the homeland. The Constitutions of Freemasonry banned the discussion of religion in lodges, even though quarrels of a religious nature sometimes broke out.

Thomas Mackay led the local militia from the late 1820s on. Starting in 1837, he was asked to serve as Lt.-Col. of the Volunteer Company of the First Battalion of Russell Militia; then, from November 1846 until his death, as Lt.-Col. of the Carleton Militia.

While British regulars served mainly on the St. Lawrence front, with a small garrison on Barrack Hill, Mackay's main duty was to guard the strategic Ottawa locks and the Rideau Canal from rebel raiders determined to blow up the locks and drain the system. He was expected to buy uniforms and supply the men with equipment partly out of his own pocket, and arrange for training with the help of the regular garrison.

The danger to the canal was real. In September 1841, the St. Catharines militia foiled an attempt by rebels to blow up the locks of the Welland Canal.

On June 30, 1838, Mackay sent his first annual return to Richard Bullock, Adjutant General of Militia in Toronto. On November 23, he asked Bullock if he could quarter his men in the Bytown barracks, noting that "there are vacant quarters for between two and three hundred men." By December 10, he had mustered three captains, two lieutenants, one ensign, three sergeants and fifty-nine rank and file.

Among Mackay's young militia officers were Jamie Stevenson, a banker; and Thomas Hannah, who was in change of a battery set up on Barrack Hill on the site of the East Block of Parliament, looking down at the Locks.

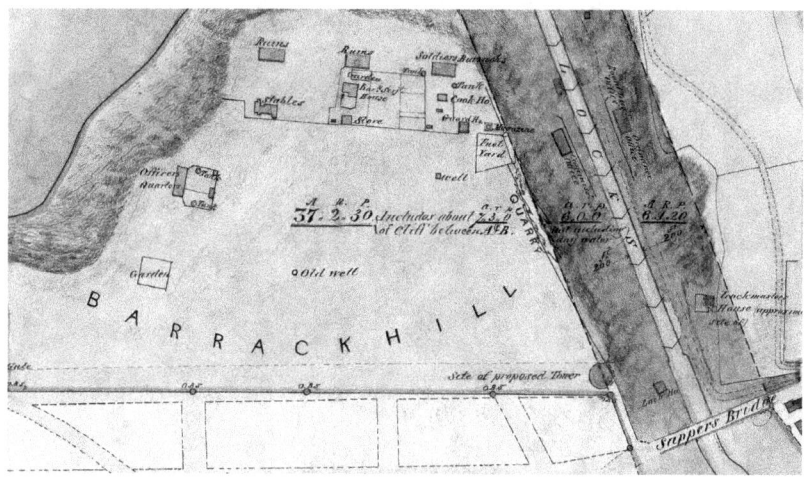

Figure 13.3. Barrack Hill buildings, 1840s.
Source: Library and Archives Canada.

At this point, Mackay ran into some resistance from the remaining British military establishment. On December 29, he complained to Bullock that Colonel Daniel Bolton, who had replaced Colonel By in 1832, had "declined to countersign the acquisition for the county of forty shillings which it was understood the non-commissioned officers and men were to receive to provide them with necessities absolutely essential to their efficiency."

There is no record of Bullock's replies.

The following June 4, 1839, he reported on four companies—New Edinburgh (252 men), Osgoode (232 men), Cumberland (75 men), and Clarence (40 men) on parade in New Edinburgh—a total of 625 men.

On one occasion, he had to sort out a problem where two of his officers, Lieutenant Mactaggart and Captain O'Connor were charged, court-martialled, and fined "one pound and costs" for non-attendance at a training parade on Barrack Hill. Mackay agreed to pay the costs of the court-martial, recognizing that their absence from the parade was based on "ignorance of the Militia Act."[2]

---

[2] Library and Archives Canada, RG9 IB1 30 and 35, Col. Thomas MacKay, Russell Militia returns, correspondence with Richard Bullock, Adjutant General of Militia, Toronto.

Figure 13.4. Volunteer militia, Montréal, 1850s.
Source: Photograph by Notman, *Illustrated London News*, March 10 1860.

Fortress Ottawa 1830–1838

Tensions between the Americans and British continued after the War of 1812, and renewed with the outbreak of rebel movements based in nearby US states. Fearing that the new Rideau Canal could be susceptible to American attack, the Ordnance in Kingston demolished the original Fort Henry and built a more extensive fort between 1832 and 1836, one capable of defending the Lake Ontario terminus of the strategic Rideau Canal. Colonel By was ordered to build wooden guardhouses along the canal.

Colonels By and Durnford had already produced a draft plan of a projected fortress in 1831, based on Durnford's previous work on the Québec Citadel.

In the plans presented to the Ordnance, the colonels made use of the existing barracks, but added bombproof casements, massive storage facilities, and ramparts, in case of a land attack on the waterway. They projected it would cost £205,450. And it was assumed Thomas Mackay, who had chosen to remain in Ottawa, and who

Figure 13.5. View of Fort Henry, Kingston, Upper Canada.
Source: Henry Francis Ainslie, Library and Archives Canada, Acc. No. 1955-128-16.

had already worked on two military forts—Île Ste Hélène and Fort Lennox—would hold himself in readiness to serve as a main contractor.

With the outbreak of rebellion in Upper and Lower Canada in 1837, Colonel By's successors were ordered to move up creation of a permanent fortification on Barrack Hill, to be renamed Citadel Hill. The fortress would stretch almost a kilometre, from the Ottawa River to what now is Queen Street, and from the canal in the east to Bank Street in the west.

John Burrows, overseer of works in the Ordnance Department's engineering office, drew the first sketch of the citadel in 1838. It shows a typical nineteenth-century Vauban-style star fort on Barrack Hill— he named it Citadel Hill. It was similar to the forts guarding Halifax and Québec City, with 6-metre-high angled stone walls bristling with cannon placements and zigzagging trenches. For further protection, it featured a water-filled moat and a "glacis" in front of the main trench, so that the walls were almost totally hidden, preventing point-blank enemy fire.

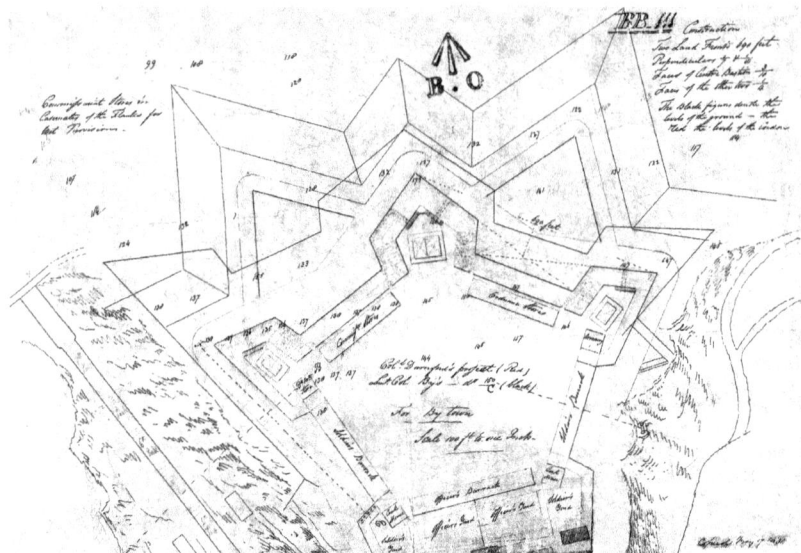

Figure 13.6. Plan for a citadel by Colonels Durnford and By, May 17, 1831. *Source*: Library and Archives Canada.

This vision of a northern fortress and twin to Fort Henry was never realized. After the rebellions were quashed and the threat of an attack from the United States fizzled out by the mid-1850s, Canada abandoned plans to fortify Bytown.

Most of all, the fortifications in Canada, from the Québec Citadel west, were rapidly becoming obsolete with advances in artillery.

Bytown never assumed more than a minor military role, but in the 1830s and 1840s, the military garrison on Barrack Hill remained a reliable pillar of the community. It supported the town with purchases of fuel, food, and living amenities, and by joining social gatherings and taking on civic duties, such as helping train the militia, keeping the peace, and attending church. In 1837, the coronation of Queen Victoria was celebrated on the Hill with a military parade, a royal salute fired from a cannon, and singing and dancing around a huge bonfire.

In 1854, the remaining military garrison at Barrack Hill was called away to the Crimean War, and the property left in the hands of a Sergeant Ritchie. He cultivated a beautiful flower garden, and delighted in giving out bouquets to young lovers. After Ritchie was recalled, the land lay fallow for several years. Farmers used one of the deserted barracks for exhibiting their cattle and produce. The grand plans for

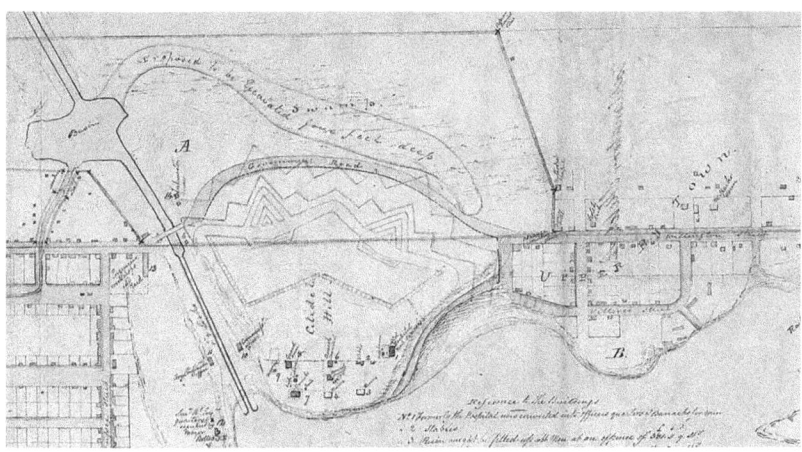

Figure 13.7. Burrows's plan for the Ottawa Citadel, 1838.
Source: John Burrows fonds, Library and Archives Canada.

Ottawa's massive stone fortress were shelved, and Citadel Hill would become the cockpit for a different kind of battle, that of politics.

Health and the Public Peace

Thomas Mackay became active in public life as a member of Bytown's first municipal council. On June 20, 1832, while the Ottawa Locks were in the final construction stage, and a few days after the Canal had been officially opened, the Governor ordered the unincorporated Bytown Council to set up a Board of Health, under Dr. Christie, to check the spread of Asian Cholera that had arrived upriver from Montréal. To isolate cases, the Board built a "cholera wharf" downstream from the locks in Sleigh Bay and a crude quarantine hospital above the Bay.

The steamer *Shannon* was ordered not to stop at the regular wharf, and passengers had to pass medical inspection before they were allowed to leave the ship and enter Bytown. Schools and public places were closed; and cattle and pigs stopped from roaming the town's streets; but still the stench of cholera hit Lower Town hard, and many died that summer.

Fifteen years later, Sister Élisabeth Bruyère and a group of Grey Nuns had just finished building a general hospital in Lower Town when typhus struck the settlement like a storm. Once again the Board of Health jumped into action, to help them save souls.

Figure 13.8. Dr. Alexander James Christie.
Source: Library and Archives Canada, MIKAN 2933576, C-115785.

The sick, mostly Irish immigrants, were isolated on the west side of the canal in crowded wooden sheds. The Sisters immediately built an addition to their brand-new hospital. By the end of the epidemic, they had treated 619 typhus victims, of whom 167 died. Shortly after, Bruyère established an orphanage for the surviving children who were without family.

Figure 13.9. Élisabeth Bruyère.
Source: Library and Archives Canada.

The Shiners' War

> *No place is better calculated to exhibit the savages of civilized countries than Bytown. All that the art of unprincipled men can devise comes under my observation every day, and a mealtime seldom passes without witnessing the determination of an important case by "wager of battle;" that is a few civil blows. The zeal with which men fight and the cordiality of their reconciliation are highly amusing.*
>
> —J. Wilson to Rev. William Bell, 1832

Other crises bedeviled Bytown. Labour unrest in the lumber industry came to a head in 1832, as many Irish labourers, newly unemployed on completion of the Rideau Canal, founded a gang called the Shiners, led by Peter Aylen, to go to war against the more experienced French Canadian "bucherons" for jobs.

The battles were more nationalistic than religious. In a rare example of Irish solidarity, many Irish Catholics joined forces with the Orangemen against the French Catholics.[3]

Aylen adopted violence as a business tactic, raiding the timber limits of his competitors, destroying the booms and rafts of his rivals, and attacking other crews. Exploiting a power vacuum, the Shiners terrorized the community, beating civilians, poisoning wells, burning stables, blowing up family homes, dumping corpses from hearses, and in one case, stripping children naked and leaving them in the snow.

In July 1835, when Aylen was arrested for assault, his enraged followers went on a rampage, destroying a canal steamer in Bytown harbour. In 1837, they disrupted a meeting of the Nepean Township Council, preventing the election of municipal officers.

When Aylen tried to seize political and economic control of Bytown, Mackay and friends on the new council sent a petition "from the principal inhabitants of Bytown" to Sir Peregrine Maitland, Lieutenant-Governor of the province, asking for the appointment of magistrates and the establishment of a court of requests, because peace was "most dreadfully disturbed and lives and property being in danger day and night by drunken and riotous persons employed on the Canal."

In 1833, Thomas Mackay was one of the four leading men who volunteered to serve as a Justice of the Peace. This was not viewed with favour by another potential magistrate, a snobbish martinet named Thomas Y. McQueen, who declined to sit on the same council as Mackay and his friend Dr. Christie.

McQueen, a young MD from Glasgow, accused Mackay and his friend Christie of "meddling" with Bytown's Roman Catholic priest. McQueen refused to associate with "most ignorant persons who have not even the rank of gentlemen—the choice of the people, Thomas Mackay, a common stone mason, Pennefeather one of the lower classes of Irish, Burgess, a clerk in Government office, and Dr. Christie (unfit for any public office, he is continually at the bottle)."

Another curmudgeonly character, George A. Rankin, also refused to let his name appear, "with two licensed tavern keepers (James Ferguson and James Black) and Dr. Christie, a person with whom no gentleman can associate without dishonour."[4]

---

[3] Benjamin Sulte, *Mélanges historiques*, XII, 27
[4] Brault, *Ottawa Old and New*; Library and Archives Canada Upper Canada Sundries, October 18, 1828.

No matter. Colonel By eventually put some of his best Royal Sappers and Miners on street patrol to help quell the violence and disorder. Mackay's militia force drilled regularly, and residents also formed their own Preservation of the Public Peace force. In 1837, they swore in armed night patrols made up of almost two hundred volunteer constables, acting under the municipal council. Aylen finally realized it was time to put aside his bully ways, and pursue peace on the river, so he moved to Aylmer, married a lumber heiress, and joined the Ottawa Lumber Association as an officer.

A proper police force was finally established by the Ottawa town council in 1863.

A Common Stonemason

With peace restored, Mackay moved from being a town councillor and justice of the peace to a member of the assembly. On October 12, 1834, in New Edinburgh, Thomas Mackay—"the choice of the people"—was declared elected by a majority of 7 votes out of 137 over Daniel O'Connor to the Legislative Assembly of Upper Canada for the county of Russell. He was re-elected in 1836, when his nominator was the same Daniel O'Connor, and held his seat until the legislative Union of the Canadas, in 1841, which he supported.

While attending the provincial parliament in Toronto, Mackay focused mainly on commercial matters. He also advocated several measures:

In 1836, he voted in favour of the use of statute labour for ablebodied men, to improve roads leading to backcountry settlements; he also worked with a young civil engineer named Samuel Keefer in preparing a report on navigable communication up the Ottawa River to Lake Huron.

He introduced a resolution to obtain an act for the erection of a new district with Bytown as county town and judicial centre, where a jail and a courthouse would be erected. On March 21 of that year, he was feted at a public dinner in Bytown. One speaker commented that many men, having made their fortune in the New World, would have carried their wealth back home to enjoy the comforts of the Old Country, but not Thomas Mackay.

Mackay also urged public ownership of the Welland Canal, which had opened in 1830. In 1837, he served on a select committee investigating navigation on the St. Lawrence River.

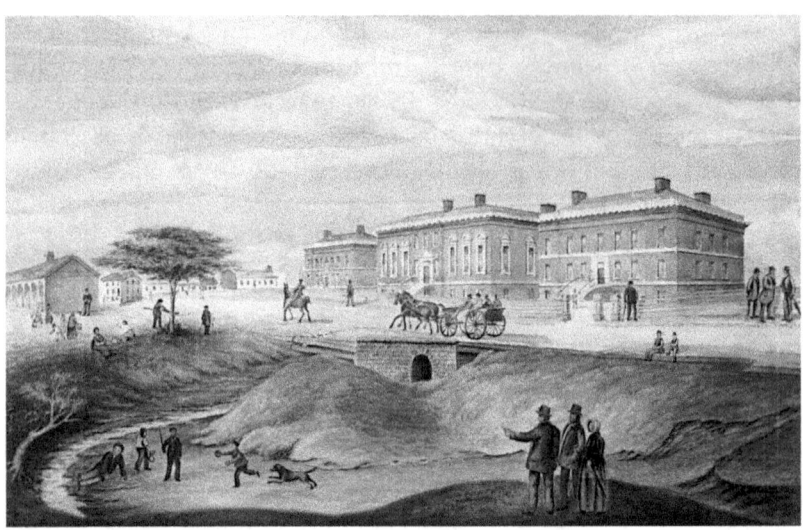

Figure 13.10. Upper Canada Parliament, Toronto, 1834.
Source: Archives of Ontario.

He also introduced a bill in April 1838 creating the District of Dalhousie, later comprising practically all of Carleton County. The first district council of Dalhousie met on August 9, 1842, in the temporary courthouse in Bytown. Mackay served as the first Dalhousie warden. He subsequently became the first warden of Carleton County, and his masons built the first county jail and courthouse.[5]

In 1841, he backed a petition from the directors of the Bank of Montreal for a charter of incorporation; and a petition from Nicholas Sparks of Bytown, praying that certain property, which had been taken by the Ordnance for the use of the Rideau Canal, be restored to him.

As a staunch Presbyterian, Mackay may have had some influence on the settlement of the clergy reserves land dispute in Upper Canada—the Governor declared that half the land set aside for Protestant churches—first defined as Anglican—would be shared between Anglicans and Presbyterians, and the other half between the other Protestant denominations.

---

[5] Brault, *Ottawa Old and New.*

Mackay by His Contemporaries

Mackay's career was multifaceted. A man of diverse talents and abundant energy, he was very much a "self made man," in the opinion of the *Montreal Witness*, and "one who amassed much property and wealth but never lost the common touch."

Indeed, due to his character and the size of his bank account, Mackay was the dominant figure in this small community.

An editorial in the *Bytown Packet* newspaper praised how much he contributed to the community:

> It is only doing justice to say that the wealthy proprietor, the Hon. Thomas Mackay, is deserving of high consideration, inasmuch as he might have retired to enjoy the quiet and ease within his reach and avoided the troubles incident to business speculations. Of all those who were engaged in the heavy contracts on the Rideau works, none have contribute[d] so much to the improvement of the country, or have employed their capital with so much benefit to this locality, as this gentleman. Capital thus employed is productive of general benefits, and we sincerely hope that his speculations may be crowned with complete success.

Mackay was known to one resident of New Edinburgh as "a ruddy faced, forceful man, who, when he had an objective, generally managed to reach it."

He was also depicted by Andrew Wilson as a straightforward, upright, and honourable man, who was accessible "even to the humblest. Nevertheless he had a dignified bearing, and knew his place as a gentleman."[6]

---

[6] J.E. Askwith, *Recollections of New Edinburgh*, 75.

CHAPTER 14

Miller Mackay, 1830–1849

With his work for the Ordnance winding down, Thomas Mackay began to invest part of his Lachine Canal profits in buying and leasing property around Rideau Falls. The gentle roar of falling water and his Scottish instincts had already led him to the same conclusion as Colonel By—that a swiftly running river could be profitably harnessed to saw lumber, mill grain, and weave blankets.

Lot Letter O

Colonel By was an enthusiastic promoter of Mackay's mill projects. In 1829, he arranged with the Ordnance to lease Mackay part of the "Lot O" military reserve, a 70-acre [28-hectare] triangle that stretched along the Ottawa River from today's Sussex Drive to the Rideau River and the Falls. The property had originally been acquired by Lord Dalhousie.

The Colonel was concerned about the two companies of Royal Sappers and Miners, to be discharged on June 8, 1831, who wished to settle in the Bytown area. Some were given positions as lock masters on the newly created canal. Others took up the promised reward of 100 acres [40 hectares] of land in the vicinity. Those who wished to farm would need an outlet for their produce. Mackay's projected milling businesses could also help provide other retired soldiers with some livelihood for their families.

Mackay and Colonel By also wanted to ease the plight of the Irish and French-Canadian labourers who were already fighting over the declining work on the canal project.

Fortunately for many of the workers, the Ottawa Valley timber boom, pioneered by Philemon Wright, was beginning to take up the slack. The Irish and French-Canadians took their battles upstream

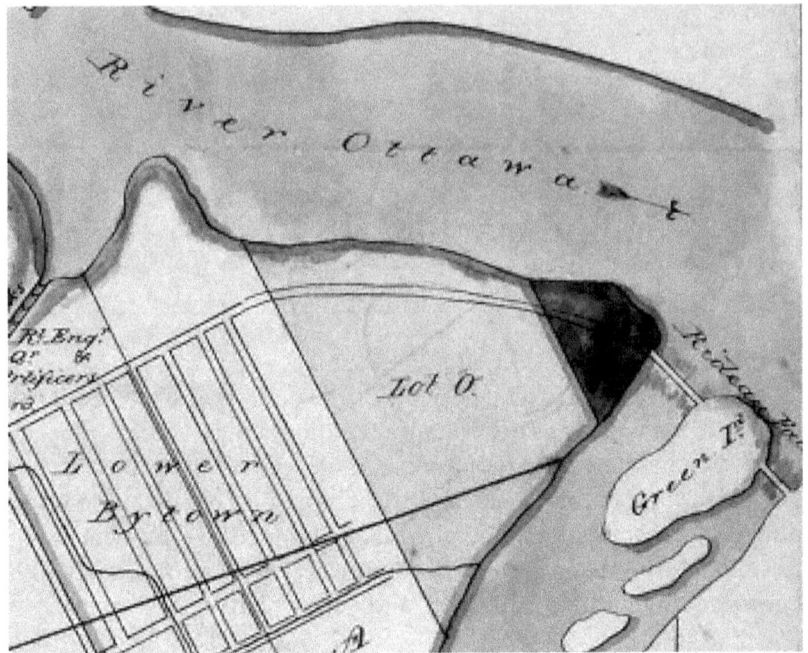

Figure 14.1. Mackay's Lot O lease in black.
Source: Library and Archives Canada.

and into the woods, where they became lumberjacks, sending immense rafts of timber down the Ottawa.

In 1830, Mackay and his masons started building a Rideau Falls sawmill that could keep his crew together. Many of them had made the decision to stay in Bytown as well—they continued working for Mackay when masonry projects were available.

Mackay also engaged a capable miller in Jean-Baptiste Saint-Louis, a francophone entrepreneur who had built the St. Louis Dam that created Dow's Lake, as well as a small grist mill on the Bywash in Lower Town.

Mackay leased him the sawmill on the west side of Rideau Falls for thirty years, at £20 a year—the lease was signed by Colonel By, because the underlying land was Ordnance property. In 1831, Mackay put his men to work cutting wood along the Rideau River for the sawmill, while he began building a grist mill on the east side of the falls. Mackay would also go on to lease Green Island and the other islands in the Rideau River from the Ordnance.

Figure 14.2. Thomas Mackay, 1830s.
Source: Topley Studio, Library and Archives Canada, C-2846.

Also in 1831, Mackay acquired all of Lots 1-2-3-4 in Gore Township, 1,100 acres [445 hectares] of choice terrain that included most of present-day New Edinburgh and Rockcliffe.

This land had originally been granted in 1797 to Captain John Munro, a United Empire Loyalist who had served in the King's Royal Regiment of New York. Munro was a member of the first Legislative Council of Upper Canada. His grant was passed in 1799, but he died in October of the following year. His heirs didn't receive title until 1815. In 1818 the lands passed to his son, Dr. Henry Munro of Montréal.

In 1826 Colonel By had tried to purchase part of Lot 3, around Governor's Bay, as a possible alternative entrance to the proposed

Figure 14.3. *Eastern and Greater Fall of the Rideau River, 1830.*
Source: Thomas Burrowes fonds, Archives of Ontario, C 1-0-0-0-2.

Rideau Canal, but the price was too rich for the Ordnance, and Sleigh Bay was already deemed superior.

So by 1831, through grant, purchase, and lease, Mackay's holdings included, on today's Sussex Street, the land on which is now the residence of the United Kingdom High Commissioner, the Pearson Global Affairs building, the National Research Council, the French Embassy, 24 Sussex, the official residence of Canadian prime ministers, Rideau Hall and its surrounding 88 acres, all of old Rideau Ward, New Edinburgh, most of Rockcliffe, part of Beechwood Cemetery, a section of Eastview (Vanier) to the Montreal Road, and the islands of the Rideau, including Green Island (by lease in 1836).

By that point, Mackay was growing annoyed about encroachment and squatters on the Lot Letter O land he was leasing from the Ordnance. In an Upper Canada Land Petition dated November 7, 1836, he asked to be allowed to purchase the rest of Lot Letter O adjoining his property "where he has erected a large and expensive establishment."

On February 16, 1837, Mackay stated that he had

expended about £15,000 in the erection of mills near Bytown,[1] that adjoining his Mill privilege is a Crown reserve marked O, that the Ordinance Dept. have applied for the same in order to have it sold in small portions, that he has experienced great annoyance from persons living on part of the property, that he considers himself entitled to a preference in the purchase of the said land for which he is prepared and willing to pay the full value of it.

The Ordnance responded a year later, allowing him to purchase some 10 acres [4 hectares] of the Letter O property.

Mackay continued pressing the argument, and the Ordnance finally caved—on February 21, 1838, they granted Mackay full title to the property.[2]

Why the change of heart? Possibly it was a reward for his militia service. Certainly, they recognized that his capital resources would ensure stable employment to laid-off masons, retired soldiers, canal workers, and new immigrants.

There is another possible reason for the grant. On August 1, 1839, Mackay and two other petitioners argued successfully that they needed Lot Letter O for building a jail and courthouse in the new District of Dalhousie.

Perhaps it was a straight swap—Lot Letter O in exchange for building Bytown's first courthouse and jail.

At any rate, Nicholas Sparks donated the land and Thomas Mackay started the buildings in the spring of 1840, but on account of a shortage of stonecutters and builders the work was delayed until some skilled workers came from Montréal. The buildings were completed in 1842.[3]

In the meantime, Mackay was becoming increasingly frustrated with the state of the two bridges, authorized by Lord Dalhousie in September 1826, across the Rideau Falls at Green Island. By 1840, they were getting rotten, and dangerous to cross.

With no action from the Ordnance, he rebuilt the bridges on his own account, added gates, and began collecting tolls—a penny for

---

[1] About a third of his fortune.
[2] City of Ottawa Archives.
[3] Brault, *Ottawa Old and New*.

vehicles and a half-penny for pedestrians. Farmers and people with business at the mills did not have to pay. The tolls were strictly enforced by the gatekeeper, a crusty old Scot known as Grandpa McIntosh.

Mackay also entered into a dispute with a neighbour, Duncan MacNab, builder of an estate called Rockcliffe House, beyond Mackay's own holdings.

MacNab demanded a right of way through Mackay's property and over the twin toll bridges, instead of taking a longer route to the east on what is now Beechwood Road. To stop MacNab from passing through his property, Mackay ordered his teams to block the road with large boulders and logs. When MacNab removed them, they were immediately replaced. This battle went on for two years, and only ended with MacNab's death in 1837.[4]

The Founding of New Edinburgh

Mackay also had some pressing domestic matters to take care of. He and his family lived for a few weeks in a tent beside the works, then in a house on Wellington Street, but while building Colonel By's residence, he had acquired property just upstream from Rideau Falls, and put some of his carpenters and masons to work building their first home—a double-frame building on the corner of what is now Charles Street and Stanley Avenue in New Edinburgh. The house had a large fireplace and a stone barn at the rear. By the late summer of 1830, he and Ann were able to move mother Christina and his four surviving children into their new residence.[5]

One of their children was not so lucky. The pain of losing a child was a reality for most people in those days—most deaths were due to illness—smallpox, cholera, scarlet fever, diphtheria, tuberculosis. The Mackays were not immune, having already lost two babies to smallpox in 1817, and a daughter, Ann, was stillborn in 1820. But in 1827, the year they moved to Bytown, they were crushed when they lost their 9-year-old boy, Alexander, born in Montréal on January 6, 1818, who fell through the ice and drowned in the Ottawa River while tobogganing with friends.

---

[4] Edmond, *Rockcliffe Park*, 6.
[5] The house was demolished by the National Capital Commission in 1954, and the stone stable in 1973.

The Mackays' heartbreak would continue. As Mackay began to develop his industrial complex on the twin falls, he wanted to help his workforce live in more salubrious lodgings than the swampy Lower Town. In late 1833, he decided to start a settlement he called New Edinburgh on the east side of the Rideau River, where he himself lived. He laid out the streets in 1834, naming them after his wife and four surviving sons. He encouraged other Scotsmen who had worked on the Rideau Canal to settle there. He also induced several family members, including his brother William, a baker, to move to the new village from his hometown of Perth, Scotland. William's son, Thomas McKay, named after his uncle, eventually started a flour mill at the Chaudière Falls.[6]

In 1840, after William's death, another Mackay relative, Alexander Scott, also opened a bakery at the corner of Ottawa and John Streets. His product was praised by the *Bytown Gazette*: "We have seen an excellent quality of Brown bread from Mr. Scott's bakery in New Edinburgh. The loaf is 1½ pence cheaper than the other, an object of consideration in a large family."

Mackay's crew also completed the five-storey grist mill on the New Edinburgh side of Rideau Falls, and soon the rasp of grinding stones joined the constant rushing sound of the millrace and the whining of the saws at the lumber mill across the Falls.

Mackay's Industrial Complex

The largest and most modern grist mill in Upper Canada went into operation on August 26, 1833, first supplied with grain from Philemon Wright's farms across the Ottawa River. A bakery was erected a year later, followed by a brewery, and finally a distillery, in 1837. In the same year, the masons completed a cloth factory and soon the clatter of looms and treadles joined the cacophony at Thomas Mackay's Rideau Falls mills.

Breweries and distilleries were important in those days when river and well water could get contaminated. When there was a surplus of grain and a shortage of clean drinking water, weak brew provided a safe liquid to drink. British soldiers were also good customers,

---

[6] According to 1861 census data, 7 percent of Scottish Montrealers were born in Perth, Scotland.

since they were often paid a daily ration in pints or "beer money." Distilled whiskies also competed with imported liquors to keep more money within the local economy. In the days before dental floss and mouthwash, some claimed that gargling with whisky every morning and night kept tooth decay at bay.

In 1834, Edward Barker of Kingston observed that Mackay's flour was "presumed to be the best in Upper Canada," superior even to the mill at Gananoque of John McDonald, whose agents also began purchasing grain along the canal. Business boomed, and long lines of farmers' wagons began arriving at Mackay's mill. By 1835, he was milling twenty-seven thousand bushels of wheat and oats, and shipping flour down the Rideau to Kingston, and up the Ottawa Valley to the lumber camps, where he found his best customers.

Prior to 1837, Mackay built a stave mill and two cooperages (barrel factories) on Green Island, along with a smithy, a carpentry shop, and a machine shop along Ottawa Street to service the mills. By 1848, the expanded mill was supplying every description of lumber and timber, planed boards, flooring, doors, sashes, shingles, and lathing.

Employees at the mills commonly worked twelve hours a day. Labourers received six cents an hour, boys got two cents an hour, and masons were paid from eight to ten cents an hour.

Mill work could be dangerous. The *Bytown Gazette* of November 29, 1837, reported that "On Monday last, while one of the labourers was employed at Mr. Mackay's sawmill at New Edinburgh, his hand got unfortunately tangled in the machinery and was so dreadfully lacerated that amputation was necessary."

In August of 1844, a distillery worker named Whitehead slipped and fell into a vat containing hot grain mash. He was so severely scalded that he died the following day, leaving a wife and seven children to be supported by the community.

On June 29, 1850, a mill worker named John Roe was crushed to death when he got caught in a spiral vent wheel.

Thomas Mackay was not immune to the danger. On June 15, 1843, the *Bytown Gazette* reported that while he was in his sawmill at the Rideau Falls, "he inadvertently got his right hand in contact with the circular saw by which several of his fingers were so seriously injured that we hear a part of one of them had to be amputated. By last accounts he was doing well."

By the late 1830s, Mackay's mills could not keep up with the growing demand for lumber products, and the business attracted

Figure 14.4. *Rideau Mills Complex*, 1840s.
Source: Library and Archives Canada.

new entrants like Isaac Smith, of Hull, as well as Philip Thompson and Daniel McLachlin, who started up competing operations at the Chaudière Falls.

Mackay continued his partnership with John Redpath in the Ottawa and Rideau Forwarding Company, the major shipper of goods and passengers on the Ottawa River and along the Rideau Canal. He also consulted on the building of the 9.6-kilometre-long Grenville Canal, built with eleven locks by the Royal Staff Corps, under Captain Henry du Vernet, to bypass the Long Sault rapids halfway between Ottawa and Montréal. While criticized for being too narrow, it was completed in 1834, making the entire Bytown to Montréal system navigable by steamboat.

In the 1830s, Mackay's masons built a number of stone buildings along the south side of Ottawa (now Sussex) Street in New Edinburgh. These he rented to various merchants. A large stone building constructed about 1835 at the corner of Ottawa Street and Rideau Road was first leased to George and Robert Lang. They carried on a general store, dealing chiefly in lumbermen's supplies and even bark canoes. One of their advertisements in April 1840 offered for sale "swords for officers, belts, buckles and metallic buttons"—a symptom of the declining military presence in Bytown.

Mackay's All-Purpose Distillery

Perhaps the most interesting industry in New Edinburgh was Mackay's all-purpose distillery, built for Isaac Mactaggart in 1837 on the present property of the Embassy of France, opposite Alexander Street.

Once the whisky was ready, it flowed down a 35-foot-long [10-metre-long] pipe to a dock below, where it was emptied into barrels that were sealed and shipped out by barges via the Ottawa River and Rideau Canal. Beer was also brewed in season.

On January 23, 1840, Mackay's old friend Dr. Alexander Christie, owner and editor of the *Bytown Gazette*, and a well-known imbiber, noted that, "In the course of last week we examined the brewery and distillery of Mr. Isaac Mactaggart, where excellent ale and whisky is produced from grain purchased from farmers."

The people of New Edinburgh benefited from the waste and surplus from the distillery, even though some regarded whisky as the devil's dram. Most residents kept a pig or two which they fed with table scraps. But the pigs also ran wild and gobbled up the grain meal from the distillery's surplus. Every autumn, the residents identified their own hogs, slaughtered them, and salted the pork away for the winter.

Hundreds of cattle and pigs were also fed from the refuse of the distillery, and the meat shipped to lumber camps, and also as far away as Kingston and Montréal.[7]

By the early 1840s Mackay's pioneer industrial complex was booming. John Robertson of Nepean described the mills as among the best in the Province:

> The proprietor, the Hon. Thomas Mackay, purchases all the wheat offered. He has likewise a large woollen factory, for carding, spinning, weaving, and finishing cloths, tweeds, blankets, flannels, etc., very extensive sawmills and shingle mill, with door-making, window, and Venetian blind factory, also, a stave-splitting machine,

---

[7] Perhaps Mackay closed Mactaggart's distillery in 1852 due to pressure from the growing temperance movement.

and cooperage—so that sawlogs, staves, hoops, and generally all kinds of farm produce, are bought and paid for in cash, at high prices. These establishments have done much to put the country around in the flourishing condition it is in at present.

Mackay's was the first large cloth factory in the Ottawa Valley, starting operations in 1841. At first all the work was done by hand looms, but in 1847 he installed a number of power looms, weaving 150 yards [137 metres] a day. In the summer of 1848, he consolidated production in a four-storey stone building.

In one year, the factory turned out 3,500 pairs of blankets, which were of such quality that they were awarded a gold medal at the Exposition of all Nations in London in 1849.

Besides weaving blankets, twenty-five people were employed producing all manner of dry goods, including cashmere, satinette, tweed, flannel (cotton warp), flannel (all wool), farmers' cloth (finished), and about 20,000 pounds of carded wool a year.

Figure 14.5. *Mackay Mills, 1851.*
Source: Library and Archives Canada.

Like British philanthropist and mill owner Robert Owen, Mackay believed in the education of children, so in 1837, he decided that a small double house intended for the builders of Rideau Hall might better serve the settlement as a school. After a search in Montréal, he hired as its first schoolteacher, James Fraser, who had been a successful "dominee" in several schools in Scotland, as well as operating his own school in Montréal.

Commercial School.

MR. JAMES FRASER, Schoolmaster, begs to return thanks to his friends in Bytown, for the encouragement they have afforded him, since he opened the above Seminary; and he now takes this opportunity of intimating, that, in order to merit a continuance of their countenance and support, he is determined to use his best endeavours to give satisfaction. To enable him to accomplish this successfully, he will avail himself of the best method of instruction which late improvements have suggested. The branches which he professes to teach are, those of an *English* and *Commercial Education*. The theory and practice of *Vocal Music* will form a part of the daily exercises of his School. Mr. F. will conduct his School upon the strictest principles of morality *alone*, to avoid giving offence to any religious denomination

Terms may be known on application at the School Room, Sparks' Street.

Upper Bytown, 29th May, 1844.   47-z

P. S.—Mr. F. will devote part of his spare time in giving lessons in music to private individuals, on the FLUTE or VIOLIN.

Figure 14.6. James Fraser's school announcement.
Source: *Bytown Gazette*, July 4, 1844.

In its issue of June 20, 1838, the *Bytown Gazette* announced, "The school of New Edinburgh is to be opened on Monday, the 25th instant under the superintendence of Mr. J. Fraser." The announcement declared the school hours to be from 10 a.m. to 12 p.m., and from 2 p.m. to 4 p.m. It is interesting to note the subjects taught—"Reading and Elocution, French Writing, Arithmetic, English Grammar, and Geography."

The old school building is still standing, at 62–64 John Street, just off Sussex Drive across from the French Embassy.

A larger school was later built at the corner of Charles and Crichton Streets.

Mackay's Religion

A God-fearing Calvinist, who with his wife Ann had suffered the tragic loss of so many of their children, Mackay put much effort into getting Bytown's Presbyterian churches off the ground.

In April of 1828, during a lull in canal construction, he and his fellow Church of Scotland elders purchased a lot from Nicholas Sparks for £200, at the corner of Wellington and Kent Streets in Upper Town. Mackay donated the stones and labour, and set his skilled masons to work building Bytown's first Presbyterian church, St. Andrew's. Their enthusiasm was so great that they completed the walls within a week. Rev. Machar of Kingston performed the first service on September 28, and the building was completed by the end of October. Mackay would serve the church for many years as an elder and trustee.

Figure 14.7. Old Fraser School House, late 1940s.
Source: City of Ottawa Archives, CA 6201.

The earliest record of Presbyterian Church activities in New Edinburgh mentions Thomas Mackay teaching Sunday School in a hall at the corner of Alexander and Charles Streets in 1845.

Mackay was tolerant of other faiths. In the fall of 1828, he also donated ground and funds in New Edinburgh for an Anglican church. In December, he was one of a committee appointed to appeal to Sir John Colborne, lieutenant governor of Upper Canada, for help towards a salary for a minister for the new church. The congregation obtained an allowance of £50 a year.

In 1839, Mackay backed the Church of Scotland and Roman Catholic churches in the Upper Canada Assembly in granting them a fair share in the clergy reserves.

A prominent elder in the Church of Scotland, Mackay failed to have the Presbyterian Church establish its proposed college in Ottawa when Queen's College, Kingston (today's Queen's University), was founded in 1841 with a royal charter from Queen Victoria. Mackay was, however, a founding trustee of Queen's.

The first classes, intended to prepare students for the ministry, were held March 7, 1842, with thirteen students and two professors. Mackay's son, John, born in 1834 in Montréal, died while a student at Queen's in the late 1840s. He likely contracted influenza, which ended in his death from pneumonia.

CHAPTER 15

Rideau Hall, 1838–1853

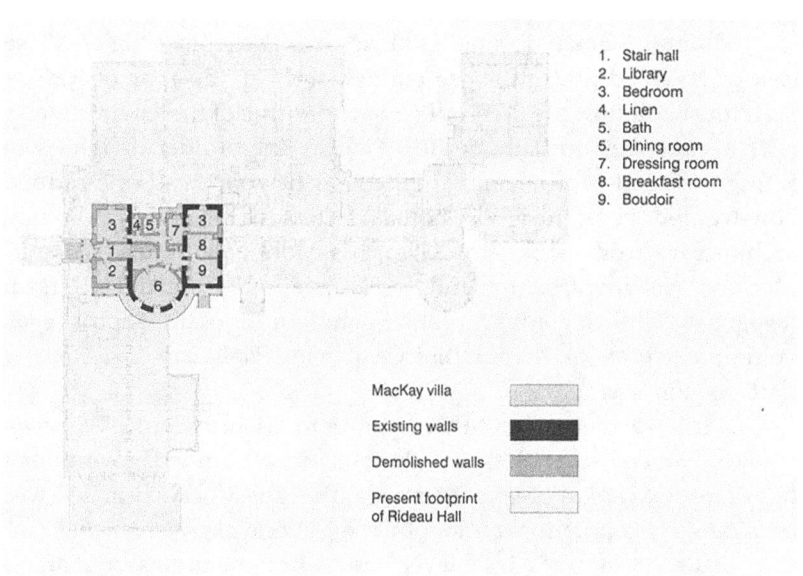

Figure 15.1. Mackay's original Rideau Hall, dwarfed by the current shaded structure.

An Amateur Architect

In 1838, Thomas Mackay and his best masons began to build the family a fine new home on a 65-acre [26-hectare] estate east of New Edinburgh that he christened Rideau Hall. It was known to the locals as "Mackay's Castle"—the Scots called any fortified house a castle.

The name was suggested by his daughter, Elizabeth,[1] clearly a lover of the Regency novels of Jane Austen. Indeed, Austen's novel *Persuasion* features two estates called Kellynch Hall and Uppercross Hall. The story contains echoes of Elizabeth Mackay's life. It begins in 1801, seven years after the broken engagement of Anne Elliot to Royal Navy Captain Frederick Wentworth. Then 19 years old, Anne fell in love and accepted a proposal of marriage from the handsome young naval officer. But her family persuaded her to reject his proposal because of Wentworth's lack of property and uncertain future.

Love finally triumphed in 1808, when Captain Wentworth returned from the Peninsular War, with £25,000 in prize money from capturing enemy vessels. Anne and Frederick married and lived happily ever after.

Thomas Mackay located Ottawa's own Regency villa on a rise east of New Edinburgh, close enough to hear the roar of Rideau Falls, the rumble of his grist mill, and the whine of his sawmills, and with a view west to Barrack Hill. Mackay the builder delighted in acting the semi-professional architect, as he conceived of a refined bow-fronted villa. Just as Thomas Jefferson mastered Palladian architecture from books, to design his Monticello house, Thomas Mackay was inspired by and freely adapted Rideau Hall from designs by English genius Sir John Soane, author of the popular 1798 volume, *Sketches in Architecture Containing Plans and Elevations of Cottages, Villas, etc.*

While serving as an MLA in Toronto, Mackay had likely seen Soane's November 1818 sketch designs for a planned government house for the capital of Upper Canada. Perhaps Mackay himself was considered as a potential builder by the provincial government.[2]

Soane, the son of a bricklayer, rose to become professor of architecture at the Royal Academy, and an official architect to the Office of Works. A strikingly original artist, he received a knighthood in 1831 for his best-known works, the original Bank of England and Freemasons' Hall, with its the Ark of the Masonic Covenant.

Soane's main legacy is his fantastic museum in Lincoln's Inn Fields, comprising his former home and office, designed to display

---

[1] Asquith, *New Edinburgh*. Both Jane Austen and Elizabeth Mackay died of tuberculosis in their early forties.

[2] There are four sketches in the Ontario Archives collection, one possibly marked up by Mackay.

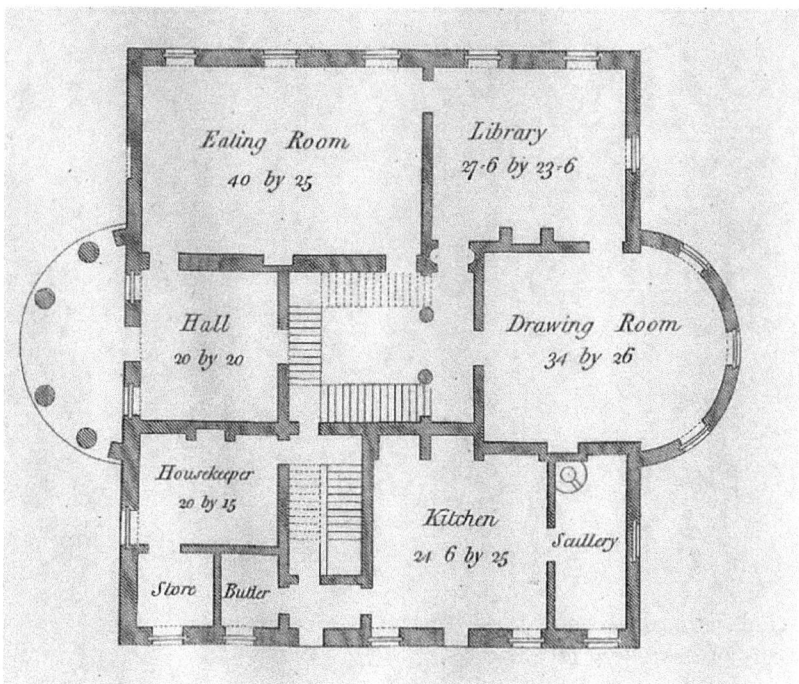

Figure 15.2. Plan of a typical Regency villa from Soane's 1798 volume.

the artworks and architectural artifacts that he collected during his lifetime. The *Oxford Dictionary of Architecture* describes it as "one of the most complex, intricate, and ingenious series of interiors ever conceived."

A Description of the House

Mackay's original villa was built with the aid of Charles Crawford, "an expert stonecutter from Montreal."[3] It was constructed on the Palladian model, with a central drum tower flanked by two wings. Crafted using fine light-grey limestone, it glowed like a jewel in the piney wood. It rose in the clearing three storeys tall, with an oval room, curved like a lady, behind a full-height, central bay, with a decorative Dutch pediment on top, crowning Mackay's third-floor

---

[3] R.H. Hubbard, *Rideau Hall*.

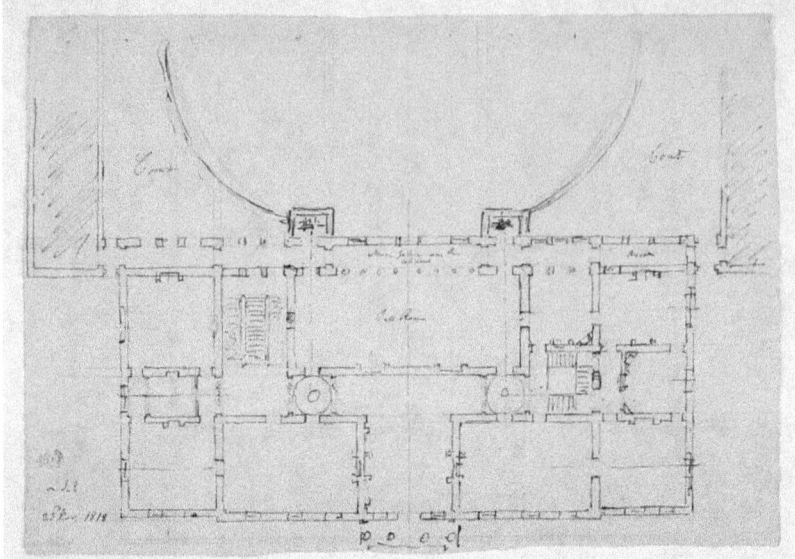

Figure 15.3. Soane sketch for Upper Canada Government House.
Source: Archives of Ontario.

drafting room. According to former National Capital Commission chief architect David Scarlett, the oval rooms were made in such a shape so as to show off the advanced skills of his masons.

Unlike today's vastly expanded Rideau Hall, Mackay dispersed rooms for entertaining, sleeping, and service throughout the three floors of the structure. This gave the family some upstairs privacy, as prominent visitors and humble petitioners often dropped by to partake of the laird's hospitality. Even before the building became a royal residence, Rideau Hall received three governors general of the Province of Canada: Lord Sydenham, the Earl of Elgin, and Sir Edmund Head.

The main entrance to the house was on the west side, and opened into a hall with stairs to the upper floor directly ahead. Along the south front were a library, a dining room, and a boudoir, all with French doors opening onto a narrow balcony. The dining room originally had three doors. Today, one opens into the Tent Room's antechamber, one into the Long Gallery, and one still opens to the outside.

The main oval drawing room on the second floor, with its thistle-encrusted plasterwork and handsome marble fireplace, is still intact.

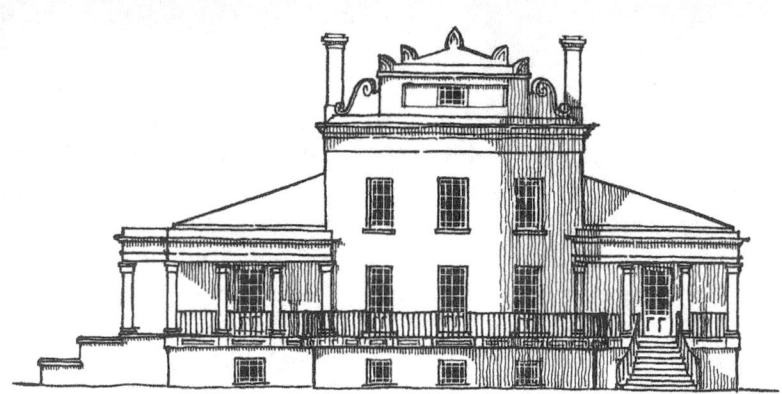

Figure 15.4. The original Rideau Hall.
Source: National Capital Commission.

It was subsequently used as a ballroom, a studio, and a study, before becoming the Queen's bedroom and royal suite when she is in residence.

Finally, Mackay had a top-floor drafting room and office, where he and his foremen would meet to plan construction of various buildings in the town, both residences and public buildings like the original Bytown courthouse and jail, built in 1842. He often

Figure 15.5. Rideau Hall, The Royal Bedroom, c. 1880.
Source: Rideau Hall.

retreated to the balcony to play the bagpipes, stampeding the local deer or alarming the Algonquins camped across the Ottawa on Gatineau Point.

Behind the house was a sunken courtyard with an elliptical pool in the centre, and a vinery from the east wing that led to the kitchen garden and barns.

Rideau Hall also featured some advanced Victorian technology, happily adapted by Mackay. A specially designed "hydraulic ram" drew water up from a spring to feed a laundry, wash house, and the ultimate in luxuries, a hot shower, all heated by a "Hot-Air Furnace," which also piped warm air through the house. A mechanical "Plate Lift" brought warmed food from a basement kitchen up to the dining room.

One luxury Mackay neglected to provide was an indoor "water closet." To answer the call of nature, family and visitors had to access ordinary privies through a covered walkway—a common indignity in those chamberpot days. London plumber Thomas Crapper had yet to popularize the modern flush lavatory, with cedar wood seats and enclosures. Crapper's innovation earned him a Royal Warrant from Queen Victoria's first son, Edward, Prince of Wales, who would himself visit Rideau Hall in 1860.

At the entrance to the Rideau Hall property, Mackay created "artificial formations," such as a winding macadamized avenue for

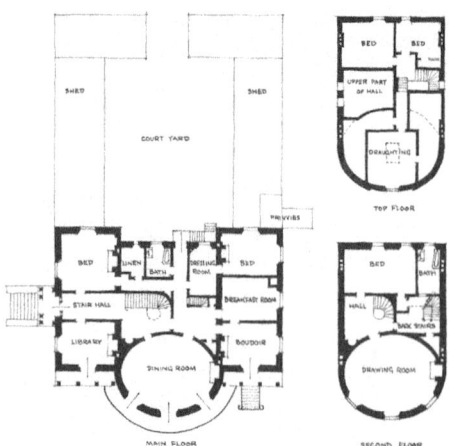

Figure 15.6. Rideau Hall plans.
Source: National Capital Commission.

carriages. Behind the house, he spent lavishly to build a terrace and a bowling green, billed as "the finest lawn in Canada."[4]

A Never-Failing Spring

In 1853, an American journalist penned a description of Rideau Hall in the *International Journal of New York and Boston*:

> Having had a letter of introduction to the proprietor, the Hon. Thomas Mackay, I accepted of an invitation to his princely mansion, which is situated at a short distance from the village on the brow of a beautiful eminence—commanding a magnificent panoramic view of Bytown and the surrounding country. A description of this charming residence may interest the reader. The estate comprises over a thousand acres [400 hectares]. Most of it is still in its primeval state. The front is laid out in parks with groves, shaded walks, a serpentine drive, and elegant hedges of cedar.
>
> There is also a ravine which will shortly be dammed and converted into a beautiful pond. Beyond these are the vegetable and flower gardens—a greenhouse, summer house, and grotto. In the background is an immense thicket of woods abounding with game—as you enter its labyrinths you are suddenly charmed with the appearance of an artificial lake of great beauty, in which trout and other kinds of fish are enjoying their revels. But it would be doing injustice to the occupant of this Elysian retreat not to mention that he combines the useful with the beautiful—and has a good many acres of arable land in a high state of cultivation.
>
> The dairy surely would make no contemptible appearance either, considering that there are eighteen milch cows of the Durham and Ayrshire breed. One arrangement on the place that I should like to see more generally introduced, was a most ingenious contrivance for raising water to a considerable height and conducting it to any part of the premises. It is an exceedingly simple piece of machinery and works something like an engine, forcing the water up a distance of about 60 feet [18 metres]. The cost of

---

[4] RG11, Public Works, Vl 426, 414. T. C. Keefer to Taché, April 21, 1864.

the machinery was about £4, and the rest of the work, including pipes, did not cost over £6—in all about £10. It was refreshing to see the cool sparkling streams dashing along in so many directions without cessation, as they issued from a never failing spring.[5]

Family Joy and Sorrow

The family happily moved into Rideau Hall from New Edinburgh in 1839.

The new house would witness many joyous celebrations, such as the marriages of eldest daughter Annie to John MacKinnon, Mackay's bank manager, on October 28, 1846; of daughter Christina to Robert Mackay, a Montréal lawyer and later judge, on June 27, 1848; of daughter Elizabeth to engineer Thomas Keefer on September 27, 1848; and of youngest daughter Jessie to Thomas McLeod Clark, insurance and commission merchant, on June 6, 1854.

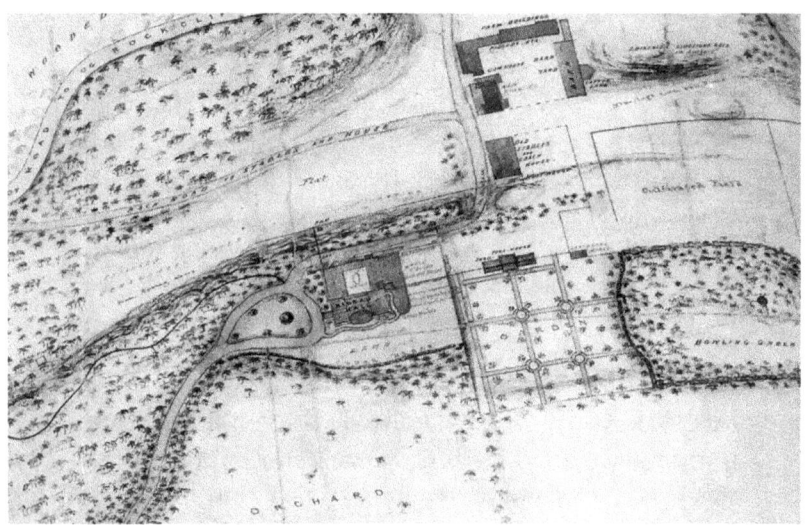

Figure 15.7. Rideau Hall domain, with stables, cow barn, garden, and bowling green. *Source*: Rideau Hall.

---

[5] Quoted in F-J Audet, "Thomas McKay, Rideau Hall and Earnscliffe," *CHA Annual Report*, 1932, 14–15.

Figure 15.8. Annie MacKinnon and Elizabeth Keefer, 1850s.
Source: Topley Studio, Library and Archives Canada.

On all four occasions, Mackay's brass cannon boomed out the glad news, as he gave a public entertainment and barbecue, with plenty of cheese and beer, to which all friends were welcome.

But with joy came tragedy. Two children died in the 1830s—Jane, born November 9, 1831, in Bytown, died stillborn; and James, born October 26, 1827, in Bytown, died of typhus on December 16, 1836, while the family were travelling through Burlington, Vermont.

On August 25, 1849, Mackay's youngest son, 7-year-old Henry, an adventurous boy, born in New Edinburgh on August 7, 1842, was "bathing" with his older brothers and friends in the Rideau River when he slipped on some loose timber at the shoreline while putting on his coat, got entangled in it, and drowned in the dark waters.

Then on August 10, 1851, Mackay's mother Christina, born in Perth in 1761, died at Rideau Hall at 88 years of age. She was buried in the family plot on Pine Hill. In 1873, she and the other family deceased were reinterred in the new Beechwood Cemetery.

Three girls survived their mother Anne—Mrs. Annie MacKinnon (later Mrs. T. C. Keefer), Mrs. T. M. Clark and Mrs. (Judge) Mackay, of Montréal. Mrs. Elizabeth Keefer died in 1869, at age 40.

Not one Mackay son survived beyond their twenties.

Mackay's mournful bagpipes often echoed through the woods from the library balcony, or the terrace below, bewailing the loss of so many children and babies. And often in the quiet, alone in his tower, he could hear the wolves howling at night, and the drumming of the Algonquins who camped every summer across where the Ottawa River meets the Gatineau. On Sunday evenings, the devout Laird of Rideau Hall would lead family and friends in the singing of old Scottish hymns and laments.

Death by Consumption: The Victorian Scourge

The Victorian malady called "consumption"—the body is "consumed" by the disease—we now know as tuberculosis, TB. It was the leading cause of death in Bytown/Ottawa in the 1800s. We can assume that one in five died of the disease, and the Mackay family was not spared.[6]

According to Mackay's friend John Mactaggart, "Consumption is also very frequent, and of the most rapid nature too." Once, he and Dr. Christie heard someone coughing in the Hull hotel and Christie said it sounded like a "churchyard cough." They went to explore the adjoining rooms, where they found "a Master Mason, a very strong healthy-looking young Scotchman." Christie predicted the lad would be dead in six weeks. "His words proved perfectly true, to the grief of a fine young woman he was going to have for a wife. I went to see him on his death-bed—she was there, and weeping over him. Dear girl! her lover died,—but she had another in a few weeks afterwards, and was married. Mr. Mackay, my worthy, gave them their outfit—of course I was at the wedding."

Five of the children of Thomas and Ann Mackay likely died of tuberculosis:

- Thomas died aged 15 in April 1837, probably of TB.
- Alexander, born in New Edinburgh in 1833, died of TB at age 24 in 1857.
- John, born July 7, 1834, in Montréal, likely died of TB-weakened lungs while a student at Queen's College in Kingston; he apparently

---

[6] In the nineteenth century, tuberculosis killed an estimated one-quarter of the adult population of Europe.

contracted influenza, which may have ended in his death from pneumonia.
- Thomas Mackay, Jr., the youngest son, born in New Edinburgh on May 3, 1838, was probably also a victim of tuberculosis, combined with an addiction to alcohol; he died in 1865, at age 27.
- Elizabeth Mackay Keefer, died in 1870 at age 40, probably of TB.

The physicians of the day were baffled by tuberculosis. The disease was curious—it did not seem to spread like fevers, colds, or influenza—in fact, only 5 to 10 percent of the people who were exposed to TB ever developed the disease. Most thought the disease was hereditary—a family curse—and that some families had a predisposition to the illness.

Sufferers did not always die within days or weeks, as was the case with cholera or typhus. They could often live with attacks and remissions that lasted for decades. The infected got married, and passed the disease on to their children.

Strangely, some Victorians dramatized TB as a romantic disease, a malady suffered by great artists. It was thought to bestow upon the sufferer heightened sensitivity, and because it progressed slowly, the afflicted could arrange their affairs and have a "good death." French writer George Sand called her lover, Polish pianist-composer Frédéric Chopin, her "poor melancholy angel." She wrote a friend that "Chopin coughs with infinite grace."

French novels, like Dumas's *La Dame aux camélias*, inspired operatic treatments of consumption, in Verdi's *La Traviata* and Puccini's *La Bohème*, where both heroines—Violetta and Mimi—die of the malady. But even after Louis Pasteur's discovery of the *tubercle bacillus*, the romantic vision of the disease remained popular.

So how did this scourge come to devastate the Mackay family, and then the Keefers, in turn?

It is entirely possible that the Mackay and Keefer family victims were afflicted by both human and bovine strains of the disease at the same time. Behind Rideau Hall was a dairy where Mackay maintained eighteen milk cows of the Durham and Ayrshire breed. It's probable that these cows were infected with bovine tuberculosis—*Mycobacterium bovis (M. bovis)*. It is commonly found in cattle, bison, elk, and deer, but can also cause the disease in people.

After Thomas Mackay's death, and before Rockcliffe Park was developed, the Mackay Estate allowed farmers to graze their cattle in

Mackay's Bush for a dollar a year. The bovine version of the disease could also have been carried by white-tailed deer, plentiful in the woods and fields.

Perhaps the unpasteurized cream the family spread on their morning porridge was the main vector—Ann Crichton Mackay often recommended oatmeal as a fine nutritious food.

The next generation was also not immune. Some of Mackay's Keefer grandchildren would also come to contract the disease, likely in the same way—there were two stone dairy barns at Birkenfels, and the Rockcliffe Manor House also had a dairy.

In 1882, German physician Robert Koch discovered that TB was caused by the mycobacterium tuberculosis. However, a treatment for the disease had to wait until the advent of antibiotics and chemotherapy in the mid-twentieth century.

CHAPTER 16

The Capital Idea, 1841–1849

Quebec was too distant from the west—any place on the St. Lawrence was too near the enemy—and wherever the capital may be, it must in the first instance be attended by a heavy expense... No part of Canada was so well fitted for the purpose of the capital as Bytown, because it was equidistant between the two extremes of the country. It was a "reasonable distance from the frontier," there was "nearly enough of building stone about it," and, it was added, "with respect also to solubriety, it is not exceeded by any place in the world."

—Hamnet Pinhey[1]

The Incorporation of Bytown

In 1839, an Assessment Roll put the population of Bytown at only 2,073. The town was still too small to incorporate, and the Ordnance Department still held property in the town's core (dividing Upper Town from Lower Town), lands that had been expropriated from Nicholas Sparks—property intended to be used for a fortress. These lands were considered by many to be blocking economic progress or being held for speculative reasons only. When a Board of Arbitration returned the lands to Sparks in 1846, at Mackay's urging, the major obstacles were removed. The Ordnance paid Sparks £27,000 for land he had bought in 1821 for £95.

Bytown was initially incorporated on July 28, 1847, and sanctioned by both the Legislative Assembly and the Governor, but this

---

[1] Courtney Bond, *Alexander James Christie, Bytown Pioneer.*

was disallowed by the Crown, possibly due to a perceived threat to Ordnance property. An act of the Legislative Assembly further eased the incorporation of municipalities, and on January 1, 1850, Bytown was incorporated as a town, replacing the military authority.

Promoting Bytown as the Capital

The choice of Ottawa as Canada's capital was Bytown's to lose.

Arrayed against it were a number of factors. An inappropriate name. No railway connections. Violence between Irish and French in the timber trade. No accommodations for civil servants. Seemingly located in the middle of nowhere.

And yet Barrack Hill, at one time perceived by Lord Dalhousie as the Edinburgh Castle of the New World, was a perfect site for a Parliament.

Figure 16.1. *Bytown Council Shield.*
Source: John Henry Walker, McCord Museum, M930.51.1.387.

Thomas Mackay was a long-time promoter of Ottawa as the capital, inspired by the predictions of Dalhousie two decades earlier, at the turning of the first sod of the Rideau Canal. It is said that Mackay heard him utter this prophecy—"I may not live so long, but whoever lives to see the Canadas united, will, from this eminence, see the seat of the United Legislature."

Mackay and his friends carried this vision in their hearts and minds, and shared it with other citizens of Bytown, in their desire to see their magnificent location become the capital of the Canadas.

Colonel By was also infected by Dalhousie's enthusiasm. When he leased lands for the creation of Bytown, he reserved the most useful and picturesque portion for public buildings, telling listeners he was well aware that this embryo village would eventually attain celebrity: "This land will be very valuable some day. It will be the Capital of Canada."

Under the direction of Colonel By, power in the region was starting to centralize in the village that would become Ottawa. On September 18, 1828, the Commissary General gave notice that all military pensions issued to residents of Richmond, Perth, and vicinity would be paid in Bytown, for, at least, the first payment of each year, this being another proof of its recognized value as a centre from its beginning.

The citizens of Bytown were more and more convinced of the important role their town could fill. At a meeting on September 4, 1828, they adopted several resolutions to create a new county town and judicial centre, with a jail and courthouse.

Thomas Mackay worked hard to make this happen, and as early as 1835 was able to tell a neighbour that it was "likely we will have a new district with Bytown as the capital," and "not unlikely that it will be the seat of government of the Canadas before many years."

On August 12, 1836, Mackay presented a petition for a new district to the Legislative Assembly, and he was successful. In 1840, the government carved out the district of Dalhousie from the district of Bathurst, with Bytown as the judicial seat and capital. This act came into force by Royal Proclamation dated March 19, 1842, after the required public buildings had been completed, including the first courthouse and jail, built by Thomas Mackay's masons.

Mackay's friend, Dr. Alexander Christie, began the public airing of the capital idea by publishing a new journal, the *Bytown Gazette,* on June 9, 1836, likely with some financial backing from Thomas Mackay.

Christie had emigrated to Montréal from Aberdeen at about the same time as Mackay, and for a time served as editor of the *Montreal Herald* and *Montreal Gazette*. The two became fast friends, and Christie followed Mackay to Bytown in 1826.

By the time of Christie's death in 1843, his newspaper had published at least twenty-five articles on why Bytown should be capital. His editorials stimulated others to respond, often in the "letters to the editor" section of the *Bytown Gazette*. He also sent editorials to newspapers in other cities, including Québec, Montréal, Kingston, and Toronto.

Even the *Montreal Herald* recognized Bytown's potential as a capital: "If Quebec is to be robbed of her diadem, Bytown may perhaps be a better substitute than any other place." A plus was that Bytown was "far removed from the risk of republican contamination."

For Christie, Bytown had it all—a central position, on the boundary of the two provinces, a natural fortification site, and distance from the American border, which meant easier defence. If the seat of government were transferred to Ottawa, the sale of Crown Lands would increase with the opening of new settlements. The towns along the St. Lawrence and Lake Ontario were increasingly defenceless, and vulnerable to republican ideas and principles. Bytown,

Figure 16.2. Dr. Alexander James Christie.

being farther away from the border, was militarily strong and surrounded by a "loyal population." A major advantage was that the choice would not excite "those jealousies which could arise from the choice of any other place."

If Bytown were to be chosen as the seat of government, new revenues would be generated for the Rideau Canal, which provided easy communication between the St. Lawrence and the west. Bytown was also blessed by the presence of an impressive government-owned site, and the grandeur and beauty of the surrounding scenery. To criticism that Bytown was but an "embryo city consisting of a few houses huddled together," Christie asked if there was "the capital of any country under the sun which was not at one time in this condition."

So convinced was Christie of Bytown's advantages for the site of the seat of government, that he seems to have assumed that his town was the only logically possible location and therefore would be selected. Although premature, Christie's musings continued to spur his fellow Bytown boosters.

Some residents of Bytown hated the name of their town, so other grander ones were suggested. In 1835, for instance, citizen Baker expressed the belief that a more classical name was needed—he suggested, "Aberdeen, in gratitude to the present Colonial Minister, despite my reluctance to the Scottish sound of the name."

The Union of the Canadas

In January 1838, Edward Ellice, the Seigneur of Beauharnois, sent Sir Henry Grey, Under-Secretary of State for War and the Colonies, a concise proposal for a federal union of the two Canadas, with a limited measure of ministerial responsibility.

But the Upper Canadians opposed federalism, and their views for a "legislative union" won out. On July 23, 1840, the British Parliament passed Lord John Russell's Bill, the *Act of Union of Upper Canada and Lower Canada*, to take effect February 10, 1841.

The *Canada Bill* followed the recommendations of Lord Durham in his report on the rebellions of 1837. It provided for uniting the two provinces under a single body, not a federal government; an elected assembly with 84 members and equal representation from Upper and Lower Canada; also assumption of £1.2 million Upper Canada debt, and establishment of a civil list.

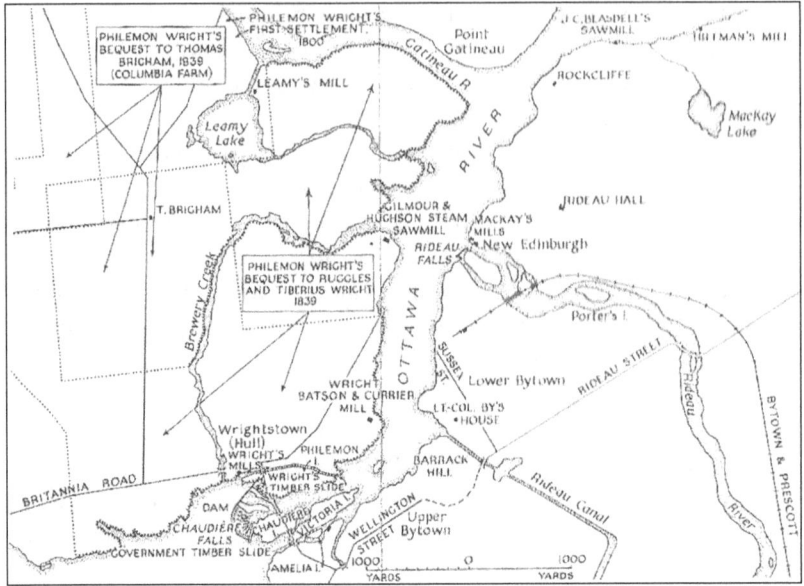

Figure 16.3. Bytown map, 1840s.
Source: C. C. J. Bond.

Thomas Mackay and his fellow citizens of Ottawa were generally pleased with the Union. According to friend Hamnett Hill:

> Situated as it was on the boundary line between Upper and Lower Canada it was so far distant from the centre of Government of Upper Canada that its interests had been sadly neglected. Dependent as it was for its prosperity and future growth on the development of the Ottawa River and the lumbering industry, it had suffered owing to the Ottawa River not being under the exclusive jurisdiction of either of the two Canadian Governments.
>
> Much needed improvements on the River had been impossible to attain as neither the Government of Lower Canada nor the Government of Upper Canada had appreciated the necessity for any joint action. On the passing of the Union Act the Ottawa River became the central artery of the United Province of Canada and the little village of Bytown from being on the outskirts became the centre of the Province, and the prospect of having one Government in control of the Ottawa River and the probability of

greater interest therefore being taken in its development brought joy to the hearts of the Bytonians.[2]

Not all Bytonians were pleased, particularly with the banning of the French language in the Assembly and in all government departments, and the dissolution of French educational and civil law institutions. As Edward Ellice suspected would happen, the Union soon became unworkable, and the province ungovernable. In 1848, the Province of Canada repealed the clause in the *Act of Union* that made English the official language of the Assembly.

Enter Lord Sydenham

Charles Poulett Thompson, Lord Sydenham, succeeded Lord Durham as Governor General of Canada. He was responsible for implementing the *Union Act* that created the Province of Canada.

In September 1840, Mackay led a committee of citizens who welcomed Sydenham to Bytown. After an address of greetings, the Governor took refreshment at Rideau Hall, where he assured his host that the town was being seriously considered as the capital of the united provinces.

In his newspaper, Christie suggested the idea of changing the name of Bytown to "Sydenham." To his credit, the Governor was not impressed by this generous suggestion. Sydenham was in Ottawa to get his favourite, Stewart Derbyshire, nominated as Bytown's first member in the new Legislature—he had already ruled out Bytown as the location for the seat of government.

To the disappointment of Thomas Mackay and friends, Sydenham shortly after rejected Bytown's arguments. On February 15, 1841, he named Kingston as the first capital of the Province of Canada, on account of its central position in the St. Lawrence Valley.

Lower Canada protested against this choice and proposed Québec or Montréal, but Upper Canada, though dissatisfied, preferred Kingston to any place in Québec and threatened the Union if the seat of government was transferred in the other province.

Meanwhile Derbyshire, newly elected member of the Assembly for Bytown, wrote to Christie that "Bytown must look to be the future

---

[2] Hamnett Hill, *Bytown Election of 1841*.

capital. She must become a numerous, wealthy, intelligent and orderly community. —Aspire to make it a capital of the Canadas—perhaps all of British America."

The choice of Kingston as the capital lasted only during one parliament. During the first session held in the General Hospital Building, J.S. Baldwin, of Toronto, moved that the seat of government alternate between Toronto and Québec because both places had government buildings suitable for the purpose. This action, he believed, would please everyone and would be an opportunity to inhabitants of both Canadas to get to know each other better, with the final result of obtaining a more united population.

After less than two years as governor general, Sydenham had a fatal accident. His horse slipped on a cobblestone and fell, fracturing his leg, and lacerating it above the knee. This led to a deadly infection, and the 42-year-old governor died on the morning of September 19, 1841, after suffering extreme pain.

Sydenham was replaced as Governor General of the Province of Canada by Sir Charles Bagot, a British politician married to Mary Wellesley-Pole, the Duke of Wellington's niece.

Bagot arrived in Canada at a time when the choice of Ottawa as the capital began to get legs. One of his first actions was to invite Thomas Mackay to serve as one of his legislative councillors.

CHAPTER 17

Mackay a Legislative Councillor

The Bagot Regime

Sir Charles Bagot was chosen for governor primarily because of his diplomatic knowledge of the United States—he was the former ambassador to Washington, and in 1818 with US Secretary of State Richard Rush was co-signer of the *Rush-Bagot Agreement* limiting armed naval vessels on the Great Lakes and Lake Champlain.

Bagot was also ordered by the British government to resist the growing demand from the colonies for responsible government. As an important concession, however, Bagot did allow the leading Canadian colonial politicians, Robert Baldwin and Sir Louis-Hippolyte LaFontaine, to form a ministry, on the basis of their parliamentary majority. LaFontaine, as a French-Canadian leader, had suffered abusive treatment by the British under Lord Sydenham. This was the beginning of what became known as representative government in Canada. Bagot's leadership was an important step forward in establishing more amicable relations between British and French.

Appointed September 27, 1841, Bagot arrived in Kingston on January 10, 1842, assuming office two days later.

Mackay took a steamer down the Rideau Canal to Kingston to attend the first meeting of the Legislative Council. On June 9, he was sworn in for life as one of twenty-four members of Bagot's Council, which was the governor's advisory body. He thus became the Hon. Thomas Mackay.

Mackay was present on June 14 as Bagot opened the first session of the first Parliament of the Province of Canada.

He lost the very first motion he put forward as the representative of Carleton, that Bytown be chosen as the capital—six voices

Figure 17.1. Sir Charles Bagot.

voted in favour and fifty-seven against. During the debate, one member quipped: "I tell you candidly, gentlemen, you might as well send the Seat of Government to Labrador." Still, opinion was shifting. The *Quebec Gazette* admitted that the site of Ottawa was a desirable one, but said that the time had not yet come for its choice. The desire to move the capital away from Kingston is easily understood when an independent witness such as Charles Dickens, visiting the place about that time, made the following comment: "Indeed, it may be said of Kingston that one half of it appears to be burnt down, and the other half not built up."

Bytown was not much better, with its unpaved streets, tree stumps, and log cabins. However, one traveller in 1854 commented on

> The quality of the substantial stone buildings in the town, and the citizens felt proud that there were already ten miles [16 kilometres]

of plank sidewalks here and there on principal streets. Many of these stone buildings may still be seen as evidence of the excellent work of the Old Country masons.

Travelling away from town was done either on foot, on horseback, in private vehicles, in stage coaches or by boat. There were now about thirty small steamers using the Rideau Canal, and others on the Ottawa, of which the *Phoenix* was the best passenger boat between Bytown and Grenville.

A covered stage coach provided a daily service to Perth. To Montréal the Press advertised "a two-way trip all in daylight" in a four-horse stage three times a week, or at least "when the roads permitted."[1]

The Draper-Baldwin Ministry had a majority in the Assembly—their bill establishing a single bank of issue for the colony was defeated, but everything else was approved, including a *District Council Act*, abolition of the pillory, public works, customs regulations, a regulated currency, municipal councils for Upper Canada, the sale of wild lands, and a system of common schools.

Bagot worked productively with this government to establish a structure for fair municipal governance in the Province of Canada, a well-defined system of three-tiered governance—federal, provincial, and municipal.

In 1842 Mackay was appointed first warden of the new district of Dalhousie, which he had promoted politically and for which he had built Bytown's first courthouse and jail, completed in 1842. Bytown then became the administrative centre of the new district of Dalhousie.

On May 23, 1843, Mackay laid the foundation stone of the Second Union Bridge, following the collapse of the Chaudière Falls wooden truss bridge ten years earlier. During the decade without a bridge, a horse-driven paddle-ferry service was the only way across the river.

On September 2, 1843, he joined a public celebration to mark completion of this magnificent 242-foot [74-metre] iron suspension bridge, Canada's first. It was designed by civil engineer Samuel Keefer, and built by contractor Alexander Christie, a son of Dr. A.J. Christie, at a cost of $60,000.

---

[1] Anne Dewar, "The Last Days of Bytown."

It was noted that the north end of the suspension bridge landed on the very stone arches Mackay and his masons had built seventeen years earlier, under the orders of Colonel By and Lord Dalhousie.

That evening, Thomas and Ann joined the festivities at the "Union Suspension Bridge Ball," held at Doran's Hotel on Wellington Street in Upper Bytown, speechifying along with John Egan, Captain Baker, Ruggles Wright, and Joseph Aumond.

Two weeks later, on September 17, Mackay cut a ribbon to officially open the bridge for traffic, "amidst the discharge of cannon, the waving of flags and the cheers of the multitude." He called it "one of the finest structures on the continent."

Back in Montréal on December 9 to attend to his parliamentary duties, Mackay witnessed with pleasure the passage of the *Ordnance Vetting Act* by the Government of the Province of Canada. The *Act* finally released the Ordnance lands in Upper and Lower Town for sale instead of lease.

In 1832, Colonel By had put in place a policy stating that no one in Lower Town could own property; rather, it had to be leased from the Ordnance for periods of thirty years. This state of affairs became a drag on settlement and development. The citizens of Lower Town had little stake in repairing or improving their homes, and in many

Figure 17.2. *Samuel Keefer's Union Suspension Bridge, 1844.*
Source: Frederick Preston Rubidge, Library and Archives Canada, C-005040.

cases tore them down and sold them for firewood at intervals. Mill and warehouse owners found it hard to negotiate long-term leases on military land—forcing many potential investors and developers to go elsewhere.

The new *Act* soon boosted growth and investment in Bytown. Ordnance control over the LeBreton lands at the Chaudière, where the owners had maintained rigid restrictions, was at last relaxed. Two lumber mills were built by Philip Thompson and John Perkins, which soon competed with the Rideau Falls mill of Thomas Mackay.

The *Vetting Act* also radically altered the balance of political power in Bytown, because it created a whole new class of property owners, primarily French and Irish.

In Montréal on November 30, 1844, Mackay was admitted as a member of the St. Andrews Society of that city. His certificate was signed by his fellow member of the Legislative Council, Hon. Peter McGill, president, and John Armour, secretary.[2]

The following March, Mackay protested against the adoption of certain resolutions on the subject of granting sessional indemnities to the members of the Legislative Council.

In September of 1846, he backed Sister Élisabeth Bruyère's request to the Commissioner of Ordnance Lands, asking for a grant consisting of sixteen lots of unsold Ordnance land for the erection of a hospital and "appurtenances thereof." In her petition, she stated that "all the Citizens of Bytown anxiously desire the advancement and stability of such a useful Public Establishment." Fourteen Bytown residents, four of them Roman Catholics, also petitioned the governor for property for the purpose of erecting a Protestant hospital, which Mackay also backed.

In 1849 he also supported Bytown's new bishop, Bruno Guigues, in helping to pass an Act of Parliament granting a civil charter to the Oblates' St. Joseph's College, turning it into the College of Bytown/Collège de Bytown, today's bilingual Université d'Ottawa. One of their prime mandates was to educate priests and laymen capable of healing the bitter divisions then rife between French and Irish Catholics.[3]

---

[2] It is noteworthy that half the members of the Upper House were of Scottish extraction—Crooks, Ferrie, Ferguson, Fraser, Hamilton, Jamieson, Macauley, Macdonald, McGill, Mackay, and Morris.

[3] Edward P. Laberge, *Bytown's own college*.

Figure 17.3. *Metcalfe Opening the Canadian Assembly*, Montréal, 1845.
Source: Library and Archives Canada, MIKAN 2895430.

In this year, the Oblates also established a mission to the Algonquins, called "La Réserve de Marie"—Maniwaki—up the Gatineau River. Today the reserve is known as Kitigan Zibo. Guigues wanted to get the Algonquin people to join the timber trade to subsidize the mission, and approved construction of a sawmill and flour mill.[4]

Mackay and Governor General Metcalfe

Governor Sir Charles Bagot had developed an amicable and productive working relationship with LaFontaine and Baldwin, but he was in failing health, and too ill to continue playing a prominent role in public affairs. He let much of the responsibility fall to the co-premiers.

Bagot submitted his resignation to Colonial Secretary Edward Stanley in December 1842. By that time he was too sick to return

---

[4] Some contemporary comments in the Bytown newspapers suggest Guigues may have clashed with Mackay and Philemon Wright, who had timber limits on the Gatineau. Mackay may have allowed them to proceed in exchange for sending their logs down to the Rideau Falls mill.

Figure 17.4. Grey Nuns' Mother House, St. Joseph's College, Cathedral, 1855. Note the chimney of Mackay's Rideau Falls sawmill in the background.
Source: Archives des Sœurs de la Charité d'Ottawa.

home, and he died at the governor's official residence, Alwington House, Kingston, Ontario, on May 19, 1843.

Bagot's successor, Sir Charles Metcalfe, assumed office on March 30, 1843. Son of a wealthy East India Company official, Metcalfe had earned a reputation as a conciliator while serving as governor of Jamaica.

Mackay and fellow members of the Legislative Council were considered to be ministers and to constitute a cabinet. Facing them, the Legislative Assembly was now dominated by one party, led by LaFontaine and Baldwin, whose main interests lay in strengthening their political support, largely by distributing patronage.

Metcalfe came to the Canadas with a reform program. He soon rejected the policy of forced anglicization, declaring that "if the French Canadians are to be ruled to their satisfaction, who could desire to rule them otherwise?"

He precluded Kingston from being a future provincial capital because it was "a foreign land" to the French-Canadians. Metcalfe also urged that the *Act of Union* be amended to give the French and English languages equal status in the legislature.

Figure 17.5. Bishop Bruno Guigues.
Source: Bibliothèque et Archives nationales du Québec, P137, S4, D10, P1.

By the end of Metcalfe's term, the imperial government had capitulated on the general amnesty for 1837 rebels, the civil list, and the language question.

Finally, Metcalfe worked on reconciling moderate Canadian conservatives like Thomas Mackay to the concept of responsible government. At the same time, he emphasized loyalty to Britain as the litmus test of colonial politicians, believing that the Mother Country must retain significant power in the internal affairs of Canada.

Figure 17.6. Sir Charles Metcalfe, 1844.
Source: Library and Archives Canada.

Metcalfe Visits Bytown

On August 19, 1843, the Hon. Thomas Mackay, as legislative councillor of the District of Carleton, welcomed Governor General Sir Charles Metcalfe on a surprise visit to Bytown.

His Excellency made his intentions known only a short time before his departure from Kingston by canal steamer up the Rideau. He explained that he wished to see the place as it really existed, without any prejudice.

Even with such short notice, the citizens of Bytown managed to put up some decorations for his reception, with two arches, one spanning Rideau Street and the other on Sappers' Bridge.

A few minutes before eleven o'clock, a courier stationed on the lookout at Hog's Back arrived on horseback with the news that the steamboat with the Governor on board was clearing the locks and was already at Dow's Lake. A few minutes later, the crowd spied the steamer, with the Union Jack flying from her mizzen, as it turned into the Deep Cut and majestically approached Sappers' Bridge, which was festooned with a large sign: "Loyal to our Queen, we Welcome Her Representative."

After passing under the bridge and docking alongside the first Ottawa lock, Thomas Mackay and friends formally welcomed His Excellency to Bytown.

Governor Metcalfe was then taken by carriage to Barrack Hill, where, in a beautiful temple in Grecian style formed of evergreens, he was presented with loyal addresses. The sheriff then announced that any gentleman who might be desirous of being presented to His Excellency would have such an opportunity after luncheon at the Dalhousie (Campbell's) Hotel.

After His Excellency spoke with a number of Bytown citizens, he was taken in a cavalcade to the Episcopal Church, where he examined the interior, then proceeded downhill to Chaudière Falls to inspect the progress of Samuel Keefer's suspension bridge, which was then being built across the Ottawa River to Hull.

The carriages then moved back up Wellington Street, and through another welcoming arch on Rideau Street, then through New Edinburgh to Rideau Hall for tea.

Bytown's cordial welcome impressed Metcalfe, but he also had hard words for its citizens—while Bytown was "the most eligible position in the country in the opinion of all persons of judgment," it was "not large enough and could not supply accommodation." His entourage also let it be known that the main impediment to the choice of Bytown as the capital was that the town did not have railway communications with the metropolis. Montréal was chosen as the new capital on November 28, 1844.[5]

---

[5] In November 1843, Thomas Mackay, along with James Crooks, Adam Fergusson, William Henry Draper, Livius Peters Sherwood, Peter Boyle de Blaquière, and seven

Figure 17.7. Samuel Keefer, 1850s.
Source: Library and Archives Canada.

Thomas Mackay and his friends took this message very much to heart, and began to pull together plans for a rail connection to Montréal.

Lord Elgin Gets the Message

By 1845, Metcalfe was beginning to suffer terribly from the skin cancer he had contracted in India. Treatment with strong acid left him blind in one eye. Lord Stanley accepted his resignation, and on November 26 he left for England, where he died the following year.

Charles Murray, Earl Cathcart, commander of the forces in British North America, took over as temporary administrator. Cathcart was another Wellington man, a Peninsular War and Waterloo veteran who had had three mounts shot from under him. But he was a naif in politics, only interested in local geology and in reforming the militia. He served quietly until the appointment of James Bruce, Eighth Earl of Elgin, who reached Canada on January 30, 1847.

Some anticipated that Lord Elgin, son-in-law of Lord Durham, but a man with Tory sympathies, would assume direction of the

---

others took the unprecedented action of walking out of council to protest the reform majority's repeal of resolutions blocking the change of capital. [Crooks, DCB]

government. Others thought that, as a governor sent by a Whig administration to bring in responsible government, he would dismiss the Draper Ministry and call the reformers to office.

Elgin did neither. He was a constitutionalist, determined not to be "a partisan governor," as Metcalfe had seemed to be. He would assume, "a position of neutrality as regards mere Party contests." He wanted to confirm in Canada what he felt certain it was his mission to ensure, what he termed "constitutional Government"—meaning government by the full body of conventions controlling the cabinet and the role of governor general as the representative of the Crown. In short, the same parliamentary system then in use in the United Kingdom.

The Responsible Government Revolution

On January 24, 1848, the Reformers led by Robert Baldwin and Louis-Hippolyte LaFontaine swept the elections in both Canada East and Canada West. On March 11, Lord Elgin called on Baldwin and LaFontaine to form a new cabinet, becoming the first governor general to allow the local, elected legislature to govern. At the same time, he would adopt a largely symbolic role, imparting wisdom where necessary.

Elgin also granted royal assent to the contentious *Rebellion Losses Bill*, passed by the Reform-dominated legislature. The act compensated those whose property had been damaged during the Rebellion of 1837—everybody except those who had been convicted of treason.

Figure 17.8. Lord Elgin, 1840s.
Source: Library and Archives Canada.

When the bill was submitted to Lord Elgin for assent, some of the English-Canadians demanded that the governor refuse assent. Lord Elgin had his own serious misgivings about the bill—making many Tory supporters confident that the governor would reject the bill—but nonetheless he signed it into law on April 25, 1849.

Many of Montréal's British population were outraged that people who had opposed the Crown in the Rebellion would be eligible for compensation. Elgin's carriage was pelted with stones and rotten eggs, and by the evening a riot had developed that would last for two days and involve thousands of people. By the time the rioting had ended, mobs had torched the Parliament building.

Despite the violent opposition, Lord Elgin's actions were supported by a majority of Canadians and by the Liberal Government in London.

In 1849, following the MacNab Ministry party line, Thomas Mackay registered his protest against the passing of the *Rebellion Losses Bill*, and also opposed:

- *An Act against the Granting of Sessional Indemnities to Members of the Assembly*;
- the adoption of the address to Lord Elgin on the subject of the destruction by fire of the Parliament House at Montréal;
- *An Act to provide by One General Law for the Erection of Municipal Corporations and the Establishment of Regulations of Police in and for the Several Counties, Cities, Towns, and Villages in Upper Canada.*

With Montréal now deemed unsafe, the search began for a new capital. Lord Elgin let it be known that he was mounting a mission in Upper Canada that September to explore the possibility of naming Kingston, Toronto, or Bytown as the seat of Parliament.

The *Bytown Packet* newspaper begged the citizens to greet the Queen's representative peacefully and loyally, to promote their own interest and push their claim for becoming the capital. Bytown had nothing to gain, and everything to lose, by partisan display.

The local reformers arranged a town meeting for Monday, September 17, in the North Ward Market (now the Byward Market) to organize a boisterous reception for Lord Elgin on his projected visit to Bytown. They also proposed sending a letter to the governor general to, among other things, express their respect for him as the Queen's representative, and to place before him the town's "wants and wishes," and to underscore the merits of Bytown as a "site for the future Capital of the Province."

The Stoney Monday Riot

One might think that a viceregal visit to Bytown would have had the support of radical Tory Loyalists, especially as they had a lot to gain from the town being selected as the new capital of Canada. However, many bore a grudge against the Governor General for signing the *Rebellion Losses Bill* into law, which they hotly opposed. According to *The Ottawa Advocate*, a Tory newspaper, the proposed letter to Lord Elgin was inflammatory.

Many extremists, particularly members of the Protestant Orange Order, including Mayor Robert Hervey, refused to join in the greetings and fully intended to disrupt the meeting. In this case, their political and religious interests were stronger than their local patriotism.

On the Sunday prior to the proposed meeting, radical supporters, "fully armed and equipped," began to pour into Bytown from surrounding farming communities in Carleton County. The main body of roughly five hundred men arrived by wagon before noon, and were met by Mayor Hervey and other leaders.

At 1:30 p.m., they marched to the Market Square, where they were confronted by an equally large crowd of Reform supporters, also armed. When local Reform MP, Edward Mallock, and Reformist leaders, Charles Sparrow and J.-B. Turgeon (both later mayors of Bytown), rose to speak from a platform erected at the south end of the square facing York Street, they were shouted down.

Within minutes, a bloody brawl broke out. Sticks and stones soon gave way to firearms. Many fled to the nearby Shouldice Hotel for safety. Up to fifty shots were fired and over thirty rioters wounded. An innocent bystander, David Borthwick, was fatally shot in the chest by a stray bullet.

Twenty minutes after the battle began, Mayor Hervey read the *Riot Act* and called out the senior military force, "A" Company of the Royal Canadian Rifle Regiment, a small British Army garrison based on Barrack Hill.

The Royal Canadian Rifles, raised in 1840 for service in Canada, was made up of veterans of service in other regiments of the British Army, spread out in detachments from St. John's in Newfoundland to Fort Wellington on the St. Lawrence to Fort Garry in Manitoba.

Because of the continuing problem of desertion, the RCRR only recruited veterans with at least fifteen years' service in the British army. Most had families and received twice the pay of other private soldiers. They were also offered pensions upon completion of twenty-one years of military service, along with free grants of land.

Led by the CO, Major Clements, the Rifles quickly marched across the Sappers' Bridge over the Rideau Canal and through Lower Town, arresting Reformer rioters before taking control of the Market Square.

The Tory supporters then passed their own resolution to write the Governor General expressing their "unqualified disapprobation of the unprecedented course pursued by Your Excellency's present advisers, whose whole system of policy in the Administration of public affairs in this Colony, from the day of their assumption of power to the present time, [they] must unhesitatingly and emphatically condemn." The draft letter was read out loud by Mayor Hervey.

According to *The Packet*, a Reform organ, the Tory letter to Lord Elgin was "steeped in the blood of fellow-citizens, and adopted at a moment when their hired bullies were butchering the peaceable Inhabitants (Reformers)."

After a series of "violent speeches," Mayor Hervey swore in special constables who, at the head of the mob, paraded through the streets. The mayor urged fellow Tories to reassemble two days hence, on the Wednesday, and to come "fully equipped for war."

The next day, Tuesday, was fairly quiet, with both sides preparing for the final battle.

Early on Wednesday the 19th, about five hundred reformers poured into Lower Town, to counter the five hundred Tory farmers from Carleton County. *The Packet* described both sides as being "completely armed as if the Country were in a state of civil war."

The Tory supporters mustered on the brow of Barrack Hill, overlooking the canal. After being addressed by their leaders, including Mayor Hervey, the mob moved eastward down Wellington Street, armed to the teeth and pulling a small brass cannon belonging to Ruggles Wright. Meanwhile, the Reformists, who had formed up in the Market Square, and were also armed with rifles, pistols, and bayonets, moved to intercept the Tories. At 2 p.m., the two groups came face to face across Sappers' Bridge, the only crossing over the Rideau Canal linking Upper and Lower Towns.

There they found the Royal Canadian Rifles holding the centre of the bridge with four pieces of cannon, staring down the combatants.

The situation grew more tense, but a Tory "proposition" to charge the troops went unanswered. After a face-off lasting two hours and a clear stalemate, the Reformists then fired a volley of shots into the air, reportedly to empty their guns before leaving. Tory supporters, their honour satisfied, marched away under a "Party Flag," to a tune played on a fife and drum, also firing a parting volley of shots into the air. Everyone eventually dispersed, and the Rifles returned to their barracks.[6]

The following day, those arrested by the Rifles on Stoney Monday appeared in court, but with a large crowd outside, their cases were adjourned. The troops also crossed to the Hull side of the Union Suspension Bridge and seized a private arsenal of arms, including Ruggles Wright's old brass cannon. They arrested Ruggles, along with Joshua Wright, Ruggles Wright Junior, and Andrew Leamy.

Figure 17.9. *The Stoney Monday Riot.*

---

[6] Michael Cross. "Stoney Monday, 1849: The Rebellion Losses Riot in Bytown."

After being detained at the guard-house, the men were released on bail. The soldiers also temporarily detained Henry Friel, editor of *The Packet*—Friel later became mayor of Bytown and Ottawa.

Mackay Yields to the Military

Where was Lieutenant-Colonel Thomas Mackay in all this disorder? As commanding officer of the Fourth Battalion of Carleton Militia, Mackay's main duty was to guard the strategic Ottawa locks and the Rideau Canal against potential raiders determined to blow up the locks and drain the system.

We can only imagine his dismay over the rioting. He was a Conservative, and a Freemason, but not an Orangeman, always having good relations with the Irish and French Catholic citizens of Bytown, many of whom had worked on his masonry crews.

As a sign of his growing tolerance, he was usually supported by the Reform-backed *Bytown Packet* newspaper.

It is likely Mackay had to proceed cautiously with involving his battalion of Carleton Militia—he did not want to expose a potential split in the militia between disgruntled Tories and Reformers. The Canadian Rifles were the senior military force, and it was their job to restore order.

If anything, he may have personally expressed his anger at Mayor Hervey using the Rifles for partisan purposes on Stoney Monday. After losing the next mayoral race, Hervey departed for the United States.

To Thomas Mackay's disgust, the infamous Stoney Monday riot again damaged Ottawa's prospects to become the capital city. It caused Lord Elgin to delay his planned 1849 visit for four years, until July 1853.

With communal riots in Bytown and the collapse of its economic mainstay, the little timber village had been through rough times. On January 1, 1850, Bytown officially became a town, its earlier incorporation having been disallowed in Britain. Now, to become the capital of the Canadas, all it needed was a railway.

CHAPTER 18

Bust and Boom, 1840–1849

The Dirty Forties

The 1840s were years of pain and plenty for Upper and Lower Canada, as British politicians whipsawed colonial grain and lumber producers by bringing in preferential tariffs and then taking them away.

As the decade began, two thirds of all exports from British North America were timber, the bulk of it from the Ottawa Valley.

In 1842, it became clear that the British Ordnance was suppressing Bytown's growth, and continuing to act as a drag on settlement. In 1842, the Ordnance decided to quadruple tolls on the Rideau Canal. This arbitrary act caused a "mighty stir," and after furious lobbying by the lumber dealers, tolls on timber were removed.

However, a year later, the timber trade collapsed, after Prime Minister Peel, infected by the new gospel of free trade, ended preferential tariffs on colonial lumber, exposing the Ottawa Valley to harsh competition. Bytown, being one of the lumber capitals of the Canadas, relied heavily on this staple industry and urgently sought out new markets in the United States.

In the back townships of Upper Canada, the market for farming produce sagged, available capital shrank, and the number of new immigrants dwindled.

Economic depression hit Bytown hard. A sharp decline in jobs in the timber industry led to the Arch Riot on Sunday, August 20, 1843, as animosity between the Orangemen and Papists of Bytown again erupted in fighting and stone throwing.

Figure 18.1. *The Arch Riot.*

The *Canada Corn Act*

On the bright side, the *Canada Corn Act*, passed in 1843 by the British Parliament and applying to all grains, allowed Canadian wheat to enter the British market at a nominal duty, and flour manufactured in Canada at a proportionate rate.

Prime Minister Peel declared, "It is desirable that we should act on the principle of treating Canada as if it were an integral part of the Empire."

Canadian farmers and millers, including Thomas Mackay, prospered as growing demand in Britain for foodstuffs led to lower duties for colonial imports, thereby promoting an imperial grain supply. These preferential rates offset the costs of transatlantic transport for British North American grain, and they built up a growing colonial stake in the export of wheat.

Famine in Ireland

The great Irish famine of 1845–1852 changed everything, as Peel's government, following the dictates of free trade, and wanting to cheapen the price of food, announced it intended to repeal the *Corn Laws*, including the *Canada Corn Act*, effective in 1849.

The repeal forced more grain onto the market, but it also boosted emigration, since small grain farmers in Britain were squeezed out by lower prices, and many left for North America.

With the removal of preferential duties on wheat, timber, and other products, economic depression hit Canada. Thomas Mackay had a large quantity of grain and wheat ready for export, but when the market collapsed, a scarcity of food developed. To Mackay's credit, he chose not to profit by raising his prices. He lowered the price of his flour, selling it at the same price for rich or poor.

Family Business

On October 28, 1846, John MacKinnon, Bytown manager of the Bank of British North America, married Annie Mackay, the family's eldest daughter, in a ceremony at Rideau Hall.

The MacKinnons first lived in the stone building situated near the corner facing the east end of the Rideau Falls Bridge, later occupied by the Street Railway company.

Figure 18.2. John and Annie MacKinnon.
Source: Library and Archives Canada, E-3525289.

MacKinnon was useful to Thomas Mackay as a junior partner and bookkeeper, and was regarded as a "front man" to represent Mackay's interests. In 1846, Mackay invited MacKinnon to leave the Bank and take charge of a portion of his business, as a partnership under the name of Mackay & MacKinnon, specifically managing the Rideau Falls milling complex.

In 1846, with MacKinnon in harness, Thomas Mackay thought that a holiday and a rest would do him no harm. Leaving aside his business, political, and militia cares and taking with him three of his daughters, he sailed for the Old Country. After visiting Perth and Edinburgh, Scotland, where he encouraged emigration to Canada, they took a steamboat to London, England, then crossed the Channel, landing at Boulogne-sur-Mer on June 25. Having obtained a "passe-port à l'Interieur" from the police authorities of the realm, they left for Paris, where they spent a few days. Before leaving the capital, Mackay went to pay his respects to the British ambassador, obtained a visa from the embassy, and returned to England via Le Havre.

On May 15, 1847, he was re-appointed president of the Bytown Emigration Society. He had been president since its founding in 1841, to encourage emigration to Canada and settlement of uncultivated territories, especially by emigrants from famine-ravaged Ireland.[1]

That year, Mackay and MacKinnon decided to replace the old Rideau Falls sawmill first erected for Jean-Baptiste Saint-Louis in about 1830. They engaged Joseph Merrill Currier, a New England mill manager of French-Canadian ancestry, to install machinery to mill laths and shingles, with an extensive window sash and Venetian-blind factory attached. Currier and Moss Kent Dickinson of Manotick also made the first attempts to supply sawed lumber to the US market, shipping it down the Rideau Canal.

The Timber Mania of 1846–1848

Boom times returned to Bytown in 1846, as an outbreak of timber mania—as frenzied as a gold rush—hit the Ottawa Valley. A record

---

[1] From 1841 to 1931, about two million Scots emigrated to North America and Australia. Today, there are more people of Scottish descent in both Canada and the US than the five million remaining in Scotland.

20.5 million cubic feet [580,000 cubic metres] of pine timber was cut in the Valley, spurred by a booming British market, and a petition by the Canadian Assembly to Queen Victoria asking for reciprocal free trade with the United States.

But two years later the boom turned to bust, as nearly 26 million cubic feet [736,000 cubic metres] of squared timber lay unsold at the port of Québec.

The timber glut of 1848 was so ruinous that Bytown saw a sharp drop in population—as many as two thousand people left the Valley. Mackay's friend William Stewart, who had replaced him as MLA, suffered a massive financial setback. Supposed to be worth £20,000 in 1846, his losses sustained as a result of a glutted market and tight credit during 1847–1848 forced him to quit the business and sell his crown timber permits to John Egan.

Mackay was luckier than most—he had the capital to survive the downturn, and he had wisely concentrated on sawed lumber rather than squared timber. In 1847, with the help of son-in-law Thomas MacKinnon, he invested heavily in building a larger Rideau Falls sawmill, renting it to Currier for £1,000 a year.

Figure 18.3. *Mackay's Mills*, 1845; Rideau Hall back centre right.
Source: Thomas Burrowes fonds, Archives of Ontario.

In 1848 the Rideau Falls mills were the first to barge sawed lumber down the canal to Kingston, where it was shipped across the border to New York State. Mackay and MacKinnon also engaged American shippers to carry surplus lumber down the Ottawa and St. Lawrence to Sorel, then up the Richelieu to the Champlain and Hudson canals. In 1849, they shipped 2.4 million board feet [5,663 cubic metres] of sawed lumber along this route.

In 1849 the Rideau Falls sawmills were expanded to accommodate value-added production of laths, shingles, staves, doors, window sashes, and blinds. During the five-month milling season, twenty thousand logs were cut up, and sixty men employed.

Once Mackay and MacKinnon had proved that shipping sawed lumber to the American market was profitable, other sawmills began to pop up in Bytown, especially at Chaudière Falls.

It did not take long for the Americans to respond—Ezra Butler Eddy of Burlington, Vermont, would arrive in 1854 at the Chaudière, where he would become one of the major figures in sawed lumber, pulp, and finally matches.

Peak Shipping on the Rideau Canal

The mid-1840s were the glory days of the Rideau Canal. During periods of high immigration, passenger traffic on the waterway grew rapidly. In 1843, thirty thousand of the more than forty-four thousand

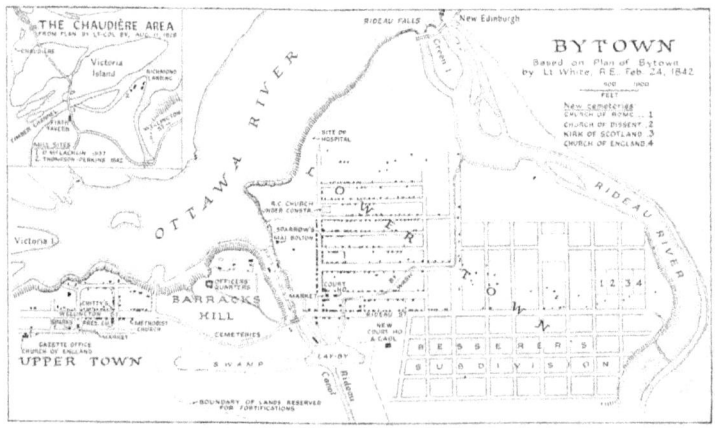

Figure 18.4. Bytown map, 1842.
Source: C. C. J Bond.

immigrants that landed in British North America moved to Upper Canada via the Rideau Canal, without paying tolls. The flow reached a peak of 89,562 in 1847, at which point the St. Lawrence canals opened for business.

Originally, it was thought that freight-laden steamboats would leave Montréal and travel up the Ottawa River to Bytown and from there to Kingston, then return to Montréal along the same route. But it was by no means an easy trip.

The Grenville canals on the Ottawa River were a major bottleneck—not wide enough for the larger Montréal steamboats, forcing shippers to use smaller barges or Durham boats. Loaded with people and freight, the barges were towed by smaller steamboats from Montréal and, after passing through the narrow Grenville canals, were attached to steamers that took them up the Ottawa to Bytown and then Kingston. There, people and goods transferred to larger lake boats and headed on to York (Toronto) and the booming Niagara and London regions.

This barge trade resulted in an unanticipated use of the dangerous (but short) downriver route between Kingston and Montréal. After passengers and imported goods arrived safe and dry from Bytown at Kingston, freight companies braved the rapids on the St. Lawrence to return the barges to Montréal.

As early as 1831, Welland Canal developer William Hamilton Merritt pointed out that both the Rideau Canal and the Erie Canal had similar disadvantages. Lake Ontario was already connected with the Hudson River by the Erie Canal—208 miles [334 kilometres] long, with 574 feet [174 metres] of lockage and 4 feet [1.2 metres] depth of water. The Rideau Canal when completed would be over 200 miles [321 kilometres] long, with over 500 feet [152 metres] of lockage and 5 feet [1.5 metres] depth of water. The St. Lawrence canals, when completed, would have just 120 miles [193 kilometres] of artificial navigation, containing less than 200 feet [61 metres] of lockage. In fact, a canal only 37.5 miles [60 kilometres] could connect Lake Ontario with the ocean.

In 1838, Lieutenant-Colonel Phillpotts of the Royal Engineers reported to Lord Durham that the only way to assure prosperity to the Canadas was by completing a series of canals between Lake Erie and tidewater, especially around the remaining rapids on the St. Lawrence:

Unless we open an uninterrupted navigation for large freight steamers capable of carrying a cargo of at least 300 tons without transshipment before they arrive at Montréal or Québec, we have no chance whatever of securing any great portion of that vast and important trade which must ere long be carried on between the Western States and the Atlantic Ocean.

By 1848, with British subsidies, new canals finally opened to bypass the St. Lawrence River rapids, and safe, direct two-way transportation became possible along that route between Montréal and Kingston.

The Rideau Canal was suddenly reduced to a regional transportation route, just sixteen years after it was completed. Five years later, just twenty-four years after its opening, the British Ordnance transferred the Rideau Canal system and properties to civilian control, to the Board of Works of the Province of Canada.

The Rideau waterway continued to serve as a lifeline for settlers in the area, as their only connection to the outside world. Those who carved farmsteads out of the wilderness depended for supplies on the small settlements that grew up around wharves on the waterway. They bought many necessities, including cloth and tools, at outpost stores; and they sold vegetables, wheat, and potash (from wood ashes) to storekeepers who used the canal to ship produce to Bytown to feed the lumber camps that were booming up the Ottawa Valley.

The Ottawa Lumbermen Turn South

By 1848, Bytown was the centre of the squared timber trade. By far the largest total output in Canada was from the Ottawa Valley. With the exception of the Gilmours, Hamilton and Thompson, whose head offices were in Québec, the local operators along the Ottawa River and tributaries were mainly dependent on the Québec shippers, who owned the timber coves in the vicinity of that city, for the necessary capital.

Cash advances were obtained by drafts on the Québec timber dealers through the five Bytown banks—The Bank of Montreal, The Bank of British North America, The Commercial Bank of Kingston, The Bank of Upper Canada, and The Quebec Bank. Mr. Noel of the Quebec Bank was the sole agent of his bank in Ottawa, and because he did not have a safe, was forced to carry his cash home every afternoon in a tin box to his house on Sparks Street, where he kept it under his bed until the next day.

By 1849, the Ottawa Valley producers felt boxed in and frustrated. While timber exports to the US were booming via Lake Ontario, and a waterway from Oswego to the Erie Canal, British demand for timber at Québec had stagnated, and millions of cubic feet of squared timber and sawed lumber had to be "wintered over" at Québec at the expense of the producers.

Mackay and MacKinnon were partly insulated against the drop in British demand, by turning their sights southward. By 1849, after investing heavily in a new sawmill with forty saws capable of cutting 40,000 board feet [94 cubic metres] a day, they shipped 2.4 million board feet [5,663 cubic metres] of sawed lumber to the New York market via the Ottawa—St. Lawrence—Richelieu River system to Lake Champlain.[2]

On October 3 and October 10, 1849, Mackay joined a convention of frustrated Ottawa Valley lumbermen as they held two public meetings in Bytown to discuss the proposed St. Lawrence and Champlain Canal, from Lac St. Louis east to the Richelieu River and Lake Champlain. If completed, it would create a deep waterway from the Hudson to the St. Lawrence, and allow the Ottawa lumbermen to bypass Montréal, sending timber directly to the New York market.

John MacKinnon chaired the meetings and Thomas Keefer supplied the analysis of their situation:

> With a good water communication between the Ottawa and Hudson Rivers, Canada would at once become a formidable competitor to the State of New York in the markets of the latter.
>
> The Ottawa is the great Lumbering district of Canada; from it four fifths of the Pine Timber and two thirds of the deals, have been supplied to the Québec market.
>
> The Ottawa river drains an area of about 75,000 square miles [194,250 square kilometres], comprising the richest and most extensive Timber district in America, if not in the world. About 10,000 square miles [25,900 square kilometres] of the unsurveyed portion is licensed for Lumbering purposes.
>
> As a necessary consequence of an improved connection with Lake Champlain the disgraceful obstruction at Grenville

---

[2] John Taylor, *Ottawa: An Illustrated History*.

(caused by two small locks within the chain of upwards of fifty larger ones, whereby the Rideau Route from Montréal to Kingston has been stultified for upwards of fifteen years), must be widened.

In addition to the Grenville locks, the meeting declared that the small Chambly Canal, up the Richelieu from the St. Lawrence, was another bottleneck that should be removed.[3]

---

[3] Proceedings of Public Meetings held at Bytown, October 3 and 10, relative to the St. Lawrence and Lake Champlain Canal. Bytown, 1849.

CHAPTER 19

Annexation and Reciprocity, 1849–1854

With Great Britain mistress both of the means of production and the means of distribution, was not the whole world her marketplace? Why bother with the expense and worry of colonies?

—Jan Morris, *Heaven's Command*

Britain in the 1840s

To understand Mackay's career in this period, we must first focus on the state of Britain in the 1840s. London, with a population of two million, had emerged as the world's largest city, and its principal financial exchange. An industrial revolution based on steam power had created a vigorous and innovative economy.

On the face of it, Britain was booming, with expanding manufacturing—especially the cotton industry. British shipping rose from 2.8 million tons to 3.6 million in the decade. Railway mania reached its zenith in the mid-1840s, and in the decade between 1841 and 1851 annual gross national product grew from £452 million to £523 million. No other nation on the globe could compete or compare with such economic performance, although the northern United States was nipping at John Bull's heels.

However, in the years from 1837 to 1843, a series of poor harvests in Britain led to a severe depression, deeper than the doldrums after Waterloo. Mass unemployment, combined with a rapidly growing population, led to poverty, misery, and starvation.

Reformers targeted the Corn Laws, passed in 1815, for a large share of the blame, as they were designed to give privileged treatment to the landed classes and the agricultural interest—the very groups that were dominant in both Houses of Parliament. The Corn Laws protected British agriculture from foreign competition, by banning imports of wheat, except from the empire.

The Corn Laws soon became the symbol of "aristocratic misrule," and the Anti-Corn Law League, founded in Manchester in 1839, turned moral outrage into a religious crusade, supported by Anglicans and Nonconformists alike. In a meeting held in August 1841, seven hundred Christian ministers proclaimed the cause of repeal of the Corn Laws to be "the politics of the gospel."

In the autumn of 1841, Sir Robert Peel's Conservatives were returned with a huge majority of over seventy seats—a triumph for his strategy of moderate Conservatism and a departure from the Duke of Wellington's hard Toryism. Peel himself was the grandson of a self-made Lancashire mill owner.

By August 1842, the stagnating economy had turned the whole central industrial area of England into a state of upheaval, racked by strikes and riots.

Peel thought himself more than up to the task, buttressed by his own article of faith—that free trade could solve the problems of the country. With the repeal of the Corn Laws, workers would have cheaper food, and so would be less likely to demand higher wages.

Peel planned to repeal the Corn Laws in 1848, just before the next general election, but in 1845, events in Ireland turned his political world upside down. By November of that year, it was clear that incessant rains, combined with a devastating potato blight in Ireland, caused by a fungus for which the scientists of the day could find no remedy, had ruined almost the entire potato crop. Peel feared that the same might well be true the following year. To avoid more social calamity and demographic disaster, he decided that the Corn Laws must be repealed immediately, so as to make available additional supplies of wheat for the Irish.

Famine and Immigration

Ireland's catastrophic famine, the greatest natural demographic disaster ever to befall the British Isles, saw the deaths of almost a million people, or an eighth of the entire Irish population, felled by starvation, malnourishment, dysentery, and typhus.

During the ten years following 1845, the British subsidized the departure of almost two million Irish, many destitute, to British North

America and the eastern seaboard of the United States, where they hoped to find a better and brighter future. In 1847 alone, a hundred thousand famine-stricken Irish emigrated to Canada. Almost twenty thousand died of typhus on refitted timber ships—the so-called coffin ships—that essentially dumped the survivors in Québec and Montréal, doubling the local population—Montréal at that time housed only fifty thousand people. The Grey Nuns and other religious organizations were able to place six thousand famine orphans with French families. The bishops insisted the adopted children could keep their family names—even today one can find French O'Neills who scarcely understand English. The remaining survivors found work as labourers in Canada or left for the United States.

The bulk of the famine refugees left for England and Scotland, where jobs were plentiful building railways and steamships. Indeed, much of the British recovery in the mid-1840s was due to a boom in railway building. Parliament passed 442 *Railway Acts* between 1844 and 1847, and more than 2,000 miles [3,220 kilometres] of track opened in those years. Railway building absorbed half the private investment of Britain, and paid a £16 million wage bill for a quarter-million navvies, most of them Irish famine refugees.

1849 in Canada

In one fell swoop, the repeal of the Corn Laws crippled the Canadian wheat and timber trades, and mills recently built to process grain before shipment went bankrupt. Jacob Keefer, who had built a number of mills along the Welland Canal to take advantage of preferential treatment, wrote to his partner William Hamilton Merritt, MPP and promoter of the canal, "The sooner the connection between Great Britain and Canada is dissolved the better."[1]

The year 1849 also saw the passage of the controversial *Rebellion Losses Bill* by the Canadian Assembly.

In February of that year, Louis-Hippolyte LaFontaine proposed a bill to repay the residents of Lower Canada who had suffered financial losses during 1837 and 1838. As if to foment trouble, the wording of the bill was deliberately designed to allow former rebels not charged with treason to qualify for compensation.

---

[1] Innis and Lower, Select Documents, II, 357: April 19, 1848.

Figure 19.1. *Burning of Parliament*, Montréal, 1849.
Source: McCord Museum, M11588.

The bill was greeted with outrage by the Tory opposition. When it actually passed into law later in the year and was approved by Governor General Lord Elgin, word quickly spread throughout the city. That evening a huge crowd gathered at the Parliament buildings, and an extreme element broke into the building and set it ablaze.

A day later, Parliament convened at the Bonsecours Market and voted to relocate to Toronto.

John Redpath in the Lead

The burning of Parliament was a symptom of real distress. Most Montrealers in the mercantile or business field felt crucified by low British demand for Canadian products of the farm and forest. Many experienced large financial losses, betrayed and abandoned by British banks who refused to issue loans or credit for Canadian investments.

The Montréal merchants were certain that the blame for their plight centred on the government in Britain, which seemed to be abandoning Canada.

Some of the more pessimistic leading citizens of Montréal decided to promote widespread discussion of annexation with the US, as a way of forcing the British to act. Thomas Mackay was not directly involved, but his old friend and partner, John Redpath, was the major driver of the movement.[2]

On December 7, 1849, the founding meeting of the Annexation Association of Montreal met in the Temperance Hall on St. Maurice Street. Redpath was called to the chair by acclamation.

The meeting concluded that the only options open to the Canadians were these, none of which was a true remedy:

1. The revival of protection in the markets of the United Kingdom.
2. The protection of home manufactures.
3. A federal union of the British American provinces.
4. The independence of the British North American colonies as a federal republic.
5. Reciprocal free trade with the United States, as respects the products of the farm, the forest, and the mine.

Figure 19.2. John Redpath.
Source: William Notman, McCord Museum, I-20963.1.

---

[2] Richard Feltoe, *A Gentleman of Substance: The Life and Legacy of John Redpath.*

Redpath put forward the motion, Resolved,

> That our state of colonial dependence can only be prolonged at the sacrifice of our most valuable interests, and that this meeting, considering the social, commercial and political difficulties of Canada, and feeling the weight of the evils that oppress our Society, believes that the only attainable measures capable of permanently improving our condition, consist in a peaceable separation from Great Britain, with her consent, and the Annexation of Canada to the United States of America.

William Molson seconded the resolution, which was put to a vote and carried without a dissenting voice.

Elected Secretary of the Annexation Association was another Thomas Mackay son-in-law, Montréal lawyer and later judge Robert Mackay, who had married daughter Christina a year earlier, on June 27, 1848. Robert Mackay would serve on the McGill Board of Governors from 1879 until December 1887, and he willed the University his extensive library.

In all, over 325 prominent Montréal citizens signed the manifesto, including John Redpath's son Peter, future finance minister Alexander Galt, and future prime minister John Abbott.

A Petulant Child

John Abbott later mused that signing the manifesto was a youthful error—"no more serious idea of seeking annexation with the United States than a petulant child who strikes his nurse has of deliberately murdering her."

But desperate times called for desperate measures, and the members of the Annexation Association were desperate men whose businesses were sorely impacted by the arbitrary actions of the British government. Redpath particularly noted that British indifference was forcing thousands of skilled Canadian artisans to leave for the United States.

The Annexation Manifesto, published in the *Gazette* on October 11, 1849, was a clear-headed summary of the ills afflicting the colonies of BNA:

LITTLE BEN HOLMES AND SOME NAUGHTY CHILDREN ATTEMPT TO PAWN THEIR MOTHER'S POCKET-HANDKERCHIEF, BUT ARE ARRESTED BY POLICE-MAN PUNCH, WHO WAS STATIONED "ROUND THE CORNER."

Figure 19.3. Anti-annexation cartoon in *Punch in Canada*, 1849.

With superabundant water power and cheap labour, especially in Lower Canada, we have yet no domestic manufactures; nor can the most sanguine, unless under altered circumstances, anticipate the home growth, or advent from foreign parts, of either capital or enterprise, to embark in this great source of national wealth. Our institutions, unhappily, have not that impress of permanence which can alone impart security and inspire confidence, and the Canadian market is too limited to tempt the foreign capitalist.

Whilst the adjoining States are covered with a net-work of thriving railways, Canada possesses but three lines, which, together, scarcely exceed fifty miles [80 kilometres] in length, and the stock in two of which is held at a depreciation of from 50 to 80 percent, —a fatal symptom of the torpor overspreading the land.

Our present form of Provincial Government is cumbrous and so expensive, as to be ill suited to the circumstances of the country; and the necessary reference it demands to a distant Government, imperfectly acquainted with Canadian affairs, and somewhat indifferent to our interests, is anomalous and irksome. Yet in the event of a rupture between two of the most powerful nations of the world, Canada would become the battle-field and the sufferer, how ever little her interests might be involved in the cause of quarrel or the issue of the contest.

The bitter animosities of political parties and factions in Canada, often leading to violence, and, upon one occasion, to civil war, seem not to have abated with time; nor is there at the present moment, any prospect of diminution or accommodation. The aspect of parties becomes daily more threatening towards each other, and under our existing institutions and relations, little hope is discernible of a peaceful and prosperous administration of our affairs, but difficulties will, to all appearances accumulate until government becomes impracticable. In this view of our position, any course that may propose to efface existing party distinctions and place entirely new issues before the people, must be fraught with undeniable advantages.

Among the statesmen of the Mother Country—among the sagacious observers of the neighbouring Republic—in Canada and in all British North America—among all classes there is a strong pervading conviction that a political revolution in this country is at hand. Such forebodings cannot readily be dispelled; and they have moreover, a tendency to realize the events to which they point. In the meantime, serious injury results to Canada from the effects of this anticipation upon the more desirable class of settlers, who naturally prefer a country under fixed and permanent forms of government to one in a state of transition.

Within ten days, more than a thousand signatures were on the petition for annexation. Most signers were British in origin and included almost every prominent merchant in Lower Canada.

Once published, the Annexation Manifesto attracted the official attention of the government. All those who signed the document were called upon to explain themselves, and were stripped of any titles or offices. John Redpath was forced to resign as a trustee of the Montreal Turnpike Commission.

Figure 19.4. Peter McGill (colourized).
Source: William Notman, McCord Museum, N-0000.6.

The Montreal Scots fought back. Peter McGill, President of the St. Andrew's Society, took the extraordinary step of removing Lord Elgin from its membership—the governor general had formerly been Honorary Patron of the society—and returned, "The paltry £10 he had given them for charity." He was also expelled from the Thistle Curling Club.[3]

On October 15, cooler heads replied, with George-Étienne Cartier and some other members of the Lower Canada Assembly signalling their astonishment and regret concerning "the avowed intention of exciting in the midst of our population a movement in favour of the separation of this province from Great Britain, and of its annexation to the United States of America."

---

[3] Doughty, Elgin-Grey Papers, 1, 350–352.

Cartier and fellows appealed to

> The wisdom, the love of order, and the honour of the inhabitants of this country, and to call upon these to oppose by every means in their power an agitation tending to subvert a constitution which, after having been long and earnestly sought for, was received with feelings of deep gratitude towards the Metropolitan government—an agitation, moreover, which can result in nothing beyond the continuation of the scenes from which this city has already so severely suffered, the disturbance of social order and a renewal of the troubles, commotions and disasters which we have had to deplore in times now past.

Lord Elgin to the Rescue

The loss of preferential duties and lower grain prices in Britain dealt a hard blow to the Canadian grain trade; but it recovered in the prosperous 1850s. The lifting of imperial economic controls also brought relief from political controls, and thus imperial recognition of responsible government in British North America.

With the British fully aware of the demands of the Canadians, they began to discuss the possibility of a free trade treaty with the Americans. This goal was promoted by the Baldwin-LaFontaine government and especially its Minister of Public Works, William Hamilton Merritt.

During the winter of 1850–1851, Merritt engaged his protege, Thomas Mackay's new son-in-law Thomas Keefer, to work with the American consul in Saint John, New Brunswick, and report on how reciprocal trade could benefit the economies of British North America and the United States. Armed with this data, Lord Elgin and US Secretary of State William Marcy were able to meet in Washington to negotiate a treaty of reciprocity.

The sun came out from behind the clouds.

The *Elgin-Marcy Reciprocity Treaty* of 1854 removed the need for Canada to join the United States to ensure access to that market. With easy and open access guaranteed, any impetus to join the US was removed. Had it not been for this treaty, the economic push to join the US might have been unstoppable.

This new British rapprochement with the US was based on more than trade—by the 1840s, the United States was taking up to 40 percent of British exports, but it was also absorbing 80 percent of its

Figure 19.5. James Bruce, Earl of Elgin, 1855. *Source*: Cornelius Krieghoff, McCord Museum, M22464.

emigrants, many of whom passed through Montréal, then turned south due to a lack of opportunity in the Canadas.

The treaty came into effect October 15, 1854. It opened the American market to the British North Americans, for wood, fish, and farm produce only, in return for freedom of operation on the Great Lakes and the St. Lawrence River and canals, and US access to the fishery along Canadian coastal waters.

Since it allowed British North American lumber into the United States duty-free, the treaty brought boom times back to the Ottawa Valley, and boosted Bytown's population. By the mid-1850s, the town boasted sixty stores, three banks, three insurance offices, three newspapers, a telegraph office, and seven schools.

Mackay & MacKinnon had already decided to go into the retail business. Lovell's 1851 Directory notes two Bytown businesses managed by the partnership:

- Mackay & MacKinnon, cloth and flour store, Sussex St. Lower Town.
- Mackay & MacKinnon, cloth factory, grist mills, sawmills, and general store. New Edinburgh—Post Office, Bytown.

Taking time out for winter play, on Christmas Day, 1852, MacKinnon refereed the first ice-shinty match between the New Edinburgh Scots and the Bytown Sassenachs ("Englishmen") on the frozen Rideau River. Shinty—also called "shinny"—was an old Irish and Scottish form of field hockey, played with a ball and a stick curved at one end, similar to a field hockey stick. The Scots won 2–1 and the laird of Rideau Hall awarded the Shintie Club winners a silver medal, now in the Bytown Museum.[4]

With most of the mill wheels freezing up, and Scots being Scots, Mackay & MacKinnon also got the workers to build New Edinburgh's first curling rink, along the shore of the Rideau River. Matches were soon arranged with the Bytown Curling Club, founded in 1851 by Mackay's friend, lumberman Allan Gilmour, with a rink on the canal.

Reciprocity with the US came too late to bolster the finances of Thomas Mackay, stressed by some unfortunate railway investments, changing demand, and competition from lumber companies based on LeBreton Flats.

In 1853, as his lumber business began to contract, Mackay began to transfer his sawmill interests to Currier, who ran it for fifteen years before the Mackay Estate sold it out to the Maclaren brothers, James and John. Currier experienced some commercial disasters, yet with the help of his brother-in-law, Alonzo Wright, managed to retain the house he had built in 1866–1868 at 24 Sussex Drive, Ottawa, which eventually became the official residence of the prime minister of Canada.

Mackay continued his interest in promoting exports from the cloth mills. In 1851, satinette from Rideau Falls won a gold medal for quality at the first Great Exhibition in the Crystal Palace in Hyde Park, London, where son-in-law Thomas Keefer served as a Canadian commissioner. In 1862 Keefer also assisted in the organization of exhibits for a second exhibition in London.

In 1877, Keefer was appointed Canada's Chief Commissioner of the Paris International Exhibition, to be held in 1878. A morale booster after the disasters of the Franco-Prussian War, the Paris expo was the biggest international show ever held to that date.

---

[4] The names of most of the Bytown players are unknown, except for James Peacock. The New Edinburgh team included John Lumsden, D. M. Grant, Allen Cameron, Peter Fraser, William McDonald, and brothers Donald and Hugh Masson.

Figure 19.6a. Mackay's silver New Edinburgh Shintie Club medallion, face, 1852.
Source: Commemorative, Bytown Museum, A203.

Figure 19.6b. Mackay's silver New Edinburgh Shintie Club medallion, verso, 1852.
Source: Commemorative, Bytown Museum, A203.

Figure 19.7. *Scots on Ice—Curling on the St. Lawrence at Montréal.*
Source: Library and Archives Canada, c040148k.

Keefer wrote and published an eighty-five-page official catalogue of the Canadian pavilion, packed with useful knowledge and statistics, with the help of financier Sir John Rose and Alfred Selwyn of the Geological Survey of Canada.

Keefer claimed that the Canadian "trophy" in Paris in 1878, opened by the Prince of Wales, was one of the most interesting exhibits at the fair.

Canada's "trophy" was a four-storey wooden tower. In spite of its appearance, it was not steam powered. At the entrance, visitors were invited to place their calling cards in baskets held by two stuffed grizzly bears. On each of the lower faces were symbols of the bounty of Canada's fields, forests, seas, and mines. Several gold ingots were on display. The balconies were inset with the coats of arms of the provinces and largest cities, and festooned with flags and bunting. And around the tower were stuffed heads of buffalo and elk, ships' wheels, farm implements, a trade canoe, and other symbols worthy of a young aspiring nation.

A large golden block at the entrance was engraved with the rounded number 333,000,000, representing the value of Canada's production of precious metals up to 1877.[5]

---

[5] "L'Exposition universelle de 1878 illustrée," *The Graphic*, July 6, 1878.

Figure 19.8. *Canada at the 1878 Paris Exposition.*
Source: *The Graphic,* July 6, 1878.

Written a decade after Confederation, Keefer's catalogue contained surprisingly little information about Canada's trading relationship with Great Britain, and more about growing relations with the United States.

PART THREE

Railway Mania

Figure 20.1. *Montreal and Lachine Railroad First Train, 19 November 1847.*
Source: John Henry Walker, McCord Museum.

CHAPTER 20

The Philosophy of Railroads, 1847–1853

> *Far away to the South is heard the daily scream of the steam-whistle,—but from Canada there is no escape—blockaded and imprisoned by Ice and Apathy, we have at least ample time for reflection; and if there be comfort in Philosophy, may we not profitably consider the PHILOSOPHY OF RAILROADS.*
>
> —Thomas Keefer, 1848

James Ferrier's Railways

From 1847 on, Thomas Mackay began to risk some of his capital in charters for potential railways. He was still mindful of the warning by one of Lord Metcalfe's staff that without railway communications to the outside world, Ottawa was not in the running as a potential capital of the Canadas. At the same time, Mackay realized the urgency of getting all-weather access to markets for the produce of his Rideau Falls mills.

Now in his sixties, Mackay was growing weary of business concerns. He already had a full plate with his Legislative Council and Militia duties, as well as running his beloved Rideau Hall, and taking care of his remaining child, Thomas, and wife Ann. But with all his cares, he was still content to support two of his sons-in-law—John MacKinnon and Thomas Keefer—with emerging railway projects.

Mackay's major partner in railway enterprises was a fellow Scot named James Ferrier, who arrived in Montréal in 1821 after several years working in a Perth, Scotland, mercantile house. Ferrier was five years younger than Mackay. The two became acquainted in the late

1830s, and during the era of railway mania in the later 1840s and '50s. Ferrier also joined Mackay on the Legislative Council in 1847.

In the spring of 1837, Ferrier was appointed to the Montréal board of directors of the newly chartered Bank of British North America, a London-based company that began operations in Upper and Lower Canada with a nominal capital of £1,000,000. Mackay moved most of the capital from his Rideau Canal profits from the Bank of Montreal to the Bank of BNA's branch in Bytown. His first bank manager was a young Scot named John MacKinnon, who in 1846 would marry Mackay's eldest daughter, Annie.

Ferrier had already served as mayor of Montréal, and sometime president of the St. Andrew's Society, as he steadily amassed a fortune in Montréal commerce and real estate. Beyond his dominant railway interests, Ferrier was also one of the 1855 incorporators of Molson's Bank and, along with John Redpath, restored McGill College to financial health.

Ferrier's first foray into railway building was the Montreal & Lachine Railroad, the first line built on the island of Montréal. On August 10, 1846, under his direction, a meeting of six thousand petitioned the government to promote more railway development in Canada. The M&L soon raised £75,000 in share capital in partnership with the Proprietors of the Lachine Canal. The enterprise attracted seventy-four co-sponsors, among them Sir George Simpson of the Hudson's Bay Company, the Sulpician Order, and William Molson, who was also interested in the Champlain and Saint Lawrence Railroad that ran up the Richelieu Valley towards Lake Champlain.

The 12-kilometre Montreal & Lachine, built to bypass the Lachine Rapids, began operating on November 19, 1847, between Bonaventure Station at Chaboillez Square in Montréal and its terminus at the Lachine wharf. With the area around the Lachine Canal seeing increasing industrial development, the line provided a commuter service, and hauled freight when the canal was closed for the winter. The line was Montréal's—and Canada's—first "rapid transit" system, running six round trips a day.

The official opening of the Montreal & Lachine Railroad took place on Friday, November 19, 1847. At one o'clock that afternoon, Thomas Mackay joined Ferrier, Governor General Lord Elgin, Louis-Joseph Papineau, Peter McGill, and a party of directors, shareholders, and politicians, as their train left Bonaventure Station for the twenty-minute trip to Lachine, with a ten-minute stopover before returning to Montréal.

Figure 20.2. James Ferrier, 1866.
Source: William Notman, McCord Museum, I-21748.1.

Figure 20.3. Montreal & Lachine Railroad token.

On July 24, 1848, Ferrier boosted the rolling stock of the line with the locomotive "James Ferrier"—the first railway engine imported from England.

Ferrier's Montreal & Lachine was never a great money-maker, but it was the first link in a chain of charters that enabled his railways to expand westward up the St. Lawrence and Ottawa valleys, and south as far as Lake Champlain and New York.

To promote the Montreal & Lachine, and other lines emerging from the imagination of railroad promoters, Ferrier hired Thomas Mackay's new son-in-law, Thomas Keefer, to write a pamphlet singing the praises of railroad building. Keefer responded with a full-scale book, *Philosophy of Railroads*, first published in 1849. It had a huge impact on communities hankering for railways, and rapidly became a North American best-seller, being reprinted four times.

In 1852, Canada had less than 110 kilometres of railroad laid down. By 1871, when his book had gone through five editions, there were thousands.

Keefer's lyrical hymn to progress set forth the main benefits of what he called "the civilizing rails"—how technology could remedy the age-old abuses of oppression, poverty, and ignorance—and for Canadians, level the playing field for a country smothered by snow and ice for four months of the year. It also promoted a strategic rail linkage between Montréal and Toronto and the west, so as to out-distance American rivals for control of the Great Lakes trade.

In 1850, he followed his *Philosophy of Railroads* with a companion volume, *The Canals of Canada* (1850), which won a prize awarded by Lord Elgin to celebrate the completion of the provincial canal system.

"The amount of the prize is not much—£50—altho' it will buy the baby shoes," he wrote his young wife, "but it is something to beat a dozen of the best writers in the Province." Thomas and Elizabeth would have three sons and four daughters.

At this stage, Keefer did not join in the creation or management or promotion of his brother-in-law's Bytown & Prescott line, but soon had his own chance to engineer a railroad.

The St. Lawrence & Ottawa Grand Junction Railway

James Ferrier was a visionary. He and his long-time partner Peter McGill were masters at obtaining railway charters from the assembly and locking up territories well before the lines were built. Thomas Mackay was a trusted associate of the partners, and used his influence and his capital to promote the lines leading to and from Ottawa.

In 1850, Ferrier also involved Keefer in launching an ambitious program of railway expansion radiating out of Montréal. On August 10 of that year, Ferrier got two amendments to the Montreal & Lachine's charter. The first gave the Montreal & Lachine permission to change its name to the St. Lawrence & Ottawa Grand Junction Railway and to build northwest from Lachine into the hinterland of the Ottawa River to Grenville or Hawkesbury, then west to Kemptville and south to Prescott on Lake Ontario. Ferrier appointed Keefer Chief Engineer of the line. The second merged the Montreal & Lachine with Molson's Montreal and New York Railroad, to go south through Plattsburgh to New York City.

Urged on by Ferrier, Thomas Mackay sat on the board of the St. Lawrence & Ottawa Grand Junction Railway, and was an early investor in his new son-in-law's railway. However, the St. Lawrence & Ottawa Grand Junction Railway was in reality a territory marker—a move on the chessboard of railway charters. It would never materialize as a viable project.

Mackay and his fellow Bytown boosters wanted to start first with a railway south to the St. Lawrence that would get all-weather access to the growing American market for sawed lumber, already being tapped using the Rideau Canal. A line to the St. Lawrence would also be able to join a railway now being promoted between Montréal and Toronto.

ST. LAWRENCE AND OTTAWA
GRAND JUNCTION RAILWAY.

President.
WM. F. COFFIN, Esq.

Vice-President.
L. H. HOLTON, Esq.

Directors.
Hon. PETER McGILL.
Hon. THOS. McKAY.
Hon. JOHN YOUNG.
Hon. CHAS. WILSON.
WM. MOLSON, Esq.
JOHN TORRANCE, Esq.
WM. DOW, Esq.
D. L. McPHERSON, Esq.
DAVID DAVIDSON, Esq.
JOHN McKINNON, Esq.
H. H. WHITNEY, Esq.

Secretary.
G. F. COCKBURN, Esq.

Engineer in Chief.
THOS. C. KEEFER, Esq.

Counsel.
A. CROSS, Esq.

Bankers.
BANK OF MONTREAL.

Figure 20.4. St. Lawrence & Ottawa Grand Junction Railway.

But Ferrier and Mackay's capital kept the valuable St. Lawrence & Ottawa charter active, and Keefer began promoting a "central" trunk line up the Ottawa Valley to Georgian Bay as potentially the first stage of a railway to the Pacific. The St. Lawrence & Ottawa Grand Junction Railway eventually became a CPR branch, and much of the track is still in use.

Thomas Keefer, Railroad Philosopher

Thomas Keefer was, like Thomas Mackay, a dyed-in-the-wool canal man making the leap to railways. He was born in 1821, the year George Stephenson put his first steam locomotive on rails between Stockton and Darlington, England.

Keefer was the eighth in a family of twenty children, fourteen of whom survived. An elder half-brother was engineer Samuel Keefer. One of his half-sisters was Laura Secord's daughter Esther.

His father, George Keefer, was a United Empire Loyalist and founder of the Niagara town of Thorold. The family was forced to trek to Canada in 1790 after the American Revolutionary War, leaving behind mills and other property in New Jersey.

During the War of 1812, George Keefer served under his friend, mentor, and fellow Loyalist William Hamilton Merritt in the Lincoln Militia. Merritt was one of General Brock's pallbearers, and received the swords of the American officers as they surrendered at Queenston Heights.

Keefer was with Merritt on December 10, 1813, when they galloped in a panic to the town of Niagara—today's Niagara-on-the-Lake—and came upon the horrifying sight of burned and frozen bodies of townsfolk, their homes recently torched by the enemy.

On November 30, 1824, as president of the Welland Canal Company, George Keefer turned the first sod to start construction of the Welland Canal, joining Lakes Erie and Ontario. Built to take advantage of Niagara water power, and compete with the new Erie Canal in New York State, the Welland Canal opened up free water transportation as far as Fort William on Lake Superior, extending the navigation of the St. Lawrence 1500 kilometres into the interior.

Eight-year-old Thomas Keefer witnessed the trial opening of the Welland Canal on November 30, 1829, as two lake schooners, the *Annie and Jane* of York, and the *R.H. Boughton* of Youngstown, New York, broke through a crust of thin ice to sail from Lake Ontario to Lake Erie.

Figure 20.5. *Opening of the Welland Canal.*
Source: J. D. Kelly, Library and Archives Canada.

After graduating from Upper Canada College in 1838, Thomas worked as an apprentice engineer on the Erie Canal in New York State. In 1840, at age 19, he began his career as divisional engineer on the enlarged Second Welland Canal, then being reconstructed with stone locks and public money.

Five years later, through the influence of his father's friend, William Hamilton Merritt, MLA for Lincoln, and of his older half-brother Samuel, first chief engineer of the Board of Works of the Province of Canada, the 27-year-old Thomas Keefer was put to work as chief engineer, Ottawa River, where he was responsible for maintaining, designing, and building water control works and timber slides to move logs downstream from remote inland camps.

In November 1845, on a tour of inspection up the Ottawa, Keefer nearly lost his life running the long Chenaux Rapids in a heavy snowstorm. "My canoe was sunk, my bowsman drowned, and the rest of our party rescued from a rock, upon which we should have frozen in a few hours, by a boat sent from the little steamer which had anchored under the islands—we were made the welcome and thankful guests of her kind hearted captain."

According to the *Bytown Gazette*, over eighty lives were lost that season:

There is scarcely a rapid the white swells of which have not proved a winding sheet for the bold voyageur or reckless lumberman; there is scarcely a portage, or cleared point, jutting out into the river where you do not meet with wooden crosses, on which are rudely carved the initials of some unfortunate victim of the resistless waters. The strongest swimmer has in broken water no more chance than a child. Some of the eddies in high water become whirlpools, tearing a bark canoe into shreds and engulfing every soul in it.

Keefer laughed off his near-death experience, but later received a stern letter from his father complaining that he had not been informed of his son's miraculous escape.

An intense young man with a Mark Twain moustache, Keefer was already forging his reputation as a firebrand, advocating engineering standards and professional ethics, raking politicians over the coals with his complaints about "pork-barrel planning and patronage," in which political expediency overruled engineering judgment about the worth of public works projects.

A Fellow Canal Man

As a fellow canal man and prophet of the new technology or railroading, Thomas Keefer was soon welcomed by Mackay as a friend and as a potential a son-in-law. On September 27, 1848, he and 18-year-old Elizabeth Mackay were married in a ceremony at Rideau Hall. Mackay's small brass cannon boomed out the glorious news.

Earlier that year, Keefer's scorn for pork-barrelling and political influence in the planning of engineering works had cost him business, and he was let go from his Ottawa River post. His brother, Samuel Keefer, then working full-time on improvements to the Welland Canal, was not able to save him. So Thomas and Elizabeth moved to Montréal, where he established himself as an independent consulting engineer, specializing in railway, harbour, and bridge engineering.

Figure 20.6. Elizabeth Mackay Keefer, 1869.
Source: Topley Studio, Library and Archives Canada.

CHAPTER 21

The Bytown & Prescott, 1847–1853

Old Winter is once more upon us, and our inland seas are "dreary and inhospitable wastes" to the merchant and to the traveller; —our rivers are sealed fountains, and an embargo, which no human power can remove, is laid on all our ports. Around our deserted wharves and warehouses are huddled the naked spars,— the blasted forest of trade,—from which the sails have fallen like the leaves of the autumn. The splashing wheels are silenced,—the roar of steam hushed,—the gay saloon, so lately thronged with busy life, is now an abandoned hall,—and the cold snow revels in solitary possession of the untrodden deck. The animation of business is suspended, the life blood of commerce is curdled and stagnant in the St. Lawrence—the great Aorta of the North.

On land, the heavy stage labours through mingled frost and mud in the West,—or struggles through drifted snow, and slides with uncertain track over the icy hills of Eastern Canada.

—Thomas Keefer,
The Philosophy of Railroads, 1848

With the British abandoning imperial preference, Thomas Keefer was fully aware that his father-in-law, Thomas Mackay, and brother-in-law, John MacKinnon, were inclined to build a railway to ship timber south to the US market, instead of east to Montréal. They had already proved their ability to serve the US market via the Rideau Canal.

In an 1847 article in the *Montreal Gazette*, Keefer noted that if a railway line from Montréal to Bytown were not built, the citizens of Bytown would first opt for a shorter line to Prescott, and ship lumber across the St. Lawrence to the US town of Ogdensburg, New York, soon to be the terminus of a railway linking the St. Lawrence River to Boston and other large cities on the Eastern Seaboard. Keefer reasoned that

> The Ottawa steamboat navigation is imperfect and tedious. The lumber trade on that river, employing a capital of £500,000 annually, is of the highest importance; the constant through travelling of the lumber would be a great source of profit to the road. If Montréal, the natural market of Bytown and the Ottawa, does not exert herself, the latter will make no great effort to avoid a connection with Ogdensburg, which can be done in less than half the distance to Montréal.

When winter navigation closed on the Ottawa River and Rideau Canal, the only way in or out of Bytown was by sleigh. A sleigh left for Prescott every day. Freight was also hauled upriver from Montréal in "traineaux"—single-horse rigs—by French-Canadian sleigh drivers dressed in red and blue toques who sang voyageur songs to hold off the cold. The trains were sometimes half a mile [0.8 kilometre] long. The return trip took a week.

Railway Mania Infects Bytown

Keefer's prediction soon came true. In May of 1848, Robert Bell's newspaper *The Bytown Packet*, today's *Ottawa Citizen*, began to promote the building of a railway between Bytown and Prescott.

A rail link from Bytown to Prescott could open an all-season transportation route for exporting lumber cut from Ottawa Valley timber, as well as finished goods such as siding and sashes and windows, to the important US markets. Such a link would be much speedier and less costly than using the Rideau Canal or the Ottawa River, locked in ice for four or five months of the year.

In June, the leading citizens of Prescott held exploratory meetings with engineers and surveyors, and pronounced the project feasible. On July 1, 1848, Thomas Mackay chaired a meeting in the Bytown Court House, to discuss the building of a railroad that would connect the town with a future St. Lawrence Valley railroad, not via the Ottawa Valley, as Keefer recommended, but at Prescott, on the St. Lawrence River. Since a Montréal to Toronto railway was in the offing, the line's backers argued that it would also give Bytown products, particularly sawed lumber, quick all-season access to the Canadian markets of Montréal and Toronto, as well as Boston and New York.

On January 5, 1850, Bytown threw off its military shackles and was incorporated as a self-governing municipality. On March 11, the first town council meeting was held, and on May 10, the charter for the Bytown & Prescott Railway was submitted to the Governor General.

The first annual general meeting of the Bytown & Prescott was held two weeks later, and the line incorporated on August 10. Thomas Mackay's son-in-law, John MacKinnon, then the reeve of Gloucester, was chosen as its first president, at a meeting in the Town Hall, then located in the Lower Town market building. Mackay's business associate, Robert Bell, a surveyor, councilman, and owner of the *Bytown Packet*, was appointed secretary of the meeting, and later the company, and Walter Shanley was chosen as chief engineer.

One of the major boosters of the railway project was Richard W. Scott, a young lawyer who had come from Prescott to act as solicitor for the Quebec Bank, and had been engaged by Thomas Mackay on occasion.[1]

The Bytown & Prescott corporate charter was given Royal Assent on August 10.[2] Early listed shareholders included MacKinnon (but not Thomas Mackay), Nicholas Sparks, and Bytown lawyer Augustus Keefer (brother of both Samuel and Thomas).[3] The citizens of Bytown, population seven thousand, subscribed for £15,000 worth of stock.

On October 12, 1850, the *Bytown Packet* published a prospectus written by MacKinnon describing the length of the line, its likely location, and its construction and outfitting costs, estimated at £150,000–200,000 (£1=C$4.87). The capital was to be $600,000, with power to increase it to $1,000,000. Shares were priced at $40 each.

The prospectus looked good on paper, MacKinnon confidently declaring that, "we cannot too highly appreciate the value of this road as an important link in the great chain of international communication."

---

[1] Richard Scott, 1825–1913; politician, Secretary of State of Canada 1874–1878, 1896–1908, born February 24, 1825, at Prescott Ontario; died in Ottawa April 23, 1913. Scott grew up in Ottawa and was elected mayor in 1852. He sat in the provincial parliament and was appointed Senator in 1874 by Alexander Mackenzie.

[2] Acts 13–14, Chapter 132 of the *Statutes for the Province of Canada*.

[3] Augustus Keefer was Commissioner of the Dominion Police (1880–1885); he died in office. One of his law students, Samuel Henry Strong, was third chief justice of Canada.

Figure 21.1. Lower Town market building.
Source: Library and Archives Canada, C-002185.

To make the line pay, he estimated that annual revenues of £21,000–30,000 were needed.

As a nod to Thomas Keefer, MacKinnon broached the possibility of extending the B&P eastward to link up with Keefer's projected St. Lawrence & Ottawa Grand Junction Railway. But Keefer's idea was placed on the back burner for the moment. No need for a battle of the brothers-in-law. By that point, Thomas Mackay's Keefer son-in-law was already working on other railway and bridge projects in Montréal.

On September 28, Bell's newspaper carried a story announcing that a line on the American side between Ogdensburg and Rouses Point on Lake Champlain would be finished shortly. Bell's editor quoted the *Ogdensburg Beacon*'s fulsome praise of the American line's "strength, workmanship, durability, and easy grade—for directness of road, superiority of construction, and economical outlay."

At that time, the *Packet's* office was at the noisy southeast corner of Rideau and Sussex, where Bell's editor publicly complained of pigs squealing "under the window of the editorium sanctum."[4]

---

[4] Brault, *The Mile of History*, 31.

The Terminus Issue

Through the winter of 1850–1851, engineer Walter Shanley, with two assistants, covered more than 400 kilometres on snowshoes and by sleigh, surveying four possible routes from Prescott to Bytown. At night, they slept in the open or in small hamlets.

Back in Bytown, investors in Upper Town began to argue that the natural location for the railway's northern terminus should be in the calm bays upstream from Chaudière Falls, on present-day LeBreton Flats, where square timber could be loaded directly, even in winter, onto trains bound for Prescott and the big American cities.

Mackay's Rideau Falls location was not nearly as practical for lumbering, as it required squared timber to be formed into small booms to transit the timber slide at the Chaudière Falls, then moved a few kilometres downstream to the Rideau Falls wharf, to be broken up and hoisted to the top of the falls for milling and finishing.

With hindsight, the wide expanse of LeBreton Flats, which later became the centre of Ottawa's lumber industry, would have been a much better location, to promote all-weather export of lumber. The river below Mackay's Rideau Falls mill was locked in winter's grip for at least three months a year.

In his memoirs, Richard W. Scott noted that the LeBreton Flats boosters made little headway against the preferences of Mackay and MacKinnon, two men with "money to spare." When it was clear that purchases of stock were far too small to pay for construction, Mackay felt it was his duty to buy a considerable slice of the shares—but only if the northern terminus was placed in New Edinburgh. A spur to LeBreton Flats would be built in future, but not for the moment.

Scott wryly noted that, "As the Honourable Thomas Mackay, and his son-in-law Mr. McKinnon, were taking a warm interest in the project, in deference to their wishes, the line was located passing through New Edinburgh."

He who pays the piper calls the tune, but this decision was based on monopoly, not economics, and would eventually cost Mackay and MacKinnon dearly. As we shall see, the B&P was a far riskier venture than they imagined.

In 1851, the Corporation of Bytown enthusiastically granted the line a loan guarantee of $60,000, to encourage an enterprise that would help make Bytown a potential site for the new capital of the Province of Canada.

On April 26, 1851, Bell's *Ottawa Citizen*, successor to the *Bytown Packet*, published engineer Shanley's recommendations for the location of the railway, which would run along the eastern shore of the Rideau River through to New Edinburgh, crossing the water on piers—still visible near Green Island—and terminate on Sussex Drive, where the Pearson Global Affairs Canada building now stands.

Workers started to clear land for the railway in early September 1851, and on October 9, Mackay joined John MacKinnon in an official groundbreaking ceremony at the Mactaggart Street station site.

As president of the line, MacKinnon gave a speech, and proceeded to put his shovel in the ground. According to the *Ottawa Citizen* reporter, MacKinnon

> tossed the first sod in first-rate style, amid the shouts and cheers of assembled thousands.
>
> Justice Burns addressed the audience, congratulating them upon the prospect presented of so great and desirable an undertaking being carried forward. Judge Armstrong being called upon, congratulated all present on the occasion of breaking ground, in commencing a work of so great importance; and in a short but very happy and humorous speech referred to some of the advantages that would result from it. G.B. Lyon, Esq. M.P., next spoke, complimenting the taxpayers, who had assented to their municipality subscribing largely on behalf of the enterprise. They were all shareholders indirectly, and were interested in its success.[5]

Bytown's mayor, members of the Town Corporation, the directors and officers of the Bytown & Prescott Railway, a senior magistrate, the area's member of Parliament, and the county sheriff, were then conveyed in carriages in a grand parade from the company offices down Sussex St., escorted by the "Sons and Cadets of Temperance" in full regalia.

That evening, MacKinnon and the directors hosted a celebratory dinner at Doran's, the top Bytown hotel. Notwithstanding the presence of temperance followers in the afternoon parade, copious amounts of champagne and wine were consumed, leading to a "number of jovial songs sung in the course of the evening."

---

[5] Omer Lavallée, *Historic review of "Bytown and Prescott Railway."*

BYTOWN & PRESCOTT RAILWAY

WINTER ARRANGEMENT.

ON and AFTER MONDAY, the 25th instant, PASSENGER TRAINS will run as follows, viz:

LEAVE BYTOWN

At SIX, A. M., *Railway Time,* — stopping at GLOUCESTER, OSGOODE, KEMPTVILLE, OXFORD and SPENCERS, and arrive at PRESCOTT at NINE, A. M., in time to connect with the Ogdensburgh Railroad Train going East.

LEAVE PRESCOTT

At 5.30, P. M., (*Railway Time,*) or on the arrival of the Train on the Ogdensburgh Railroad, stopping at the Way Stations above mentioned, and arrive at Bytown at 8.30, P. M.

PASSENGERS for MONTREAL, BOSTON, and NEW-YORK can proceed via OGDENSBURGH RAILROAD, ARRIVING in Montreal the SAME EVENING or Boston and New York the Day following.

R. HOUGH,
Supt. B. & P. Railway.

B. & P. Railway Office,
Bytown, 22nd December, 1854. (45u)

Figure 21.2. The Bytown & Prescott.

Richard W. Scott to the Rescue

Construction was initially slow, but for the most part straightforward —Shanley had done a good job siting the tracks. The most difficult part was crossing a swamp north of Prescott. Here the engineers laid down a wooden causeway as a bed for the train tracks.

By 1852, the company was running into serious trouble. The *Ottawa Citizen* reported that:

The directors of this company have now expended about £100,000 on this road, and in addition have purchased and paid for the iron. The locomotives and cars are likewise purchased and principally paid in stock; and now if they could obtain £75,000, the road could be completed and cars running to Kemptville, this fall and early next spring to Bytown. This being their situation, the directors can see no way of finishing the road without aid from the Corporations of Bytown and Prescott, and the municipalities through which it passes.

Even with this infusion of cash, there was not enough money; further funds were eventually raised from the towns along the proposed routes, which would be paid to the railway as a bonus on completion. These bonuses were highly controversial, as they were raised by local taxes.

More funds to build the railway came from subscription from private shareholders, and partly through loans from the rail suppliers in England and Canada. Unfortunately for the railway's backers, the line, only 52 miles [83 kilometres] long, was too short to qualify for a provincial subsidy under the 1849 *Guarantee Act*, for railways of at least 75 miles [120 kilometres] in length.

The 75-mile rule may have been aimed at the Bytown & Prescott, as many Quebeckers shared Keefer's opinion that Ottawa Valley products should be shipped through Montréal Island, and not directly to the US.

Elected mayor in 1852, Richard W. Scott was finally able to engineer a £50,000 loan guarantee from the provincial government's new Municipal Loan Fund, a godsend for towns like Ottawa trapped by railway mania and a $200,000 railway debt. Tiny Prescott, with a population of only 2,000, provided another £8,000 in capital and got £25,000 in loan guarantees. The township of Gloucester chipped in a further £5,000.

In 1852, Mackay dissolved his management partnership with MacKinnon, so the younger man could concentrate pretty much all his resources on the Bytown & Prescott Railway. The capital-burning railway was now out of his hands, and in 1853, Mackay transferred most of his milling interests to his Rideau Falls mill chief, Thomas Currier, who proceeded to expand the mills to meet projected demand.

By 1853, the rapidly developing sawmill industry at Chaudière had eclipsed the one at Rideau Falls. Overnight, LeBreton Flats and

Figure 21.3. Richard W. Scott and grandchild.
Source: Topley Studio, Library and Archives Canada, PA-025786.

the Chaudière sector of Ottawa became the more logical terminus for a lumber railway, which would certainly be built in opposition to the Bytown & Prescott.

Even with Currier's major expansion of the Rideau Falls mills, the Bytown & Prescott did not generate enough traffic, and bled money from the beginning. At least, marvelled an *Ottawa Citizen* editor, it was built with economy in mind—"a singular fact in connection with this enterprise, unprecedented I believe in the history of railroads and other large contracts, consists in the cost of the work and materials falling below the actual estimate of the engineers."

Once the rails arrived from England from the Ebbw Vale Iron Company in late 1853 and early 1854, the pace of construction picked up. The railway company laid down a narrow 4 ft. 8½ in. gauge track, commonly used in the United States and elsewhere, rather than the broad 5 ft. 6 in. "provincial" gauge typically used in Canada at that time. The carriages and locomotives were sourced in the United States, with the help of Richard W. Scott.

In May of 1854, the first locomotive, the "Oxford," was delivered by barge to Prescott. Two more engines, the "St. Lawrence" and the "Ottawa," arrived in July, with carriages. They were put into service

Figure 21.4. Ottawa & Prescott share certificate with corporate seal and Bell and MacKinnon signatures.

to Kemptville by August, and reached Gloucester, just 3.5 miles [5.6 kilometres] from Bytown, by November 11.

On December 29, the first train, pulled by the "Oxford," arrived in New Edinburgh. As the bridge over the Rideau had not yet been completed, the passengers were ferried across to Cumberland Street and they walked to the station on Sussex Street, where was held an inauguration ceremony that ended with a banquet.

On January 1, 1855, Bytown became the city of Ottawa. The Bytown & Prescott Railway shortly after changed its name to the Ottawa & Prescott.

Richard W. Scott and others were able to get provincial funding to keep the O&P afloat until April 1855, when the first train crossed the bridge over the Rideau River to the station at Mactaggart and Sussex Streets, a hundred yards from Earnscliffe.

May 10 marked the official opening of the line, exactly five years after the railway company was incorporated. With the O&P line finally completed, goods could be loaded on a train at Mactaggart Street station in Lower Town and shipped to Prescott, where they

Figure 21.5. Ottawa & Prescott locomotive, "the Ottawa," 1861, Sussex Street Station. *Source*: Library and Archives Canada, C-005288.

could be unloaded and then either barged across the St. Lawrence to the US, or reloaded onto Grand Trunk trains to be distributed all over Ontario and Eastern North America.

At least the O&P was running, albeit at a huge loss to the investors. That was enough to convince the Queen's advisors to keep Ottawa in the running to become the capital of the Province of Canada.

After the opening of the O&P, the new Ottawa town council began pressing bondholders for the interest on the railway loan. They brought the railway venture to the brink of insolvency, a matter that weighed heavily on Thomas Mackay, then 63 and in failing health.

Around the time of his death that October, the City of Ottawa defaulted on the O&P loan. The company went into receivership shortly after.

Charters, Consolidation, and the Grand Trunk

> *The greatest speed possible was 9 miles [14 kilometres] per hour. At some places, he says, children jumped on the foot-board to sell berries to passengers. The train could be signalled to stop anywhere, even in the forest, just by pulling a cord. The company was then in a very poor financial state, if one may judge by the figures for 1864 when the Company carried 32,943 passengers and 34,028 tons of freight for a total amount of $32,472, the expenditures being $70,640.*
>
> —L.-P.-E. Duvergier,
> "Huit mois en Amérique," 1865,
> on the Ottawa & Prescott Railroad

While the O&P limped along, all the remaining railway mania centred around the Grand Trunk Railway, linking Montréal with Toronto and the Ontario Peninsula.

In 1850, James Ferrier began to step away from the presidency of both the Montreal & Lachine and St. Lawrence & Ottawa Grand Junction Railways. To attract the British financiers and contractors eager to build the Grand Trunk Railway, he and Peter McGill chartered two lines, the Montreal & Kingston Railway Company, to run from Lachine to Kingston, and the Toronto & Kingston Railway Company. They appointed Thomas Keefer as chief engineer of both lines. Keefer published his "Report of the Preliminary Survey of the Toronto and Kingston Section of the Grand Trunk Railway" in Toronto in 1851.

To satisfy his Ottawa friends, and rescue their railway, Ferrier also chartered the Montreal, Ottawa and Kingston Grand Trunk Railroad Company, and issued a paper prospectus, "to raise among themselves, a capital sum, not exceeding one million of pounds, currency, to be divided into forty thousand shares of twenty-five pounds, currency, each." Both Thomas Mackay and John MacKinnon appeared on the prospectus, MacKinnon on the executive committee:

> The line was to pass through several Townships, Parishes, or places following to wit, across Isle Jésus by the Villages of Saint Thérèse or Saint Eustache to the Village of Saint Andrews, recrossing the Ottawa River at a point between Carillon and Grenville, thence through Hawkesbury, L'Orignal and Caledonia Springs to the Town of Bytown, and thence through Richmond, and Perth to Kingston.

Opposition to these lines was mostly theatrical—the Toronto & Kingston was leverage against a line from the west presided over by Sir Alan MacNab of Hamilton, whose Kingston & Toronto Railway Company was backed by John A. Macdonald and his Kingston law partner Malcolm Cameron.

Grand Trunk Follies

> *In Canada, with many of the bank incorporators themselves leaders in legislative councils, bribery was, in general, superfluous.*
>
> —Gustavus Myers, *History of Canadian Wealth*

In 1850, the Assembly of Canada passed an act with a conditional provision that the Grand Trunk Railway could be constructed as a public work by the Canadian government joining with the municipalities. The British government was agreeable to assist with financing of the line.

As a first step, the government sent Francis Hincks, Inspector General [Finance Minister] as Canadian envoy to England to negotiate with the British on financing.

It soon became apparent that the British had changed their attitude. Capital was available in London, but only on condition that the contract for building the Grand Trunk was turned over to the huge English contracting firm of Peto, Brassey, Betts, and Jackson, builders of railways and the new Parliament buildings at Westminster.

Thomas Keefer later wrote that "propositions were made to Francis Hincks by English contractors of great wealth and influence. The course of the Canadian envoy can only be defended on the assumption that a refusal was inevitable, and that a proper appreciation led him to appreciate it." Keefer eventually found that in exchange for Hincks's change of heart, the contractors eventually set aside $250,000 of stock for Canada's finance minister.

A committee of the Legislative Council whitewashed Hincks, reporting that the stock had been put in Hincks's name "without his knowledge," and that he had no personal interest in it.

Keefer also charged that provisions of the Grand Trunk subcontracts were either not enforced or were but meagrely complied with:

> Not only did the contracts fail to provide every essential to the perfect completion of the road, but the provisions they did contain were either not enforced or so loosely complied with, that the efficiency of the road has been impaired, its working expenses increased, and all the available resources of the company have been required to supply deficiencies, and to repair damages consequent upon this state of things. The bad quality of rails east of Toronto, with the deficiency of ballast and sleepers under them, have led to a destruction of rolling stock and property (fortunately hitherto unaccompanied by loss of life) which is unprecedented in the history of railways.

In 1854, British capital markets contracted, due to the outbreak of the Crimean War, and Peto, Brassey, Betts, and Jackson were forced to suspend operations because of bankruptcy.

Keefer went on to blame Canadian naiveté for the disaster that was the Grand Trunk in its formative days:

> It does not rest with the English public to charge upon Canada all the disastrous results of the Grand Trunk. The prospectus was not prepared in the province, nor did any member of her government see it until it was issued. Canada was not a stockholder in

the company; but as the endorser for it, not of it, put four of her ministers on a board, composed of eighteen directors, of whom six were in London and twelve in Canada, eight of the latter being really nominees of the English contractors.

The Canadians, as novices in railway matters, could not be censured if they even believed all they were told by the promoters of the railway; nor could they be worse than other people if they gave it a trial without believing in it; but there must have been many men, and many editors in London well versed in railways, not only English but American, who thoroughly appreciated the scheme, as one originated and promoted for the money which could be made out of it by men whose mission it is to prey upon their fellows.[6]

Unfortunately for Thomas Keefer, Hincks and the English contractors would soon have their revenge.

---

[6] Thomas Keefer, *Eighty Years' Progress of British North America*, 209.

CHAPTER 22

The Keefers in Montréal, 1850–1859

Thomas Keefer and the Victoria Bridge

In April 1850, Keefer mentor William Hamilton Merritt accepted the cabinet post of chief commissioner of Public Works. Samuel Keefer then returned to Ottawa as chief engineer of the department, while Thomas Keefer remained in Montréal to oversee building the world's longest bridge.

In June of 1851, Montréal's maverick Harbour Commissioner John Young, then Chairman of the St. Lawrence and Atlantic Railway, engaged Keefer to survey a railway route to Kingston and prepare a plan and estimates for the construction of a railway bridge across the St. Lawrence from Montréal. It was a major undertaking for a young man barely 30 years old.

The bridge was proposed because Montréal interests wanted a direct railway connection with the St. Lawrence and Atlantic line that ran from Longueuil Saint-Lambert on the south shore of the St. Lawrence, to the ice-free harbour at Portland, Maine. Montréal was unable to benefit from transatlantic trade for six months of the year by ice, whereas the port of New York was ice-free all year round.

Young agreed to pay Keefer $6,000, from the St. Lawrence and Atlantic account, then another $600 from the Montreal Harbour Trust.

Young had earlier engaged another engineer, in 1847, who stated that a bridge at Pointe-Saint-Charles was impractical. Keefer turned this conclusion upside down. In the autumn of 1851, he worked on soundings for a hydrographical chart of the river, showing the outline of both shores and the navigable channel, between the head of Nuns' Island and the foot of the St. Mary rapids. Over the winter he performed

Figure 22.1. Thomas Keefer, 1848.
Source: Library and Archives Canada.

a more accurate sounding of the riverbed through the ice, and fixed the location of the potential bridge between the Pointe-Saint-Charles shoals, where the water was generally not more than 20 feet [6 metres] deep, over Moffatt Island to the Saint-Lambert shore near the Champlain & St. Lawrence Railway Terminus.

By the following spring, Keefer had completed his master plan. His chart showed a bridge over 2 kilometres in length—the longest ever built. To reduce the length of the main bridge, he proposed two long approach embankments, jutting out 1,350 and 1,710 feet [411 and 521 metres] from either shore. This would diminish ice flows along the shore—a skill he had perfected during his Ottawa River timber slide work.

Most of his bridge consisted of twenty-three timber truss spans, each a wooden tube 250 feet [76 metres] long, resting on stone piers 70 feet [21 metres] above low water. For the 360-foot-deep [110-metre-deep] centre section of the river, he proposed a wrought-iron tubular span so as to provide a wide channel for timber rafts and steamboats to pass. This was similar to the Menai Straits tube bridge built by Robert Stephenson in England.

Keefer also recommended sinking cofferdams in the river for building the piers. To protect the cribwork from ice action, he proposed wedge-shaped upstream extensions having a sloped solid face, which would deflect ice floes past each pier, dissipating the energy of the ice. His so-called "timber shoes"—soon dubbed "Keefer shoes"—had already proved useful in protecting warehouses along the river from ice damage. They were elastic enough to absorb the grinding of ice and could be easily and cheaply repaired.

Keefer estimated the cost of this stupendous bridge to be $1,600,000. It would have a lifespan of fifty years, after which the timber spans could be replaced by wrought-iron tubes.

Keefer's *Report on a Survey of the Railway Bridge over the St. Lawrence, Surveyed in 1851–52*, was soon published as a pamphlet, with an enclosed map titled *The Railway Bridge over the St. Lawrence at Montréal, Surveyed by Order of the Committee of the Montreal & Kingston R. R. Hon John Young, Chairman. Thomas C. Keefer, Engineer, 1851*.

In 1852, quite suddenly, Thomas Keefer's bright future in bridge engineering came to an abrupt halt, as George-Étienne Cartier engineered passage of a bill to charter the Grand Trunk Railway (GTR) Company of Canada as a private company. Finance Minister Hincks

REPORT
ON A SURVEY FOR THE
RAILWAY BRIDGE
Over the St. Lawrence
AT MONTREAL,

SURVEYED IN 1851-52, BY ORDER OF THE COMMITTEE OF THE MONTREAL AND KINGSTON RAILWAY.

Hon. John Young, Chairman.

THOS. C. KEEFER,
ENGINEER.

MONTREAL:
PRINTED BY JOHN LOVELL, AT HIS STEAM-PRINTING
ESTABLISHMENT, ST. NICHOLAS STREET.
1853.

Figure 22.2. *Report on a Survey of the Railway Bridge over the St. Lawrence.*

got financing for the line in England, and the GTR was able to take over the charters of the Montréal and Kingston, and Kingston and Toronto railways.

Without warning, at age 31, Keefer found himself unceremoniously dumped from his projects before construction had even started.

In an atmosphere of political chill—Keefer had dared to criticize Premier Francis Hincks for corruption—the Grand Trunk, now financed and controlled by British interests, replaced him with an

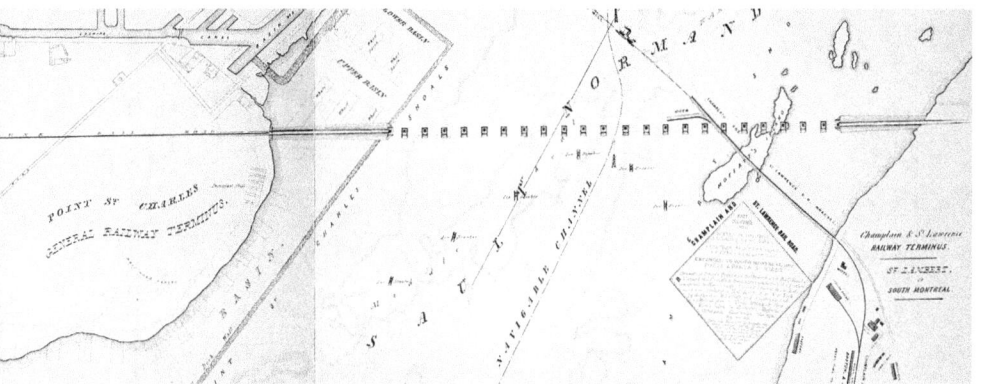

Figure 22.3. Keefer's map showing the approach embankments and piers.

English engineer, Alexander Ross, of the contracting firm of Peto, Brassey, Betts, and Jackson.

Ross took over all of Keefer's engineering plans on the Victoria Bridge, and made them his own, not deigning to recognize Keefer's contribution. He even published a second chart, now in the McGill Library, that completely scrubbed Young's and Keefer's names from the document.

A subsequent map (in the McGill University Library) was identical to Keefer's, except his name and Young's were scrubbed, as below. Keefer was not invited to the bridge opening, nor was his name put on the commemorative plaque on the finished structure that honoured the bridge builders and engineers.

Robert Stephenson, son of the inventor of the locomotive, who was named joint chief engineer of the Victoria Bridge, later recognized Keefer's role in the location and foundation design for the bridge, in a letter published after his untimely death in 1859. But, in fact, Stephenson was a mere figurehead to reassure nervous British financiers. Ross was the main contractor.

Young Keefer remained unbowed and unbroken, though the Grand Trunk initially refused to pay his $2,000 account against the Montreal and Kingston Company for estimates for the bridge.

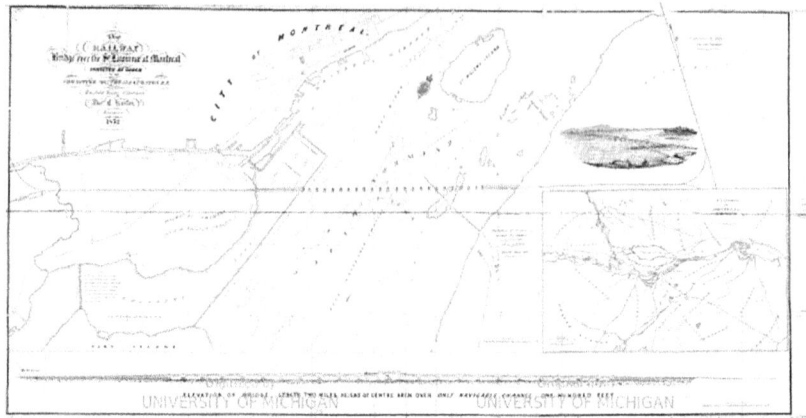

Figure 22.4. First version of the chart, with the names of Keefer and Young featured, top left.[1]
Source: The University of Michigan Library.

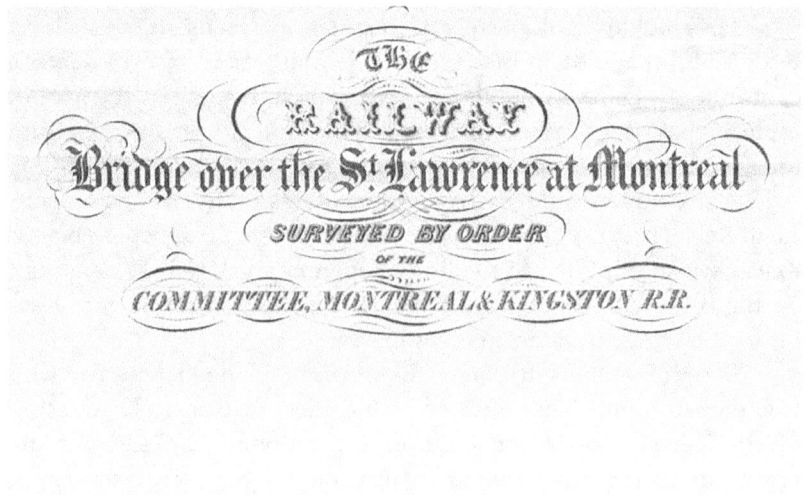

Figure 22.5. Later chart missing "Hon. John Young, Chairman. Thomas C. Keefer, Engineer, 1851."

---

[1] The University of Michigan Library has this first version of the railway bridge chart, with Keefer and Young's names included, in its collection. The author is attempting to get a full-size version of the chart.

Keefer and Waterworks

Keefer's many supporters rallied to help him obtain other engineering jobs. In 1853, John Young appointed him to the position of chief engineer of the Montreal Harbour Commission.

Another opportunity came his way when he was asked to make a preliminary survey for the water supply for the city of Montréal. A few months later he was appointed chief engineer of the Montreal Waterworks.

Keefer was well aware of the dangers of untreated water in causing typhus and other diseases. One of his cousins, Dr. Charles Keefer, a surgeon at the Montreal General Hospital, died of typhus during the 1847 epidemic.

Keefer's innovative solution was to draw clean water, upstream from the Lachine Rapids, to provide the city with pure water for drinking, as well as fire protection. In 1853, he set to work building the system. Rather than relying on steam engines using costly imported coal, his waterworks used St. Lawrence River energy to both supply and raise the water, using hydraulic pumps, up to a reservoir at the foot of Mont Royal that would in turn pressurize water mains in the city below. However, the rapidly growing city outgrew the capacity of the system, and more powerful steam pumps were installed in the late 1860s.

In 1856, he also proposed a municipal waterworks system for Hamilton, Ontario. As Keefer noted in a wry letter to an ally on Toronto City Council: "I see Hamilton Water Com[missioners] have adopted my report & plan in its entirety—but nothing can be considered decided until the bylaw is submitted to the Citizens—a few large fires will settle the matter both with them and you."

Over the next thirty years, Keefer would design municipal waterworks systems for Ottawa, St. Catharines, Toronto, London, Québec, Dartmouth, and Halifax.

Keefer's third waterworks project—that of Ottawa—was described by a visiting Englishman as the finest he had seen on the continent. The *Ottawa Daily Citizen* of December 7, 1874, gave details about its six single-action plunger pumps of 19-inch [48-centimetre] diameter. Each was capable of delivering a million gallons [4546 cubic metres] a day. A Liffiels turbine water wheel of 60 inches [152 centimetres] diameter, weighing 8,800 pounds [4 metric tons], drove each set of pumps, ensuring enough pressure to fill firehoses and deliver a safe supply to a thirsty city used to buying water from barrels on horse-drawn wagons, or taking it from a well in the Bytown market.

Keefer's Fleet Street Pumping Station, with its open aqueduct flowing from an inlet above Chaudière Falls, has been restored, with its Victorian garden, and still plays an auxiliary role in the city's water system. In addition, its outlet rapids are now being used as a kayak slalom course.[2]

Keefer also began to lecture in civil engineering at McGill College, arguing for more engineering education and a new status for the engineer. "The engineer," he said, "though an indispensable agent, is generally a junior partner in the firm of Grab, Chisel & Co." He proposed that engineers, like lawyers and doctors, should be a "self-sustaining" profession and that their technical advice should prevail over political and business considerations.

In 1857, McGill created an engineering professorship, and engineering education emerged at four other Canadian universities—New Brunswick, Toronto, Royal Military College, and École Polytechnique. He helped found the Canadian Society of Civil Engineers (CSCE) in 1887, and served as its first president.

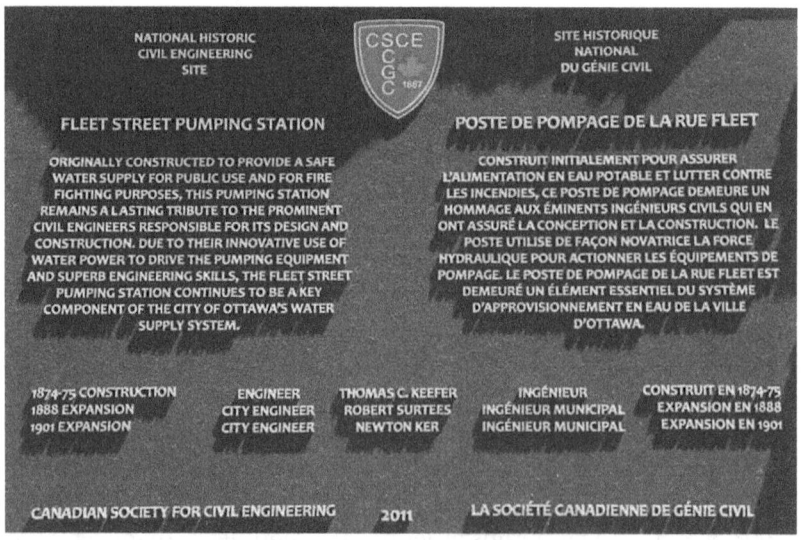

Figure 22.6. Keefer's Fleet Street pumping station plaque.
Source: Photo by Alastair Sweeny.

---

[2] http://www.capitalgems.ca/kayak-slalom.html.

Keefer himself was made a fellow of the Royal Society of Canada in 1890 and its president in 1898–1899. He received an honorary doctorate from McGill in 1905, and in 1912, in recognition of his long life of professional leadership, he was named an honorary member of the Institution of Civil Engineers of Great Britain.

The Grand Trunk and Samuel Keefer

In 1853, Keefer's old patron James Ferrier was appointed chairman of the Canadian board of directors of the Grand Trunk, serving until his death in 1888. One of his first acts was smoothing the political waters by hiring Thomas Keefer's brother Samuel, head of the Department of Public Works, as the Grand Trunk's resident Montréal engineer.

As chief engineer of Public Works, Samuel Keefer had laid out the Beauharnois Canal, directed the enlargement of the Lachine Canal, rebuilt the lock at Sainte-Anne-de-Bellevue and the canal at Saint-Ours on the Richelieu River, and carried out preliminary surveys for a canal at Sault Ste. Marie.

Samuel Keefer also designed the suspension bridge over the Chaudière Falls at Bytown (Ottawa), completed in 1844, and introduced

Figure 22.7. *Enlargement of the Lachine Canal, 1840s.*
Source: Canadian Illustrated News, © National Archives of Canada, C-066176, 1877.

economical solid-timber gates on the St. Lawrence locks in 1850. From 1846 to 1848, he was placed in direct charge of enlarging and realigning the Welland Canal.

In 1853, Samuel essentially took over his brother's work-in-progress, supervising construction of the GTR between Montréal and Kingston (which Thomas had surveyed for the government in 1850–1851), including a bridge at Sainte-Anne-de-Bellevue, which took the railway off Montréal Island, and another crossing the Gananoque at Kingston Mills. He engaged more soundings of the river and recommended moving the location of the Victoria Bridge farther upstream at right angles to the current. In 1856, he served briefly as superintendent of the railway's eastern division, while acting as chief engineer for the projected Brockville and Ottawa Railway.

The Grand Trunk Railway Company of Canada—today's CN—was incorporated to build a line from Montréal to Toronto, with authority to unite small railway companies to build a main trunk line, built to the broad, or "Provincial" gauge of 5' 6"—nine inches [22 centimetres] wider than the Lachine line. British financiers were prepared to provide capital of $60,000,000 for the project.

In 1853 and 1854, with George-Étienne Cartier lining up substantial capital investment from British financiers and contractors, Ferrier and his board amalgamated the Grand Trunk Railway Company of Canada East (Montréal to Rivière-du-Loup), with the Toronto & Guelph Railway Company, the St. Lawrence & Atlantic Railroad Company (Montréal to Island Pond, Vermont), the Quebec & Richmond Railway Company, and the Grand Junction Railroad Company (Belleville to Peterborough). In addition, the Atlantic & St. Lawrence Railroad Company (Portland, Maine to Island Pond, Vermont) was leased, to give the Montréal railway access to an ice-free winter port in Maine.

Mackay and MacKinnon's copycat Montréal, Ottawa, and Kingston Grand Trunk Railroad Company charter was premature, but it locked up more territory, prevented competition, and steered investors to the Grand Trunk.

April 1854 saw the start of construction on the Victoria Bridge, but the outbreak of the Crimean War dried up British capital for a time. On February 23, 1855, Parliament granted a £900,000 loan guarantee to the railroad, and for a time, the economy of the Canadas recovered. The first freight train passed through the tubular bridge on December 12, 1859.

The Grand Trunk consolidation led by James Ferrier and George-Étienne Cartier effectively ended railway mania in Canada. The Great Western amalgamated with the Grand Trunk in 1884. The Northern Railway of Canada and the Hamilton & North Western were absorbed in 1888, giving the GTR—today's CN—control of all of the important railway lines in Ontario except for the Canada Atlantic (Parry Sound to Ottawa and Montréal) and those owned by the Canadian Pacific.

All this feverish activity in the St. Lawrence Valley pretty much bypassed the Ottawa & Prescott Railway, as Cartier brought his political muscle to bear on protecting the Grand Trunk's hinterland. His actions completely ended any chances of a railway bridge across the St. Lawrence, to Ogdensburg, New York, which would bleed Canadian commerce away from Montréal.

CHAPTER 23

The Queen Approves of Ottawa, 1853–1857

At the present moment the condition of Ottawa is, to say the least, peculiar. Perhaps never in the history of any country has the fate of the city been so placed. Years ago it was declared to be the Capital of Canada by no less authority than that of the SOVEREIGN. Since that declaration was made, interests that are influential and powerful have been employed against it. Time and again we have heard that the carrying out [of] the Royal decision was doubtful; and these rumours have been regarded as truthful. At present, however, we have every prospect of a realization [of] our long-deferred hopes. We have every reason now to think upon the removal of the seat of Government here as certainty. No later then Saturday week, it was declared by the Executive Council that the removal would take place next autumn, under any circumstances.

—*Ottawa Citizen*, May 24, 1864

The Capital Campaign

With the rioting and burning of Canada's Parliament in 1849, Montréal's misfortune should have been Bytown's golden opportunity. But the town nearly blew it with its own 1849 riot—Stoney Monday—in homage to their fellow partisans in Montréal a few months earlier.

Lord Elgin quickly cancelled his proposed scouting trip to Bytown that September—announcing that Canada's capital would now alternate every four years between Toronto and Québec City.

By the summer of 1853, tensions had died down. Lord Elgin—his term as governor soon to end—decided to see if the leading citizens of the rowdy lumber town were capable of civilized behaviour. He was primed to do so by a member of his council, Thomas Mackay, who invited him officially to open the first exhibition of the Bytown Mechanics' Institute and Athenaeum, forerunner of the Ottawa Public Library. Mackay had served as founding president of the Institute in 1847.

Arriving by Ottawa River steamboat on July 28, Lord Elgin was met by throngs of well-behaved well-wishers. They were all of them eager to impress upon Victoria's top Canadian designate that the Queen should make Bytown—soon to be renamed Ottawa—her permanent, picturesque, "metropolis" of British North America.

In the West Ward Town Hall, Institute president Dr. Hamnett Hill delivered a glowing welcome to Lord Elgin — "with the liveliest feelings of pleasure and satisfaction"—and invited him to cut the ribbon opening the institute's special exhibition showcasing Ottawa's resource wealth and intellectual sophistication.

On display were tweeds from the Rideau Falls Mill, window blinds from Currier, Dickinson and Company, hemp canvas from Hull-grown flax, and even a fine set of false teeth from a local dentist.

Dr. Hill noted that the society had dedicated itself to "developing the Ottawa Valley's natural resources and spreading knowledge about science, nature, industry and the arts among all classes of citizens... Here alone do we find the two provinces really and geographically united."

In his closing speech, Lord Elgin expressed his gratitude, "for giving me so admirable an opportunity of seeing how rapidly the Arts which accompany and adorn civilized life advance along the banks of the Ottawa."

Thomas Mackay hosted Lord Elgin at Rideau Hall, and the following day arranged for a volley of mortar fire to go off as the Governor's steamer started downstream past New Edinburgh. A wooden cannon built for the occasion unfortunately exploded, but no one was injured.[1]

Elgin's speech buoyed the citizens of Bytown, soon-to-be Ottawa. In the better-behaved years that followed, lectures were a staple of the Mechanics' Institute, as improving the mind of the common man was

---

[1] Wilson, *History of Old Ottawa*, 80.

Figure 23.1. Mechanics' Institute lead cornerstone, 1853.
Source: Ottawa Public Library.

the ultimate goal. Like-minded women also attended the lectures in good numbers.

By 1856, the Institute had 1,004 volumes, and subscribed not just to the local daily papers, but also tri-weeklies, including two French, as well as one from Dublin, and one from Glasgow. There were also twenty-nine weeklies, including *Scientific American* and *Canada West* weeklies, as well as four illustrated papers, including *Punch* and *London Illustrated News*, and several United Kingdom periodicals, including *Blackwood's Magazine*.

Somewhat relieved by the kind words of Lord Elgin, Dr. Hill and other civic leaders were infused with newfound confidence as they carried their "Capitol" campaign forward through the mid-1850s. Their enthusiasm for the cause grew after the Parliament Building in Québec was consumed by a fire on February 1, 1854.

For Thomas Mackay, his dream was coming to fruition, but sadly, the stress of railway losses was starting to tell. The Bytown & Prescott was bleeding money, and he was beginning to feel the effects of the stomach cancer that would kill him two years later.

Sir Edmund Head Takes Charge

Lord Elgin recommended New Brunswick Lieutenant Governor Sir Edmund Head as his successor. Head had North American roots—his grandfather had immigrated to South Carolina in the 1760s, but returned to England after losing his holdings as a Loyalist sympathizer during the American Revolution.

Head accepted the Canada appointment with delight, and travelled from Fredericton to Québec, where he was sworn in on December 19, 1854.

As a former commissioner of the Poor Law, an accomplished scholar, and a man possessed of keen political instincts, Head was a brilliant choice. Lord Grey declared that his appointment "was the best hit he had made since he had been in office."

Head's clear-headed vision of federalism was linked with the idea of a new nation that should extend from sea to sea. It would thrive under a British constitution, where the inhabitants should "stand in conscious strength and in the full equipment of self-government as a free people bound by the ties of gratitude and affection."

In his commonsense dispatch to Grey on the annexation movement, Head wrote that separation from Britain was not an inevitable consequence of progress in democratic government.

While visiting Bytown after his appointment, Sir Edmund visited an ailing Thomas Mackay at Rideau Hall. He and Lady Head were also entertained at a luncheon under canvas on Major's Hill. Lady Head drew several watercolours of the scenery, one of which she presented to Queen Victoria—which it was said influenced Her Majesty to consider Ottawa as the capital.

At this point, George-Étienne Cartier, Chairman of the Railway Committee, lawyer for the Grand Trunk and counsel for the Sulpician Order, emerged as an open supporter of Ottawa as the capital.

Cartier saw Ottawa as the essential location for the capital because it was on the border of the two provinces and was a place where French-Canadians could feel at home—at this time Ottawa had a French majority. As Minister of Militia, he appreciated its distance from the American border. Montréal had been deemed indefensible by the British army, but as a Montrealer of long standing, chief solicitor of the Grand Trunk, and a visionary regarding a railway to the Pacific, Cartier knew that the Ottawa Valley was key to making Montréal the entrepôt of a transcontinental trading system.

Figure 23.2. Edmund Walker Head.
Source: Mediawiki Commons.

In fact, the Queen's approval of Ottawa as the capital was engineered by Cartier and Head as a way to break a deadlock.

Bytown Becomes Ottawa

The petition of the Town Council of Bytown of 1854 asked that "The Town of Bytown be proclaimed a city by the name and style of the City of Ottawa and that the Said City may be divided into the Same Number of wards and with the Same divisions as the Town of Bytown is now constituted under the General Municipal law."

In the petition, the population was estimated at ten thousand "being the number required under the municipal law to entitle it to city corporate powers." It was a gross exaggeration, as the correct number was 7,760 persons.

Nonetheless, on January 1, 1855, Bytown was formally incorporated as the city of Ottawa—a proper city possessed of a bankrupt railway.[2]

---

[2] Thomas Mackay's secretary George Hay was the first to suggest changing the name of Bytown to Ottawa. Louis Le Jeune, *Dictionnaire général*, 392.

On March 17, 1856, opposition leader John Sandfield Macdonald argued that the time had come to assemble Parliament in a permanent capital. The approximate cost of the necessary buildings was estimated at £300,000 by the Assistant Commissioner of Public Works. As soon as this amount to be spent was known, Montréal, Québec, Kingston, and Toronto all clamoured for the exclusive privilege.

Attorney-General Lewis T. Drummond, seconded by George-Étienne Cartier, suggested that the names of Hamilton and Ottawa be added to the proposed cities, to vote upon. Ottawa was supported by fifty-six yeas against sixty-four nays.

Figure 23.3. *First City of Ottawa Crest.*
Source: John Henry Walker, McCord Museum, M930.50.1.71.

Arms—Quarterly (1) a locomotive and tender; (2) a lake, with a tree between two stags in the foreground, the dexter one lodged, and in the background, a range of hills and the sun issuant; (3) the locks of the Rideau Canal; (4) Chaudière Falls and the Suspension Bridge with a boat in the foreground.
Crest: "A hand holding a cleaving knife."
Motto: "Advance."
Supporters: Dextra, a workman with a hammer in right hand standing behind an anvil, and sinistra, justice.

Then followed a huge number of votes on the subject—forty-eight in a single year—but no city won the support of a clear majority.

Head broke the deadlock by suggesting to Prince Albert that the Queen be invited to approve the choice. And who would dare to contradict Queen Victoria?[3]

In March 1857, government leaders convinced the legislature to approve the process to refer the question to London, and to appeal to the Queen to break the political deadlock. Both houses of the legislature addressed Queen Victoria, asking her to exercise her royal prerogative and choose "some certain place" for the capital.

Governor General Head invited the five principal cities (Kingston, Montréal, Ottawa, Québec, and Toronto) to send in statements of their claims. Publicly he said it would be inappropriate for him to appear to offer any advice on behalf of the Executive Council on a matter specifically referred to the Queen's discretion. In fact, the fix was already in—military governor Sir John Michel had persuaded Head that advances in artillery made Québec, Montréal, and Toronto indefensible.

The municipal council of Ottawa approved an address, written by Mackay's lawyer and former mayor Richard W. Scott, to be laid before Her Majesty, in which the following points were stressed:

- the distance from the frontiers, making it safe from hostile attack in wartime as well as from foreign influences in peacetime;
- the natural advantages for defence; the communications with Montréal and Kingston by water and with Prescott by rail, and eventually with the Red River Valley in the future;
- the equal distance from Québec and Toronto, Montréal and Kingston, extending as from a radiating centre;
- the possibilities of colonization and of attracting emigrants in the interior of the country;
- the beautiful scenery and healthy climate;
- the extensive property of Government in the city, which might be used for Parliament buildings;
- the abundance of building materials in the vicinity;
- the site on the border of the two provinces on the Ottawa River;

---

[3] Alastair Sweeny, *George-Etienne Cartier*, 168.

- the loyal English and French population setting at rest feelings of jealousy;
- the only bridge uniting Canada East and Canada West, making intercourse convenient for both Upper and Lower Canadians;
- the promise by Sydenham to choose the capital city within Upper Canada.

Scott's address promoting Ottawa was unique, in that he did not rely on bringing attention to other cities' negatives to bring positive reflection to its own case.

Privately, Head—in England at the time—wrote a confidential memorandum coming down strongly on the side of Ottawa, and lobbied hard in person. He praised the future site of a Parliament on Barrack Hill as magnificent—commanding, "an uninterrupted view on the Ottawa River, the Chaudière Falls, the entire city and the surrounding country for many miles."

It was on the strength of Head's arguments that the Colonial Office recommended Ottawa as the Canadian seat of government to the Queen in October of 1857. After reviewing the matter with her advisors, the Cabinet, and her husband, her decision was firm—Ottawa would be the capital!

On December 18, Prince Albert wrote Colonial Secretary Henry Labouchere that "Ottawa must indeed be a beautiful situation and all the detached descriptions must tend to confirm the impressions that the choice is the right one. We must now trust that the Province will look upon it in the same light, when it becomes known."

In a New Year's Eve despatch, Colonial Secretary Labouchere informed Governor General Head, that

> I am commanded by the Queen to inform you that in the judgment of Her Majesty, the City of Ottawa combines greater advantages than any other place in Canada for the permanent seat of the future Government of the Province, and is selected by Her Majesty accordingly.

Some boosters in the major cities were furious at the Queen's choice. Legislative turmoil followed, and there were fourteen separate votes on the motion. Ottawa was finally confirmed by a vote of sixty-four to fifty-nine. Finally, on January 27, 1859, George-Étienne Cartier proclaimed Ottawa the capital of the Canadas. Later that year, the assembly voted the sum of £225,000 (about a million dollars) for a Parliament Building, two departmental buildings, and a residence for the Governor General.

The royal decision was supposed to put a stop to the rivalries—Québec and Toronto would each hold the Parliament for four years, until permanent buildings were built. But Ottawa would not hold its first session of Parliament for another eight years.

By the time the Parliament buildings were erected and the legislature officially opened in June 1866, the Province of Canada was already committed to a Confederation pact that would, on July 1, 1867, see Canada East and Canada West join with New Brunswick and Nova Scotia to form the Dominion of Canada—the sprawling nation destined to stretch from Atlantic to Pacific to Arctic. Its capital, too, would be Ottawa.

As for the losing cities of Québec and Toronto, they were soon satisfied by the establishment of provincial parliaments on their own turf.

Did the Queen Choose or Approve?

In actual fact, the so-called Queen's Choice was engineered by Head and the vote was delivered by George-Étienne Cartier—the most powerful politician of the day in Canada. According to Cartier,

> It is true that Ottawa is in Upper Canada, but in terms of business, it is a Lower Canadian city, linked to Québec by the timber trade, and to Montréal by its demand for imports. There, the French Canadians will feel themselves in a sympathetic environment, because they number 5,000 out of a total population of 12,000, the majority of whom are Catholics. They will find colleges, convents, churches and all that is especially dear to them in Lower Canada. For all these reasons, Ottawa is an excellent choice, not only as our capital city, but as a means of increasing prosperity and attracting colonization to the region. It is a fortunate choice, a disinterested one, one that must satisfy all reasonable men.[4]

---

[4] Tassé, 170–174; the French were the majority in Lower Town until the late nineteenth century.

Head's argument to Foreign Secretary Carnarvon pretty much mirrored Cartier's:

> Ottawa is the only place which will be accepted by the majority of Upper and Lower Canada as a fair compromise. With the exception of Ottawa, every one of the cities proposed is an object of jealousy to each of the others. Ottawa is, in fact, neither in Upper nor in Lower Canada. Literally, it is in the former; but a bridge alone divides it from the latter. Consequently its selection would fulfill the letter of any pledge given, or supposed to be given, to Upper Canada at the time of the Union. The population at present is partly French, and partly English and Irish. The settlement of the valley of the Ottawa is rapidly increasing, and will be at once stimulated by making it the capital.
>
> This circumstance is an incidental advantage of great value. Canada is long and narrow; in fact, all frontier. The rapid extension of settlement up the Ottawa, and on each side of it, would give breadth and substance to the country.
>
> The main objection to Ottawa is its wild position. But this wild position is a fault which every day continues to diminish.
>
> Ottawa is accessible by water from Montréal and from Lake Ontario. In the former communication there are still some difficulties, but they are not important. It is accessible too by a branch railroad from Prescott, where the line joins the Grand Trunk. The distance from Montréal may be called 100 or 120 miles [160 or 193 kilometres], but its connection with Montréal is such as to cause its selection to be readily acquiesced in by that great city. I have heard persons of influence at Montréal say that they would as soon have the seat of Government at Ottawa as at Montréal itself. The latter city considers itself as the natural outlet to the Ottawa country, and believes that the opening of the valley of that river would establish its own communications with the western lakes, independently of Lake Ontario.
>
> In a military point of view (I speak of course with submission to higher authorities), Ottawa is advantageously situated. Its distance from the frontier is such as to protect it from any marauding party, or even from a regular attack, unless Montréal and Kingston, which flank the approach to it, were previously occupied by the enemy. Stores and troops could be sent to Ottawa

either from Québec or Kingston, without exposure on the St. Lawrence to the American frontier.

A secondary consideration, but one of some importance as affecting the popularity of the choice, is the fact that the Rideau Canal, now handed over to the Provincial Government, would probably increase its traffic, and become more productive by the transfer of the seat of Government to Ottawa. At present this great work is a dead loss so far as money is concerned.[5]

Building Parliament—Samuel Keefer's Contest

Two years after his death, one of Thomas Mackay's most ardent wishes came true, as Ottawa was selected as the permanent capital of the Province of Canada. The strategic hill overlooking the Ottawa River and Rideau Canal, where Mackay and Redpath had built barracks for the Royal Sappers and Miners, was selected to be the site of the Parliament buildings.

Forgetting that the British had burned Washington with ease in 1814, a cynical American journalist mocked the Queen's choice— "The new Capital could not be captured even by the most courageous soldiers; the invaders would inevitably be lost in the woods trying to find it."—precisely.

And Toronto's Goldwin Smith quipped that the site was a "sub-Arctic village converted by royal mandate into a political cock-pit"— yes, but a village with a beautiful view.

Ottawa Mayor Moss Kent Dickinson told his fellow citizens that they should be "greatly indebted to Sir George-Étienne Cartier for its success."

On April 6, the town council offered the Union Government temporary accommodations. The following year, on May 7, 1859, Samuel Keefer, back in Ottawa as inspector of railways and deputy commissioner of public works, issued a notice inviting architects to compete in furnishing designs for the new Parliament buildings on Barrack Hill and Government House across the Rideau Canal on Nepean Point.

Architects were told what space was needed, what materials to use, and then were given free rein to design buildings in a "plain, substantial style of architecture."

---

[5] Carnarvon papers, vol. 69, 44–46.

The sum of £225,000 (about a million dollars) had been voted in the 1859 estimates for the Ottawa projects, including landscaping and extras. Interested architects should aim at a cost not exceeding the following figures:

The Parliament Building—$300,000
Two departmental buildings—$240,000
Residence of the Governor General—$100,000

The drawings were to be submitted anonymously to prevent favouritism. The final date set for considering plans submitted by architects was August 1, 1859.

Keefer and government engineer Frederick Rubidge, then at work in Québec City, were to judge the entries, advised by John Morris, an architect who would serve as clerk of works overseeing the construction.

For the best approved set of designs, £250 was to be awarded as the first prize, and £100 as the second. In September, 298 drawings of the thirty-three submitted designs went on display at the Parliament buildings in Toronto. The entries were judged on ten requirements—cost,

Figure 23.4. Samuel Keefer, 1860s.
Source: Topley Studio, Library and Archives Canada, PA-197756.

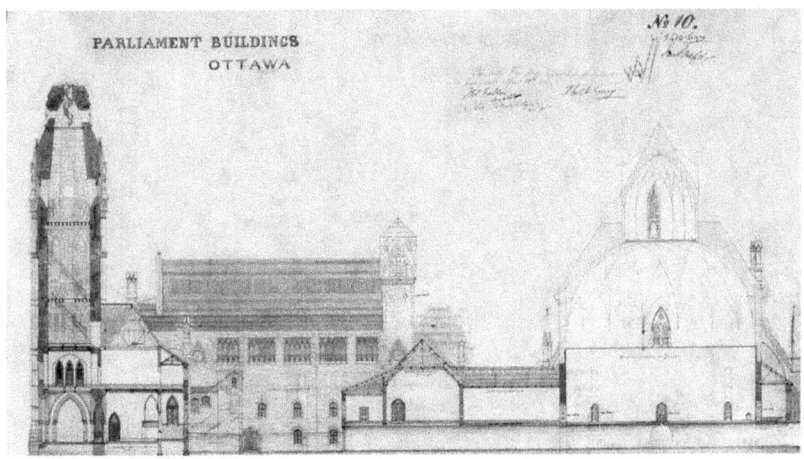

Figure 23.5. Fuller and Jones design for Centre Block and Library, 1859.
Source: Library and Archives Canada, RG11M 79003/29.

beauty, layout, fireproofing, and so on. The judges had narrowed the winners down to three, but Keefer and Rubidge could not agree on who came first and who second.

Keefer preferred the centre block design by Thomas Fuller and Chilion Jones. Their design featured a Gothic Revival tower and a circular domed library. Rubidge agreed it was excellent, but felt it was too expensive and unsafe. They also disagreed on the east and west block designs, by Thomas Stent and Augustus Laver, and Rubidge did not feel that the designs for a palatial Government House by Frederick Cumberland and George Storm were at all suitable.

Keefer asked Governor General Sir Edmund Head to break the tie, with a strong argument in favour of his own design preferences. The winners were announced on August 29. To the sound of cannon fire, the half-frozen sod was broken by John Rose, Commissioner of Public Works, on a cold and stormy December 21, 1859, and the first stone laid on April 26 following, after crews cleared the site of stunted cedars and shrubs.

The buildings were constructed out of local sandstone, quarried at the property of Mr. Augustus Keefer in Nepean Township; the arches over the windows and door lintels were red sandstone from Potsdam, New York, and the dressings were of grey Ohio freestone. The roofing was dark slate from Vermont, decorated with a band of light green slate from the same place.

Figure 23.6. *Prince of Wales Lays Cornerstone of Parliament.*
Source: *Illustrated London News.*

Queen Victoria's eldest son Edward, Prince of Wales, later Edward VII, laid down the white marble cornerstone at the northeast angle of the Senate on September 1, 1860. Then, for the Prince's amusement, he descended the Government Slide at the Chaudière on a crib of timber. A Citizen reporter wrote, "Crowds lined the river to watch and ladies tastefully arrayed occupied the most prominent position. As the royal crib passed a large wave struck the raft, and rebounding, deluged the admiring females in its vicinity."

The following day the Prince drove through the grounds of Rideau Hall, and his staff informally evaluated it as a potential viceregal residence.

Before he departed downstream on his steamer, the Prince was entertained by a Lumberers' Regatta in the Ottawa Locks basin.

As for government engineer Frederick Rubidge, he returned from Québec City in 1863 to supervise construction of the Parliament buildings and sort out competing claims by the architects and builders. On completion, in June 1878, the cost reached the $4,000,000 mark, four times the original estimates. Any plans for a Government House on Nepean Point were scrapped, and Rubidge turned to designing and overseeing renovations and additions to Rideau Hall, now to be used as the residence of the Governor General of Canada.

Figure 23.7. *The Lumberers' Regatta.*
Source: George Henry Andrews, Library and Archives Canada, C-013285.

British novelist Anthony Trollope visited Ottawa in 1862, and marvelled at the nearly completed buildings:

> The glory of Ottawa will be—and indeed already is—the set of public buildings which is now being erected on the rock which guards the town from the river. I know of no modern Gothic purer of its kind or less sullied with fictitious ornamentation. Our own Houses of Parliament (in London) are very fine, but it is, I believe, generally felt that the ornamentation is too minute; and moreover, it may be questioned whether perpendicular Gothic is capable of the highest nobility which architecture can achieve. I do not pretend to say that these Canadian public buildings will reach that highest nobility, they must be finished before any final judgment can be pronounced; but I do feel very certain that the final judgment will be greatly in their favour.[6]

---

[6] Smallery and Booth, *Trollope, North America*, 72.

American journalist Charles Dudley Warner, co-author with Mark Twain of *The Gilded Age*, visited Ottawa when the three buildings were completed, and wrote:

> The situation on the bluffs of the Ottawa River, is commanding, and gives fine opportunity for architectural display. The Parliament House and the Departmental Buildings, on three sides of a square, are exceedingly effective in colour, and the perfection of Gothic details especially in the noble towers. There are few groups of buildings anywhere so pleasing to the eye, or that appeal more strongly to one's sense of dignity and beauty.

But dignity and beauty came at a cost. In 1861, the Parliament of United Canada ordered all construction work to cease on Parliament Hill. The government blamed skyrocketing costs, largely from having to blast foundations out of solid rock.

The three building sites stood as empty shells for two years. The economy of Ottawa was devastated—more than 1,700 men were put out of work; families lost their only source of income; skilled craftsmen left Ottawa in droves; and many merchants filed for bankruptcy.

Construction resumed in 1863, and in 1864, Ottawa was designated as the new capital of the Province of Canada, and subsequently of the Dominion of Canada. However, plans to house the Governor General in a Government House on Nepean Point were put on hold, to save costs. This palatial residence would have stood across the canal from Parliament Hill where the National Gallery of Canada now stands.

At that point, the Great Coalition ministers concluded that an enlarged Rideau Hall might have to fit the bill, even if only temporarily. George Brown of Toronto was delighted by the Parliament buildings alone, declaring them "fit for the British, French and Russian empires, were they all confederated."[7]

---

[7] Library and Archives Canada, Brown Papers, George Brown to Anne Brown, Aug. 15, 1864.

PART FOUR

Thomas Keefer and the Mackay Estate

Figure 24.1. *Thomas Keefer, 1863.*
Source: *Canadian Illustrated News.*

CHAPTER 24

The Thomas Keefer Regime, 1855–1865

Mackay's Death and Burial

The stress of seven years of railway mania undoubtedly shortened Thomas Mackay's lifespan. In 1854, his gut began to pain him, and his doctor diagnosed stomach cancer.

Holding his bagpipes and grimacing with pain as he climbed the stairs to his drafting room at the top of Rideau Hall, he then felt his strength failing, and slowly limped back down.

On September 8, 1855, with the help of family lawyer Richard W. Scott, Thomas Mackay made his last will and testament. He left his estate to his four sons, an annuity and the use of Rideau Hall to his widow, and various Montréal properties to his four daughters.[1]

Unlike John Redpath's fortune, which had blossomed with savvy Montréal real estate investments, Thomas Mackay's fortune, battered by railway losses, had diminished considerably in the years since 1832. His 1,100-acre [445-hectare] Mackay Estate—consisting of raw land, buildings, machinery, and mills, was still valued at £100,000—about C$15,000,000 in 2020—with yearly rentals near $12,000—about C$400,000 in 2020.

Scott set up a family holding company, Mackay & Company, to administer the will and oversee the leasing and selling of properties. Mackay chose son-in-law Thomas Keefer as his executor.

On October 9, after suffering from painful stomach cancer for almost a year, Mackay succumbed to the disease, and died at his beloved Rideau Hall, where he had lived since 1839.

---

[1] RG 22, ser.155, will of Thomas McKay.

Figure 24.2. A world-weary Thomas Mackay in the 1850s.
Source: Topley, Library and Archives Canada, PA-125208.

With Mackay's death the sound of bagpipes no longer disturbed the woods.

After a ceremony at Rideau Hall, Mackay was buried with his deceased children and other relations in the family burial ground at Pine Hill, a wooded triangular enclave at Princess Street and Lisgar Road. With the creation of Beechwood Cemetery in 1873—part of the land was a gift from his estate—the graves were moved there and interred in a Mackay family plot.

Thomas Mackay was survived by four sons, four daughters, his wife Ann, and his old mother Christina, born near Perth, Scotland, in 1761. She died at Rideau Hall on August 10, 1857, at age 88.

The family lived in Rideau Hall until 1863. By 1865, all of Mackay's sons had died young and unmarried.

Charles Mackay

Charles Mackay was the youngest but one of the four sons who survived their father. Born in Montréal on April 21, 1836, he was educated at the Montreal High School and the University of Edinburgh, Scotland. When the Crimean War broke out he insisted on enlisting, and his ailing father obtained for him a commission in the 9th Regiment, which had a high number of death vacancies.

Figure 24.3. Militia Corporal Charles Mackay.
Source: Library and Archives Canada.

In 1856, after his father's death, he sailed for Balaklava, arriving after the fall of Sebastopol and the cessation of hostilities. On his return from the Crimea, he paid a visit to his widowed mother in Canada, which was abruptly terminated by the breaking out of the Sepoy rebellion, in 1857.

He arrived in Calcutta in November 1857, serving as an officer in the 97th Regiment of Foot. With the Indian Mutiny raging, he was sent up, in December, to Benares, where his regiment formed part of General Frank's division, in the march to lift the siege of Lucknow. He survived hails of bullets and cannon shot, but was felled by virulent smallpox at Banda on February 13, 1859, at age 23, after three days' illness.

In announcing his death to his family, a brother officer wrote of Lieutenant Mackay, "He was mentioned in the despatches by our colonel for his conduct at the capture of Lucknow, which was beyond praise."

The Lease of Rideau Hall

With the developing government interest in Rideau Hall, Ann Crichton and son Thomas Jr.—likely under the prodding of family lawyer Richard W. Scott—sent for Mackay son-in-law and executor Thomas Keefer to take over active management of the Mackay Estate. He did so, under an agreement registered in the Carleton County Registry Office. He agreed to take a salary for his services as estate manager.

One of Keefer's first acts was to work with lawyer Joseph Sherwood to sell the New Edinburgh house for the benefit of Annie MacKinnon and Tom Junior.

In the fall of 1864, Thomas and Elizabeth Keefer moved to Ottawa from Toronto and lived for a short time with Elizabeth's mother Ann and brother Thomas in the family white elephant, Rideau Hall.

Keefer's first challenges as manager of the Mackay Estate were to pay off the creditors, clear mortgages, improve returns on the Rideau Falls mills and property, then sell them, and then wind up family interests in the mills.

Keefer's second challenge, in 1864, was to negotiate with the Board of Works of the Province of Canada, whose deputy minister was his half-brother Samuel Keefer, for the lease and possible sale of Rideau Hall.

In 1854, an ailing Thomas Mackay had financed the sale of his Rideau Falls sawmill to an employee, a young American of French-Canadian ancestry, Joseph Merrill Currier, by taking back a mortgage.

Figure 24.4. Thomas Keefer, 1860s.
Source: Library and Archives Canada.

Currier, a machinist by trade, modernized the mill, and added product lines. Mackay always found him to be a capable manager.

An ad in the June 29, 1854, *Bytown Gazette* announced a major upgrade to the "New Edinburgh Saw Mills Sash, Door and Blind Factory":

> The subscribers having ordered a complete set of the most improved machinery for the manufacture of doors, blinds and

sashes, beg to notify the Public that they will hereafter be prepared to fulfill all orders in this branch of manufacture with greater despatch than formerly and no interruption in the business will occur consequent on the removal of the old machinery now in use. Will also keep on hand a large supply of seasoned, sawed lumber, Dressed Flooring, Laths, etc.

When Thomas Mackay died in October 1855, Currier was one of his pallbearers.

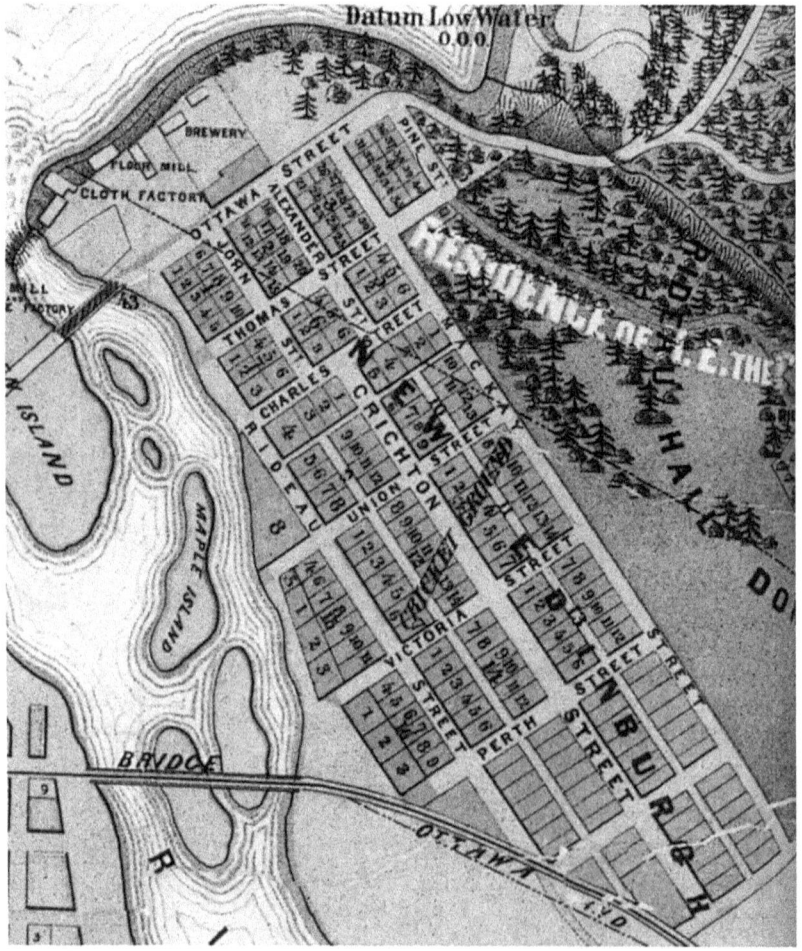

Figure 24.5. New Edinburgh, cloth and flour mills and brewery, 1864.
Source: Thomas Keefer, Mackay Estate Prospectus, 1864, Library and Archives Canada.

Mackay & Company

From 1856 to 1865, the Mackay Estate, operating as Mackay & Company, also carried on the family flour milling operation under different names. The mill was partially burned in May of 1857, and rebuilt in 1861. A note in the New Edinburgh census returns for the year 1861 stated that repairs to the flour mill in New Edinburgh cost $16,000, and that the capacity of the new structure would be twenty thousand barrels per year.

In 1865, a new firm, S. H. Waggoner & Company, took over management of the New Edinburgh Flour Mills, offering:

> All Kinds Of Gristing and Merchant work
> Constantly on hand Flour, bran, Shorts and Provender
> Cash paid for good wheat and other kinds of grain[2]

In 1856, Mackay & Company also passed on management of the New Edinburgh cloth factory—into the hands of Henry O. Burritt, originally a carder—and in 1858 a new company called the Rideau Falls Woollen Mills was established.

From the census returns of 1861:

> Capital invested – $50,000
> Capacity–90,000 pounds of wool – value $30,000
> Employees – males – 20; females – 20
> Total amount of salaries paid per month – males $350; females $200
> Production per year – 1500 pair of blankets
> 80,000 yards of cloth and satinette
> 5,000 yards of flannel
>
> Total Value – $70,000

---

[2] Shorts consist of fractions of endosperm, bran, and germ, and are richest in proteins, vitamins, lipids, and minerals; provender is dry animal feed.

The Sale of the Mills

With the passing of the last male Mackay heir—Thomas Junior—Thomas Keefer became head of the family. With the successful lease of Rideau Hall, and seeing the surviving family members well housed, he turned his attention to selling the Rideau Falls mill properties.

In 1865, Keefer dissolved the family firm of Mackay & Company, and in 1866 sold all the remaining interests in the three New Edinburgh lumber mills to James and John Maclaren, of Buckingham, for $82,000, taking back a mortgage of $61,500 at 6 percent.

Thomas Currier took his share of the sale, crossed the river to Hull and became a partner in Wright, Batson, and Currier, helping them build a steam sawmill that by 1871 was producing 30 million board feet [70,792 cubic metres] of lumber a year.

From 1872 to 1877 Currier was president of the Citizen Printing and Publishing Company, which owned the *Ottawa Daily Citizen*. He was involved in a host of other companies, being president of the Ottawa and Gatineau Valley Railway Company and of the Ontario

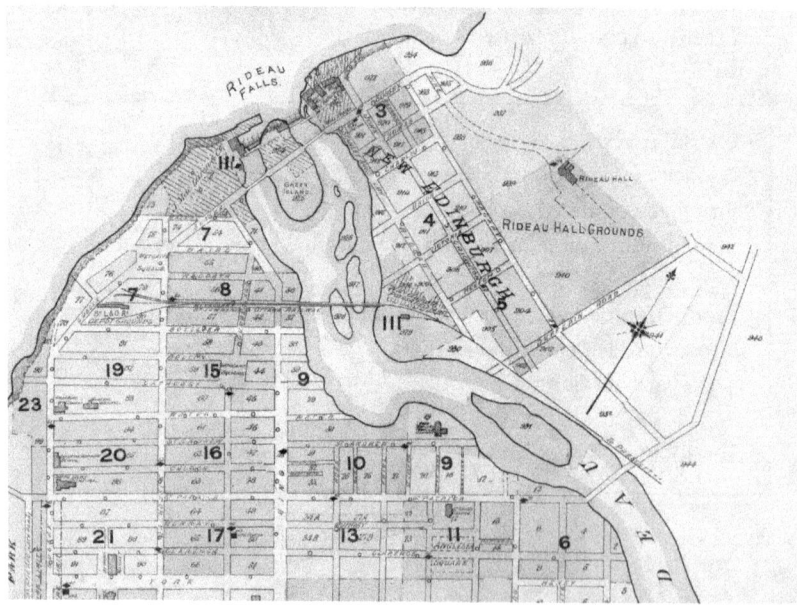

Figure 24.6. Lower Town and New Edinburgh, 1875, with the Ottawa & Prescott Railway and Maclaren Mills.
Source: Library and Archives Canada.

and Quebec Railway Company, and a director of the Ottawa City Passenger Railway Company.

In 1878, Currier's business career foundered and when the mill in Hull burned down, he was, according to his friend Alonzo Wright, "hopelessly bankrupt." He still managed to retain the mansion he had built from 1866 to 1868, at 24 Sussex Drive, which in 1951 became the official residence of the Prime Minister of Canada, then Louis St. Laurent.

As for the Rideau Falls cloth factory, sawmills and flour mills, the Maclaren brothers sold them to the W. C. Edwards Company in 1894. On July 25, 1907, the entire Rideau Falls complex of mills was destroyed in a fire.

CHAPTER 25

The Sale of Rideau Hall

Their house is of stone, built in the old English style, solid and substantial. It is approached through a long avenue of noble trees, and is surrounded by what is said to be—and there is little doubt of it—the finest lawn in Canada.—Constant cropping, manuring and rolling, have given to it the true velvety appearance, and that elasticity to the tread so much prized by gentlemen at home. A cedar hedge runs along one side of the lawn, furnishing a very good substitute for hawthorn and making a capital fence.
Then there is the garden, covering several acres of ground, cultivated with the greatest care, abounding in fruits and flowers, with nicely gravelled, well-bordered walks; and from the arbor at the upper end, a splendid view of the Ottawa and the surrounding country is obtained. No gentleman's seat in England is more neatly kept or more tastefully laid out. The Prince of Wales and suite rambled about it for hours on the day before their departure, all expressing great surprise that so much taste and refinement should exist so far in the Canadian woods.

—Ottawa Tribune, *November 10, 1860*

The Lease of Rideau Hall

With the successful winding up of the family milling business, Keefer turned his attention to government feelers regarding the lease and sale of Rideau Hall to serve as Government House. It had become clear to all that with massive cost overruns on the Parliament buildings, the proposed viceregal palace on Nepean Point was never going to get built.

Figure 25.1. Anne Langton, *From Behind Rideau Hall*, 1870s.
Source: John Johnston, Mediawiki Commons. This file is licensed under the Creative Commons Attribution-Share Alike 4.0 International license (https://creativecommons.org/licenses/by-sa/4.0/deed.en).

His Excellency Viscount Monck, appointed twenty-first Governor General of British North America, arrived at Québec after the outbreak of the US Civil War. He took office on November 28, 1861, just as war between Britain and the United States seemed inevitable over the Trent Affair, in which the US Navy illegally captured two Confederate diplomats from a British ship.

Throughout his term, Monck worked closely with Lord Lyons, the British minister at Washington, to cool the outrage of Union politicians at Confederate use of Canadian territory after the St. Albans raid in 1864. In this he was aided by his secretary and confidant, Dennis Godley, quickly nicknamed "Almighty Godley" by the Canadians.

Monck and Godley arrived at the New Edinburgh station on October 8, 1862, at about two in the afternoon. After Ottawa MLA Richard W. Scott read a civic address of welcome, His Excellency was driven to nearby Major's Hill, where a tent pavilion had been erected. Before entering, Scott took the party to the lookout at Nepean Point, to view the entrance of the Rideau Canal and the half-completed

Parliament buildings on the opposite cliff. Afterwards the party were treated to a "sumptuous luncheon."

In proposing the toast to "His Excellency the Governor General," Scott noted that on the spot where they were assembled, Col. By had first pitched his tent in the year 1826, before there was a tree cut on the site where the city of Ottawa now stands.

Monck replied in kind, saying that, "for the last five or six weeks I have been engaged in visiting a country which I believe to be unsurpassed for natural beauty, but I was unprepared for the magnificent

Figure 25.2. Viscount Monck.
Source: Library and Archives Canada.

spectacle with which my eyes have just been feasted and which I can say with truth, I have seldom, if ever, seen equalled."

Confederation—and getting funding to complete the Parliament buildings—soon became Monck's principal aim, and two years later, in the spring of 1864, he paid another inspection visit to Ottawa. Arriving late one evening in the pouring rain on the Ottawa & Prescott Railway, Lady Monck's first impression was not good; she was

> much disgusted with the squalid look of Ottawa, though we only saw it by lamplight, which was scarcely any light, such wretched gas. The streets were so rough, like dirt roads. I went on wondering how we could ever live there, when the seat of government is moved there. The enormous signs over the shops amused us: just opposite our room at the hotel (Russell) hung an enormous boot. We all groaned over Ottawa; it looks as if it was at t'other end of nowhere. The hotel was third-rate and the food looked and tasted uncivilized.

The next day the Moncks visited the nearly built Parliament buildings, which were finished enough to permit the civil servants to move in from Québec City when the session closed in September. Monck and Godley also visited Rideau Hall, where they toured the domain and sat down with Thomas Keefer to discuss the sale of the property as a potential viceregal residence.

Figure 25.3. First photo of Rideau Hall, circa 1865; to the left is the frame garden building, to the right a new guard house and construction shed.
Source: National Capital Commission.

On August 2, 1864, Monck signed a lease arrangement for the Mackay Estate's eleven-room Regency villa for $4,000 per annum, for up to twelve years, with an option to purchase the property within three years.

Under the terms, Rideau Hall would have to be cleared completely—lock, stock, and barrel. The unfeeling Board of Works was not interested in purchasing any mahogany and New Brunswick black walnut furniture made especially for the family.

Keefer immediately went to work, with the help of Richard W. Scott, to pay off three Mackay mortgages totalling $29,000.

On July 1, 1864, with government architect Frederick Rubidge's workmen swarming over Rideau Hall, he moved with his wife Elizabeth and mother-in-law Ann Crichton into a new stone house, Birkenfels, originally built for the last Mackay male heir, Thomas Mackay Jr. Birkenfels is Celtic for "a rocky hill of birches"—possibly recalling the name of a ruined castle in Alsace, ancestral home of the Keefers.[1]

To make way for the family, Tom Junior was installed at nearby Elmwood Farm, where he died on November 11, at age 27, probably of TB.

Figure 25.4. Thomas Keefer and family at Birkenfels.
Source: Library and Archives Canada.

---

[1] The family name was originally spelled "Kieffer."

Birkenfels was originally built of limestone in the sturdy style of the old Scottish farm houses. Above its fireplace was carved the Cross of St. Andrew.

After only four years at Birkenfels, heartbreak hit the family again, with the death of Keefer's beloved wife, Elizabeth, likely of tuberculosis, at age 40. She was survived by seven children—four boys and three girls—but eldest daughter Anne died shortly after.

The Governor General Moves In

> *We are inclined to take Government House for granted. We think of it as an old house where the Governor General lives ... actually it is Canada's most historic residence. Physically parts of it go back to the very beginnings of the community, and as the home of every Governor General since Confederation, it has associations with our national story such as no other country can boast.*
>
> —Ottawa newspaper clipping[2]

Following the lease agreement, Keefer and Scott ensured that the Rideau Hall mortgages were discharged that August, so the property was free and clear.

The Board of Works did not move as quickly. When it came to collecting the rent due to widow Mackay, no monies were forthcoming from the government, who let cows roam over Ann's abandoned garden, and left the house unheated over the winter—not a wise course of action if you want to preserve plaster work from frost.

"Mrs. Mackay," complained Keefer to deaf ears, "has been unable to obtain any advances from the Bank of Montreal and has been much inconvenienced."

Keefer's white-knight approach failed to move the hard-hearted functionaries, but he found some small leverage when the Board of Works discovered that it had overlooked renting a small triangle of land near the estate gates, with access to the Ottawa River. Keefer suggested that the estate was prepared "to include this piece of ground in the Domain agreement if the Govt will undertake within a reasonable time to exercise their option of purchase." This at least had the effect of locking down the eventual selling price.

---

[2] Dated October 14, 1935 (Library and Archives Canada).

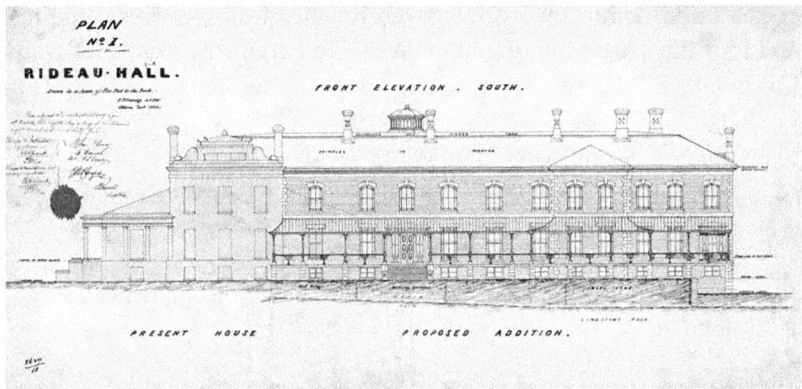

Figure 25.5. Rubidge plan of the Mackay Estate with the original villa, 1865.
Source: Library and Archives Canada, MIKAN 2171391.

During 1865 and 1866, while Monck supervised the renovations and furnishings, Board of Works architect Frederick Rubidge started to remodel Mackay's original villa. He began by adding a long, two-storey, forty-nine-room wing to the east, in the French Norman style of Spencer Wood, who designed the governor general's residence in Québec. A long verandah with greenhouse overlooked the famous lawn, gardens, and bowling green. To harmonize with the original, Rubidge clad the exterior walls in the same local ashlar limestone masonry and the roof in cedar shingles. He also enhanced the gatehouse and built a red-brick house, Rideau Cottage, for the secretary to the governor general.

George Brown opposed the additions, grumbling to John A. Macdonald that Rideau Hall was "a miserable little house, and the grounds those of an ambitious country squire."

Macdonald shared his opinion, complaining that "more had been spent on patching up Rideau Hall than could have been used to construct a new royal palace." When he was in his cups, Sir John A. would also growl that the Rideau Canal should be paved over and used as a railway line.[3]

Monck, on the other hand, came to appreciate Rideau Hall, telling his son, "we are all agreeably surprised by this house; everything

---

[3] Even as late as 1970, having got rid of streetcar service, barbarians on the Ottawa City Council seriously considered filling in and paving over the Canal to make an expressway.

is clean and comfortable." However, the city was a different matter, and four days after moving in, he wrote to Foreign Secretary Edward Cardwell:

> It seems like an act of insanity to have fixed the Capital of this great country away from the civilization, intelligence and commercial enterprise of this province, in a place that can never be of importance, and where the political section of the community will live in isolation and removed from the action of any public opinion.[4]

Monck moved in with his family in August 1866, at which point rental monies began to flow into the account of the Mackay Estate. Monck also allowed the new Ottawa Cricket Club to take advantage of the splendid lawn at Rideau Hall to establish its first cricket pitch.

Monck, however, hated the dust and potholes and noisy millworks of Sussex Drive, the street leading from Rideau Hall to the Parliament buildings. Until the road was macadamized, he often demanded a six-oar cutter, with a Royal Navy crew, to transport himself to and from a wharf below Rideau Hall to the Ottawa locks.

Figure 25.6. Lord Monck and family, Rideau Hall, 1866.
Source: Library and Archives Canada, MIKAN 3192017.

---

[4] Brault, *The Mile of History*, 9.

Keefer Makes the Sale

Keefer's next burden was to negotiate the outright sale of the property. It took two more years of bargaining, this time with the Minister of Public Works of the new Dominion of Canada, who claimed to be scouting several other viceregal sites. At one point, Keefer and Richard Scott threatened to sell off the Rideau Hall Domain as building lots if the government did not exercise its option to purchase after three years.

Finally, the government blinked, agreeing to acquire from the estate for the sum of $82,000, a domain with four parcels of land amounting to 87 acres [35 hectares].

Not included in the offer were 57 acres [23 hectares] of woodlands and 100 acres [40 hectares] of pastureland. Fortunately for the family, this property would increase in value, as it became a major part of the future Village of Rockcliffe Park.

Monck left Canada on November 14, 1868, after seeing to the final purchase of Rideau Hall as an official residence for succeeding governors general.

Before leaving, he laid the cornerstone of St. Bartholomew's Anglican Church in New Edinburgh, facing Rideau Hall, on land donated by the Mackay Estate.

The Estate also granted funds to another Anglican church, St. Albans, after the *Canadian Churchman* newspaper argued for creation

Figure 25.7. Rubidge addition, 1870s, with original Rideau Hall (left) and new greenhouses.
Source: National Capital Commission, Rideau Hall.

of a new parish in Sandy Hill, "so that the souls of civil servants, soon to be arriving from Québec City, might not be lost."

John A. Macdonald was one of the first parishioners to have his soul saved, in what is now Ottawa's oldest surviving church.

Within a decade, Rideau Hall had become the social centre of Canada's capital—a regular Downton Abbey. On February 23, 1876, Governor General Lord Dufferin and Lady Dufferin hosted a fancy dress ball for 1,500 guests.

The MacKinnon Tragedy

> *It is an unhappy but perhaps significant fact that Annie MacKinnon, who remarried, was never known to refer in later life to her first marriage.*
>
> —Norman Reddaway,
> British High Commission historian[5]

Keefer continued to grapple with family creditors after the death in 1865 of brother-in-law Thomas Mackay Jr., and the death of his other brother-in-law John MacKinnon a year later.

Figure 25.8. Old Rideau Hall entrance in 1889; to the right is the Tent Room built by Lord Dufferin in 1872.
Source: National Capital Commission, Rideau Hall.

---

[5] Norman Reddaway, *Earnscliffe*.

Tom Mackay once held promise as an up-and-coming successor to his father. But he remained a bachelor, and did not long survive the move from Rideau Hall, dying at age 27 at Elmwood Farm, likely from a combination of TB and alcohol.

An official obituary declared that "if he had lived to take that place in his country's service to which his position, his education, and his talents entitled him, he would speedily have been acknowledged as one of the foremost speakers in Parliament, and as a debater of no ordinary merit."

Unofficially, family lawyer Richard W. Scott pronounced to a friend that he was "a drunken stupid fellow, who could not take care of $5."[6]

John MacKinnon's death was equally tragic. In 1854, the year before he died, Thomas Mackay sold MacKinnon, recently retired from the presidency of the Ottawa & Prescott Railway, about two hectares of land on a height overlooking the Ottawa River. In 1855, Mackay-trained master masons Donald Dow and Peter Fraser built John and Annie a beautiful three-storey gabled villa on the site, on what was then Metcalfe Square, only a short distance west of Rideau Falls. The MacKinnons moved into the house in 1857 from a nearby apartment.[7]

In the years following Thomas Mackay's death, John MacKinnon led a quiet life, nursing his financial wounds after the embarrassing bankruptcy of the O&P Railway. He ran for Parliament for Renfrew, but was defeated by the then Premier, Sir Francis Hincks.

Depressed and morose, MacKinnon withdrew from society, except for teaching Sunday school in New Edinburgh and serving as treasurer of the Protestant Hospital Board, which he founded. Ashamed by the losses suffered by his fellow citizens, he was no longer an active public figure, held no municipal offices, and no longer appeared in the city directories as a merchant. He may have retained an interest in the woollen mill on the Rideau Falls, but Keefer eventually sold all remaining mill properties to the McLaren brothers.

By the 1860s, MacKinnon had little or no income, and was repeatedly forced to mortgage the property after he moved in. It was rumoured that he may have been speculating with Mackay's money

---

[6] RG11, Public Works, vol. 426, Scott to [illegible], July 17, 1865.
[7] Lady Veronica Goodenough, *Earnscliffe*.

Figure 25.9. Earnscliffe today.
Source: John Johnston, Mediawiki Commons. This file is licensed under the Creative Commons Attribution-Share Alike 4.0 International license. (https://creativecommons.org/licenses/by-sa/4.0/deed.en).

before his father-in-law died. There is no evidence he cooked the books or cheated Mackay, but it is not beyond the bounds of possibility. That Mackay was at the very least disappointed with his abilities is clear, since he made Thomas Keefer the executor of his estate, not MacKinnon.

On June 19, 1866, John MacKinnon died suddenly at the young age of 51. The cause of death was due to "inflammation of the bowel," possibly due to stress, or virulent influenza, or the same cancer that had killed Thomas Mackay in 1855. But based on his behaviour, it might very well have been self-inflicted—suicide by poison. One of the major effects of arsenic is cramping and stomach pain.

Suicide is often associated with shame and guilt. Perhaps this was a dark family secret. Perhaps this was why Annie Mackay, touched by tragedy, would never talk about her first marriage.

MacKinnon left no will, and the affairs of his widow were put before the local Surrogate Court. On October 30, the court issued a ruling that Annie MacKinnon should be the guardian of the three children and that the house should be sold. The mansion was accordingly put up for auction on November 7. Keefer took charge, acquired the property, cleared the outstanding mortgage of $6,000 due to Neil Robertson, an Arnprior lumber merchant, and paid $48 for the transfer and taxes, putting the house in the name of the MacKinnon's oldest son, Thomas.

Keefer let widow Annie and her grieving children Thomas, William, and Flora, live there until the spring of 1868, when they could comfortably move to Rockcliffe House, the residence of the late Duncan MacNab, newly acquired by Keefer as a residence for the widow Ann Crichton. Keefer would add a second storey to the house, built in the same year as Rideau Hall, converting it from a Regency cottage into a Victorian Gothic villa.[8]

Four years later, on July 19, 1872, Thomas, the eldest MacKinnon son, died at the age of 24. William and Flora also died at comparatively young ages, William in 1877 and Flora in 1897.

After Annie and her children had moved to Rockcliffe House, Keefer offered the MacKinnon house to Thomas Reynolds, a Grand Trunk superintendent and Canadian agent of the rail suppliers Abbw Vale. Reynolds had recently purchased the bankrupt Ottawa & Prescott Railway for ten cents on the dollar, and reorganized it in 1867 as the St. Lawrence and Ottawa Railway, with improved access to the Chaudière mills.

On June 3, 1870, Reynolds acquired the MacKinnon property for $7,500, and occupied it from 1872 to 1879. He loved the house and spent lavishly on improvements, but was soon forced by ill health to retire to England. The house was used for a short time by the Royal Engineers as a military hospital. Sir John A. Macdonald, Prime Minister of Canada, became a tenant, and in 1882 he bought the house, christened it Earnscliffe, and died there, on June 6, 1891. In the 1930s, it was sold for $130,000 to become the residence of the British High Commissioner.

The MacKinnon tragedy also had a happier ending. In 1872, three years after his wife Elizabeth died, Thomas Keefer remarried, to Mackay's eldest daughter Annie, John MacKinnon's widow. A Unitarian by conviction, Thomas Keefer was not overly concerned by

---

[8] Thomas Mackay had attempted to buy the house after MacNab's death, but his widow refused to sell.

salacious gossip about marrying his deceased wife's widowed sister. The wedding was officiated by a cousin, the Rev. B.B. Keefer, of London, Ontario.

The couple raised their new MacKinnon/Keefer extended family at Birkenfels until widow Ann's death in 1878. Annie and Thomas then moved into Rockcliffe House and Birkenfels was sold.

They enjoyed more than thirty years together; she died in 1906, he passed away in 1915.

Keefer's other brother-in-law, Thomas McLeod Clark, married to Elizabeth's twin sister Jesse, ran a successful brick-making enterprise in Rockcliffe. Keefer backed Clark, and involved him in the Mackay Estate as an agent. Following Jessie's death in 1880, Clark moved his family to Crichton Lodge, a stone villa opposite the gates of Rideau Hall. It serves today as the residence of the Norwegian ambassador.

The Death of Widow Mackay

Saddened by the death of her husband and almost twenty children and grandchildren, Ann Crichton remained a forlorn figure until her own passing on August 21, 1878, at the age of 85. She had outlived her husband by more than twenty years, and thirteen of her sixteen children, leaving only three surviving daughters.

The obituaries spoke of "a gracious kindly person, who brought happiness to the homes of many a distressed family, being noted for her charitable disposition and warm-heartedness."

Ann Crichton's funeral took place on August 24 at four in the afternoon in Rockcliffe House. After religious services, conducted by Rev. Mr. Haney, her remains were interred in the family vault in Beechwood Cemetery. The pallbearers were mostly old friends and colleagues of her husband—Allan Gilmour, H. V. Noel, R. Blackburn, W. Clegg, John Durie, G. P. Baker, J. M. Currier, and A. Drummond.

After her death, the *Ottawa Citizen* published an interview with a Mrs. Furneval regarding her years of service at Rideau Hall under Lady Lansdowne and Princess Louise. She recalled Mrs. Mackay's last years of residence at the Hall, when she was a maid of ten years old:

> Mrs. McKay had a fruit and vegetable garden on the "Castle" grounds, and each year in the fall, she made it a practice of

Figure 25.10. Ann Crichton Mackay, 1873.
Source: William Notman, McCord Museum.

sending for the children of the employees of the mills, and loading them with gifts from the garden.

She sat in the sun in a big arm chair and imparted homely advice with the gifts. She told us of her frugal up-bringing in Scotland and extolled porridge as the best food in the world for everybody, young and old, with the added advantage of being cheap.

A thrifty Scot to the end.

CHAPTER 26

Keefer Develops Rockcliffe Park

Rockcliffe Park is so quintessentially Canadian: water, forest, rock.

—Humphrey Carver

Keefer's Development Program

With Rideau Hall leased, the Rideau Falls mills sold, and the estate debts cleared up, Thomas Keefer embarked on an ambitious program to develop the remainder of the Mackay Estate as a rural Eden, somewhat like several communities he had seen while consulting in the US. He called it Rockcliffe Park.

According to Martha Edmond, author of *Rockcliffe Park: A History of the Village*, "Keefer was the perfect embodiment of the Victorian Renaissance man. He had a practical knowledge of mills, railway surveying, navigation, water power, land management, and early conservation principles. He would transform Mackay's Bush into a planned suburb, one that was truly innovative for its time."[1]

Keefer had been pondering for several years how to profit from developing and marketing the Rockcliffe property to business owners and government officials.

He originally surveyed and divided the 1,000 acres [404 hectares] of Mackay's Bush into four shares, one for each surviving Mackay daughter and one for the MacKinnon heirs.

---

[1] Martha Edmond, *Rockcliffe Park. A History of the Village*, 22.

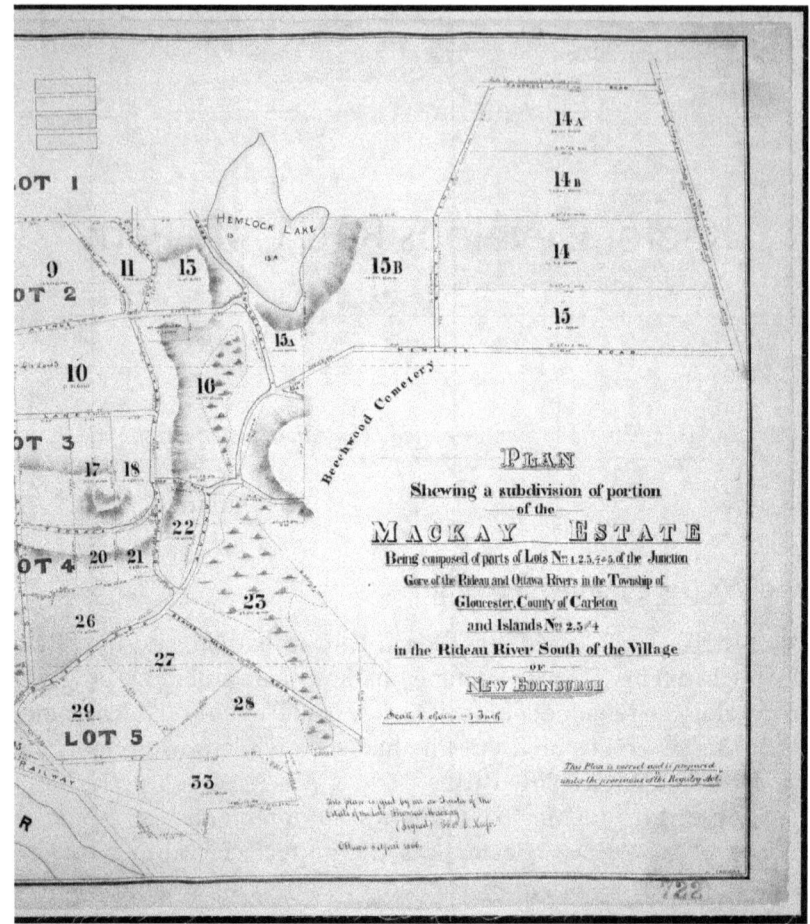

Figure 26.1. *Mackay Estate, West Side*, 1866, by T. C. Keefer.
Source: Library and Archives Canada.

In 1864, he published a prospectus on the Mackay Estate:

> It embraces upwards of One Thousand Acres en bloc, in Gloucester, immediately adjoining the City of Ottawa but in a separate municipality in which there is but a nominal taxation. It has a frontage of more than a mile [1.6 kilometres] upon each of the Rivers Ottawa and Rideau, the latter entering the former, upon the Estate, by a perpendicular fall of forty feet [12 metres], forming a curtain, from whence the name Rideau is derived. The grounds offered for sale have commanding

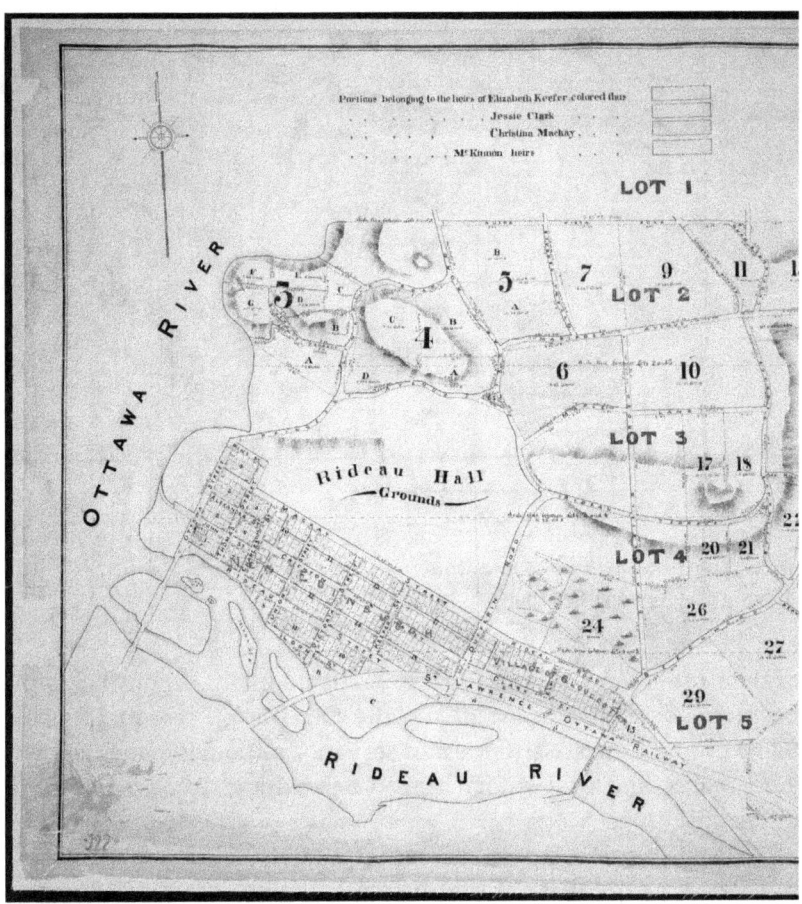

Figure 26.2. *Mackay Estate, East Side*, 1866, by T. C. Keefer.
Source: Library and Archives Canada.

situations, at elevations sixty to one hundred and twenty feet [18 to 36 metres] above the water level of the Ottawa River, giving fine views of the City of Ottawa and Parliament Buildings, the Hull Mountains, the Gatineau River in both directions... Many of the sites are wooded with evergreen and deciduous shrubs and trees. The position of this estate is more advantageous than that of any other suburban property about Ottawa.

In 1865, the first Province of Canada civil servants arrived in Ottawa from the old capital of Québec City, bringing the contents

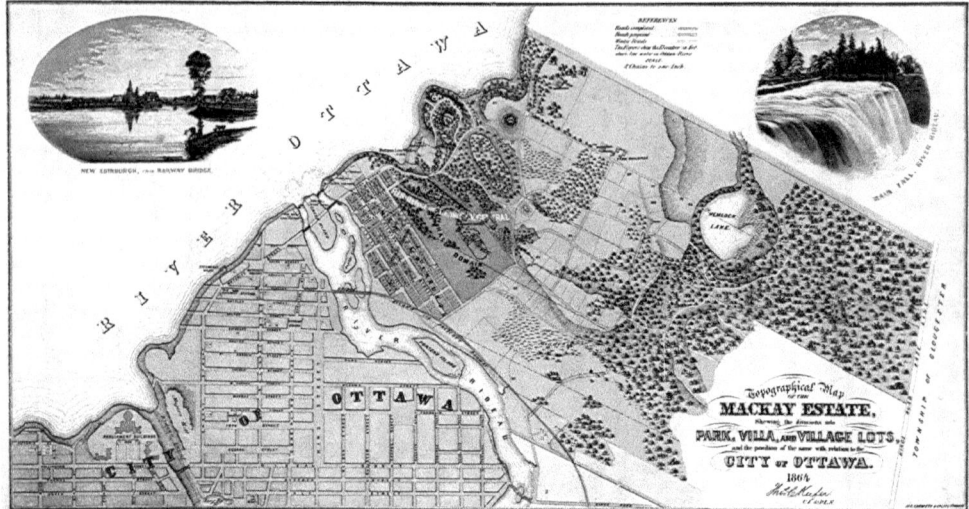

Figure 26.3. Thomas Keefer, *Mackay Estate Prospectus*, 1864.
Source: Library and Archives Canada.

of their offices to new lodgings on Parliament Hill. About 350 families arrived by steamboat or via the Ottawa & Prescott Railway. Some brought their assistants and servants, although many messengers, pages, and charwomen stayed behind and were replaced by Ottawans.

Most of the newcomers were not at all delighted with leaving the old capital for a rough lumber town in the wilderness. They quickly found that Ottawa lacked the sophistication of Québec City. Police services were provided by unsalaried constables, paid by the number of arrests they made. Ottawa had only one school for senior students, on Kent Street in the Upper Town. Drinking water was still delivered by wagons from barrels filled from the as-yet-unpolluted Ottawa River or from a well in Lower Town.

One newcomer, senior government functionary Edmund Meredith, kept an energetic diary. His entry on November 17 probably summed up the feelings of many fellow exiles: "The more I see of Ottawa, the more do I dislike and detest it."[2]

---

[2] Quoted in Sandra Gwyn, *The Private Capital*.

Meredith was especially disgusted by the odour of Ottawa—the smell from outdoor privies, stagnant water, and a festering sewer running into the Rideau Canal "nearly knocked me down."[3]

To escape the stench, the family enjoyed taking long walks in the countryside, to Chelsea or Aylmer and back. Finally, in 1874, the Merediths and their fellow citizens breathed a sigh of relief, as Thomas Keefer's first piped water supply came on line, and modern sewage systems were finally installed, replacing the crude wooden drains, outhouses, and privies of a frontier town.

The civil service move from Québec City added about 1,500 new inhabitants. Keefer had hoped to sell many of the Mackay Estate properties in Rockcliffe to the more prominent government officials, but he was premature in his optimism—most settled in Upper Town and in the new neighbourhood of Sandy Hill. One person who did appreciate Rockcliffe was Meredith, who found the building lots "very rough and rocky but decidedly picturesque." But he still chose to live in Sandy Hill, where he was able to walk to work in the East Block. In winter he took Keefer's new horse-drawn railway to work. Once there, he often froze, the wood furnace struggling to raise the temperature in his office above 10°C.

To give the Rockcliffe lots more romantic appeal, Keefer gave some of his streets names like "Buena Vista" (Lovely View), "Mariposa" (Butterfly), and "Acacia" (a flowering tree), probably inspired by a visit to Mexico on an engineering contract. The names Coltrin Road, Coltrin Place, and Coltrin Lodge came from his middle name—commemorating Dr. Asa Coltrin, an American army surgeon, who fell in love with his older sister Elizabeth Keefer during the War of 1812, as the pair tended the wounded in the Keefer homestead commandeered by invading Yankees as an army hospital. A true romance of the War of 1812—the couple married under a flag of truce at Queenston.

His brochure on the Mackay Estate noted that:

> The Executors have expended several thousand dollars, under the direction of Thomas C. Keefer, Esq., Civil Engineer, in laying out and firming roads which give access to the different terraces, blocks and highways, as well as to the Ottawa and Rideau Rivers.

---

[3] Sandra Gwyn, "The Inescapable Stink of Early Ottawa," *Ottawa Citizen*, October 29, 1984.

These roads have been made as much like private avenues as possible, by preserving the trees, and by adopting curved lines; thus they convert the greater portion the Estate into a large park, with a pleasing drive some four miles [6.5 kilometres] in extent, which will be increased with the extension of the roads.

The Mackay Estate's Rockcliffe Park investment would eventually pay off, as more and more members of the growing diplomatic corps acquired properties. Keefer's grandson, Alan, an architect, was able to design and build several of the new houses in the village, including Waterstone, now the residence of the Japanese ambassador, and Stornoway, residence of the Leader of the Opposition.[4]

Neighbouring New Edinburgh attracted some of the more modest civil servants, who converted and improved many of the old cottages in the village, some that had been owned by old servants and employees of Mackay. By 1870, the total population reached about 2,400, including many new immigrants from Scotland and some of the growing staff of the Governor General.

By 1875, St. Andrew's Presbyterian church had outgrown its quarters. Thomas Mackay's grandson, William MacKinnon, had helped raise funds for a new Presbyterian Church in New Edinburgh, and donated two lots at the corner of Mackay Street and Dufferin Road for a church building. MacKinnon died two years later.

Keefer Family Tragedies

By 1880, the extended family consisted of Thomas Coltrin Keefer and his second wife Annie, and Thomas's three daughters Jessie, Christina, and Mary Falding, who was aged 27 and married. Her two sons James, aged 3, and Harry, aged 2, were also living in the house, as was Flora MacKinnon.

The Mackay family tragedies were soon revisited on the Keefers. All of Thomas and Elizabeth Keefer's seven children died in their prime, except for Charles Henry. Anne died first, perhaps of TB, followed by Ralph in 1886. Flora may have been a victim of TB as well (she died in 1897).

---

[4] *Dictionary of Architects in Canada*: http://www.dictionaryofarchitectsincanada.org/node/1544.

The family was also afflicted by more drownings. To compound the Keefers' grief, 28-year-old son, Harold, a lieutenant with the Princess Louise Dragoon Guards, perished in the Lachine Canal in 1887, after falling off a bridge.

Even more heart-wrenching was the drowning death of daughter Jessie and her two young nephews, James and Henry Falding, aged 11 and 9, near Seguin's Ferry in June of 1888. According to Martha Edmond, in her history of Rockcliffe Park,

> Jessie had accompanied them while they "bathed" in the Ottawa River below Rockcliffe Manor House. The swell from a passing steamer apparently carried the boys beyond their depth and Jessie drowned trying to reach them, weighed down no doubt by the voluminous skirts and petticoats of the day. She was found still clutching the branch of a tree. Passengers on board the *Empress* bound for Montréal later recalled seeing the three waving exuberantly from the shore.[5]

T. C. Keefer and his wife Annie, visiting in Montréal, immediately returned on a private rail car provided by CPR President Sir William Van Horne.

Figure 26.4. Jessie Keefer.
Source: Topley Studio, Library and Archives Canada.

---

[5] Martha Edmond, *Rockcliffe Park. A History of the Village*, 33.

As a vestige of the tragedy, generations of Keefer children were strictly forbidden from venturing down that same ferry road. As Keefer's great-granddaughter Nini Keefer was warned, "It led straight to hell."

Mary Keefer Falding, Jessie's sister and mother of the boys, never recovered from the shock; she died in 1899, and her sister Christine in 1903.

Promoting Rockcliffe with Light Rail

Keefer's 80-by-100-foot [24 by 30 metre] lots in the village of Rockcliffe Park were bound by a bylaw that stated, "no person shall erect or use any holding for any purpose other than as a single detached family dwelling." Rental apartments and even doctors' offices were excluded, which led to the growth of a commercial strip along Beechwood Road.

In 1866, to ease access to downtown Ottawa and the Chaudière flats, Keefer incorporated for the Mackay Estate the Ottawa City Passenger Railway Company (OCPRC), the first public transportation system in Ottawa.

One of Keefer's original board members was flour miller William Hutchison, the son of Robert Hutchison, a Scottish immigrant who worked as a foreman for Thomas Mackay. Hutchison's mother was Mackay's niece Mary Mckay.

Other board members included sawmill owners William Goodhue Perley and Joseph Merrill Currier, lumber merchant Joseph-Ignace Aumond (also a board member of the Bytown & Prescott Railway), and Robert Blackburn, Reeve of New Edinburgh and later Liberal MP.

The first president of the line was George B. Lyon-Fellows, MLA for Russell County from 1848 to 1861, and in 1876, Mayor of Ottawa.

The OCPRC's inaugural run, at 5 a.m. on July 21, 1870, started with ten wooden twenty-passenger tramcars riding on iron rails, each drawn by a two-horse team. In winter, fifteen sleighs followed the route.

Fares cost five cents for a seventy-minute round trip with service every twelve minutes. Each teamster worked a fourteen-hour day (with a forty-five-minute break) for $1.25. He also collected the fares, proceeding through the car, making change from a small leather pouch over his shoulder, while handing over the reins to a passenger—the horses were familiar with the route, and continued on their way without any problem.

Figure 26.5. Keefer's Ottawa City Passenger Railway Company, 1871.
Source: Library and Archives Canada.

Beginning near Rideau Hall Gate, the track ran for 4 miles [6.4 kilometres] through the village of New Edinburgh and across Green Island to Metcalfe Square. It continued along Ottawa Street (Sussex Drive) south to Rideau Street, then up Rideau over Sappers' Bridge, west on Sparks Street to Bank Street, up Bank Street to Wellington Street, then west across Pooley's Bridge to Queen Street, along Duke Street to Bridge Street (Booth Street), and thence north to the Union Suspension Bridge.

The line operated with fifteen sleighs when snowfall was heavy. In the winter, the floors of the sleighs were covered with straw and heat was provided by a tiny coal stove in the centre of the car.

To cope with the spring thaw, the company mechanics would lift the whole tram body off its chassis and bolt it to a large flangeless-wheeled wagon that rode above the mud.

The OCPRC carried 273,000 passengers in its first year of operation. By 1891, it had twenty-five horses and fifteen employees, carried over 500,000 passengers and expanded to serve Hull with a track across the Union Suspension Bridge.

The lumber barons also used the OCPRC's horse-drawn trams and sleighs at night, as a convenient way to move lumber from mills at the Chaudière Falls and New Edinburgh (now part of Ottawa) to shipping points on the Rideau Canal and the Ottawa & Prescott Railway.

Figure 26.6. OCPRC East.
Source: Library and Archives Canada.

After 1900, Rockcliffe Park village came into its own with the arrival of the automobile. Well-to-do families, doctors, lawyers, and retired mandarins partly gave way to a growing number of embassies. Currently over seventy ambassadors and their staff have residences in Rockcliffe.

At this time, Keefer applied to the city to convert the OCPRC to electricity, but was refused. So he took steps to transfer the Mackay Estate's tramway franchise to two passionate young Ottawa entrepreneurs, members of his board of directors—Thomas Ahearn and Warren Soper.

Thomas Ahearn,[6] born in LeBreton Flats in 1855, was the co-founder of electric rail in Ottawa. As a young man, impassioned by

---

[6] In 1877, Thomas Ahearn devised a rudimentary telephone system based upon an article in *Scientific American* about Alexander Graham Bell's pioneering efforts. Ahearn used two homemade cigar boxes, magnets, and wire and, using existing telegraph lines, rigged up a routing from Pembroke to Ottawa. This was Ottawa's first long-distance telephone call. Ahearn was threatened with legal action for his

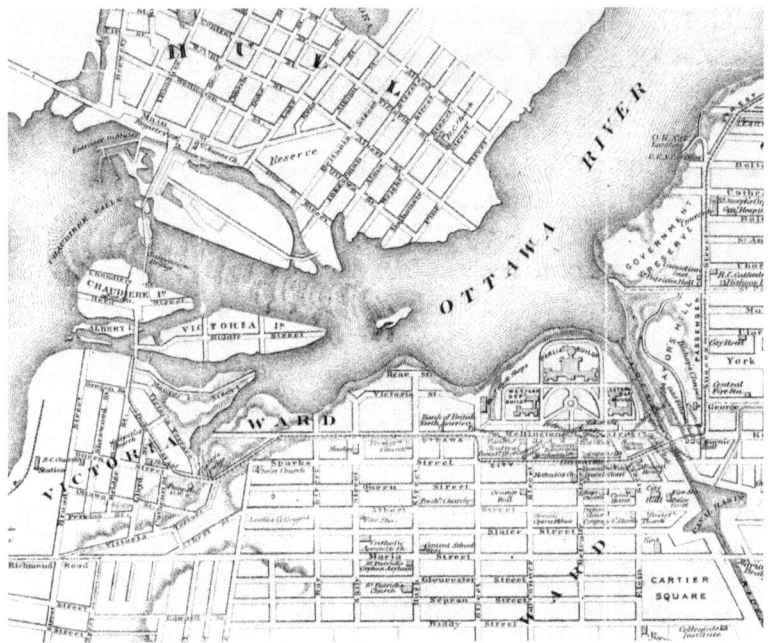

Figure 26.7. OCPRC West.
Source: Library and Archives Canada.

electricity, he offered to work for free for the J. R. Booth Company so that he could learn telegraphy. His friend, Warren Soper, Manager of the Dominion Telegraph Company, also shared this passion for electricity, and in 1881 they founded Ahearn & Soper, electrical contractors at large. In 1882, their Ottawa Electric Light Company installed a series of sixty-five arc street lamps—invented by Ohio engineer Charles Brush in 1878—powered by a small water wheel at Chaudière Falls on the Ottawa River—the first hydroelectric generator in Canada.

Ahearn & Soper installed the Parliament buildings' new electric lights, and turned them on for the first time on January 17, 1884. Three years later, they illuminated Parliament buildings with thousands of electric lights, to celebrate Queen Victoria's Diamond Jubilee.

Soon lauded as "The Canadian Edison," Ahearn is famous for inventing the world's first all-electric oven and stove. On January 17,

---

unauthorized use of Bell's patented technique, but instead was appointed manager of Bell Telephone Company's first Ottawa office.

1884, he cooked the first dinner with the appliance in Ottawa's Windsor Hotel before a collection of VIP journalists. The oven was over 6 feet [2 metres] in height and width and in the words of the *Ottawa Citizen*, "It was hot enough to roast an ox." The dinner consisted of Saginaw trout, potato croquettes, sugar-cured ham, lamb cutlets, stuffed loin of veal, strawberry puffs, chocolate cake, and apple pie.

In 1891, Keefer transferred the Mackay Estate's passenger railway charter to Ahearn & Soper. On June 29, starting with four electric trams, their new Ottawa Electric Railway Company (OER) introduced electric streetcars to Ottawa a year before both Toronto and Montréal's systems came into action. They installed the first electric powered hot-water heating for the streetcars and also developed a rotating brush sweeper to clear the track of snow.

In its first eleven months, OER ridership hit 1.5 million, almost tripling the ridership of the horse-drawn streetcars that came before it. The OER connected people across town, and also created family destinations for passengers to relax during their days off. Keefer established a park at the Rockcliffe Buena Vista terminus, and the OER lines were expanded to Lansdowne Park in the south centre, and Britannia Park on Lac Deschenes in the far west.

Rockcliffe Park, now the property of the National Capital Commission, was renowned as "Canada's first playground." Keefer

Figure 26.8. Thomas Ahearn, 1903.
Source: Topley Studio, Library and Archives Canada, PA-012222.

sited the Pavilion and Lookout to capitalize on breathtaking views of the Ottawa River, the Gatineau Hills, and picturesque Gatineau village.

Streetcar service brought a wide range of Canadians to the park, for family gatherings, swimming, and picnicking. Winter recreation included toboggan runs, ski hills, and a renowned ski jump. Indeed, Rockcliffe Park was the birthplace of skiing in the Ottawa region.[7]

On the other side of the river, the Hull Electric Railway was developed by another group of private entrepreneurs, and opened in 1896. The line originally ran from Hull to Aylmer, but in 1901 the first trip was made between Ottawa and Hull in an electric streetcar across the Alexandria Bridge, making the passage between provinces that much simpler. The company was taken over by Canadian Pacific in 1902.[8]

Historic Rockcliffe Houses

In his will, Keefer left the Rockcliffe Manor House, at the corner of Acacia and Mariposa, to his son, Charles Henry Keefer, who leased it to a succession of tenants, until the Manor House was purchased by Senator Cairine Wilson and her husband in 1929. The Wilsons remodeled the place, adding a plaster "cobweb ceiling" in the library, installed by a Keefer grandson, architect Allan Keefer.

Since 1962, Rockcliffe Manor has served as the Nunciature or Embassy of the Holy See, and the residence of the Apostolic Delegate to Canada.

The Birkenfels house went through several owners before it was purchased by Warren Soper in the 1890s. In 1908, Soper built a summer cottage on the property, and this humble edifice later made way for another spacious residence. In 1935, the property was divided. One half became the official residence of the American Ambassador to Canada.

---

[7] *Rockcliffe Park redevelopment plan: the restoration of a picturesque pleasure park.* Wilfrid Laurier University Press, 1999; The Free Library. (2014).

[8] In 1924, the OER introduced buses unsuccessfully, and then again in 1939. Eventually, in 1947, a referendum led by a group of Ottawa city councillors was held and the City of Ottawa took over the OER in 1948. It then became the Ottawa Transportation Commission, or what is now known as the OC Transpo. At that time it ran with 130 streetcars and 61 buses.

Another house, Stornoway, designed by Allan Keefer, was built for Mr. and Mrs. A. J. Major in 1914. The house became a sanctuary for Her Royal Highness Princess Juliana (now Queen Juliana) of Holland and family when her country was overrun by Hitler's Wehrmacht.

On June 16, 1943, while living there Princess Juliana entertained Madame Chiang Kai-shek, wife of the Chinese leader in the war against Japan. Since the war, the house has been the official residence of the Leader of the Official Opposition.

Another property, Elmwood Farm, was owned by J. McLeod Clarke, who married Thomas Mackay's daughter. Later acquired by the Keefer estate, it became the residence of Charles Keefer. Elmwood School is now on the site of part of the old farm.

Keefer's Final Years

During Keefer's later years, he devoted himself to the advancement of engineering as a profession.

After bitter experiences in the 1850s with railway promoters and politicians, he argued for expanded engineering education. In a lecture at McGill in 1857, he proposed creating an engineering professorship at McGill. "The engineer, though an indispensable agent, is generally a junior partner in the firm of Grab, Chisel & Co." Instead, he proposed that engineers, like lawyers and doctors, should be a "self-sustaining" profession and that their technical advice should prevail over political and business considerations.

During the 1880s, with contemporaries Sir Casimir Gzowski and Walter Shanley, he lent his name to the movement to organize Canadian engineers into a society to seek these goals. On February 24, 1887, he presided at the founding meeting of the Canadian Society of Civil Engineers in Montréal, and served as president again in 1897. He was the first Canadian to become president, in 1888, of the American Society of Civil Engineers and the only person to date to be president of both bodies.

Keefer also argued that engineers should be learned gentlemen, not just technicians, and in the forefront of cultural, scholarly, and educational initiatives. He was invited to become a fellow of the Royal Society of Canada and served as its president in 1898–1899. He received an honorary doctorate from McGill in 1905, and in 1912 was named an honorary member of the Institution of Civil Engineers of Great Britain.

Figure 26.9. Thomas Coltrin Keefer, c. 1910.
Source: Topley Studio, Library and Archives Canada.

Two of his sons, a nephew, and a grandson followed him into the field, driving the CPR through the Rocky Mountains, building infrastructure in Vancouver, and developing mining operations. Eldest son Charles Henry Keefer, born in Rideau Hall, followed his father's career closely. He apprenticed as a surveyor of the Canada Central Railway (Ottawa to Carleton Place), and worked on the Chaudière branch of the St. Lawrence and Ottawa Railway, the Canadian Pacific Railway (Yellowhead and Kicking Horse passes), and the Canada Atlantic Railway. Between 1872 and 1875, he helped his father engineer the Ottawa Water Works, and worked on the Montreal Harbour Works between 1881 and 1885. He was an engineer for the construction of the Tay Canal, and joined the Canadian Society of Civil Engineers (CSCE) in 1887.

Thomas Keefer was active in his profession into his 80s and 90s. He was almost 80 years old when he delivered a keynote address to the Royal Society of Canada. He spoke of water power, or Canada's newest resource, which he called "white coal." He foresaw high-speed railroads operating on electricity, and with some foresight, hoped for cleaner manufacturing plants and an end to the "poisonous smoke" associated with coal operations.

Thomas Keefer died in the Rockcliffe Manor House at age 92 on January 7, 1915, leaving an estate of $610,000. He was predeceased by his second wife, Annie, and three of his children, and was buried in the family vault at Beechwood Cemetery.

Appendix A: Rockcliffe Arms

Figure C.1. Granted May 31, 1994, to the Corporation of the Village of Rockcliffe Park.

Arms—Per fess enarched Argent and Vert resting on the fess line a Sugar Maple tree (*Acer saccharum Marsh*) between two Eastern White Pine trees (*Pinus strobus*) Vert in base a bar wavy Argent bordering a base Azure;

Crest—A mural coronet Argent masoned Azure charged in the centre with a maple leaf Vert;

Supporters—On grassy mounds rising above a representation of water, dextra a Pileated Woodpecker (*Dryocopus pileatus*) sinistra a Green-backed Heron (*Butorides striatus*) environed of reeds all proper;

Motto—INTER ARBORES FLOREMUS ("We flourish among the trees").

Source: Martha Edmond, *Rockcliffe Park: A History of the Village.*

Appendix B: Lines on Thomas Mackay

The following poem is from "Recollections of Bytown and its Old Inhabitants" by William Pittman Lett, Ottawa's city clerk for many years.

>Thomas Mackay, who's worthy name
>Is well known even to modern fame,
>The worth which honest men revere
>Deserves a fitting record here.
>With mighty gangs he excavated
>The ancient quarry situated
>On west side of "the Major's Hill,"
>Which modern hands find hard to fill;
>The stones from thence by powder rent
>To build the seven Canal Locks went.
>The Sappers' Bridge, too, was erected
>by blocks of limestone thence ejected.
>Like many another rising man,
>Mackay for ancient Russell "ran"
>To use a term, which means to-day
>That he runs best who best can pay!
>The declaration found him seated
>And his antagonist defeated.
>New honors came his name to greet,
>A Legislative Councillor's seat
>Was given next to Russell's pride.
>Clad with dignity he died.
>And no more upright man has e'er
>Deserving of the post sat there.

"Lines on the Death of Hon. Thos. McKay"

By Andrew Wilson[1]

A seraph came to Rideau Hall,
Sent by tho God of love,
For a harp of a thousand strings,
That was required above.

The heavenly chariots from above,
They bore this harp away;
They took it from its prison here,
To realms of endless day,

This golden harp of a thousand strings,
That hall will hear no more —
It's left a circle of loving friends,
For its home on Emmanuel's shore.

The great Supreme has called him home
From this sad vale of tears,
To wear a brilliant, starry crown
Throughout eternal years.

"In Beechwood Cemetery"

A Sonnet by Archibald Lampman, 1894

Here the dead sleep, the quiet dead. No sound
Disturbs them ever, and no storm dismays.
Winter mid snow caresses the tired ground,
And the wind roars about the woodland ways.
Springtime and summer and red autumn pass,
With leaf and bloom and pipe of wind and bird,
And the old earth puts forth her tender grass,
By them unfelt, unheeded and unheard.
Our centuries to them are but as strokes

---

[1] Andrew Wilson, *History of Old Ottawa*, 83.

In the dim gamut of some far-off chime.
Unaltering rest their perfect being cloaks—
A thing too vast to hear or feel or see—
Children of Silence and Eternity,
They know no season but the end of time.[2]

Thomas Keefer's tombstone reads as follows

Figure C.2. Mackay-Keefer graves, Beechwood Cemetery, Ottawa.[3]

---

[2] Lampman was a cousin of the Keefers from Niagara.
[3] Find a Grave, memorial page for Thomas MacKay (1 Sep 1792–9 Oct 1855), Find a Grave Memorial no. 185599015, citing Beechwood Cemetery, Ottawa.

Sacred to the Memory of
Thomas Coltrin Keefer
CMG LLD [1821–1915]

ELIZABETH HIS 1ST WIFE [1830–1870]
Aged 41 Years

ANNE HIS SECOND WIFE [1825–1906]
Died 1906

Jessie [KEEFER] [1861–1888]
Aged 27 Years [drowned in 1888 attempting to rescue James and Henry Falding]

Christina Mackay [Keefer] Fleming [1867–1903]
Aged [36] Years

Mary B. [Keefer] Falding [1853–1899]
Died 1899

JAMES AND HENRY [sons of Mary FALDING drowned 1888]
Aged 11 and 9 Years

HAROLD WALDRUF KEEFER [1856–1884]
Aged 28 years [d. 1887 falling off Lachine Bridge]

CHARLES HENRY KEEFER CE [1851–1932]
Aged 81 Years
[married Lucy Mabel Jones on February 13, 1877, at Prescott, Ontario]

LUCY [MABEL JONES KEEFER] 1855–1925
Aged 71 Years

FLORA MACKINNON [1849–1897]
Died 1897

RALPH DELAMERE KEEFER [1858–1886]
Aged 28 Years

All of whom are buried here

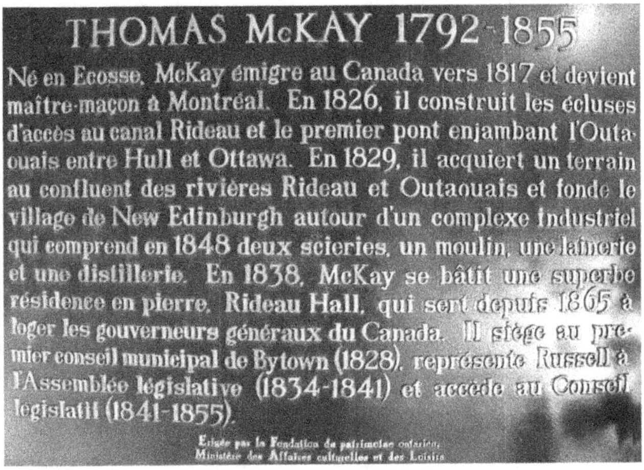

> **THOMAS McKAY 1792-1855**
> Né en Ecosse, McKay émigre au Canada vers 1817 et devient maître-maçon à Montréal. En 1826, il construit les écluses d'accès au canal Rideau et le premier pont enjambant l'Outaouais entre Hull et Ottawa. En 1829, il acquiert un terrain au confluent des rivières Rideau et Outaouais et fonde le village de New Edinburgh autour d'un complexe industriel qui comprend en 1848 deux scieries, un moulin, une lainerie et une distillerie. En 1838, McKay se bâtit une superbe résidence en pierre, Rideau Hall, qui sert depuis 1865 à loger les gouverneurs généraux du Canada. Il siège au premier conseil municipal de Bytown (1828), représente Russell à l'Assemblée législative (1834-1841) et accède au Conseil législatif (1841-1855).
>
> Érigée par la Fondation du patrimoine ontarien,
> Ministère des Affaires culturelles et des Loisirs

Figure C.3. Mackay French plaque.

Select Bibliography

Collections

Library and Archives Canada—Library and Archives Canada Thematic Guide

http://www.bac-lac.gc.ca/eng/discover/maps-charts-plans/Pages/thematic-guides-rideau-canal.aspx

1. Surveying—Field work, 1818–1849 Jones Falls, 1821, 1831.
2. Canals—Design and construction, 1821–1831 Davis Mills, 1849–1876.
3. Ottawa (Ont.)—Canals, 1818–1871 Smiths Falls Station, 1870–1871.
4. Cholera, n.d. Gloucester (Canada West: Township), 1818–1849.
5. Locks (hydraulic engineering)—Design and construction, 1821 Nepean (Canada West: Township), 1818–1849.
6. Piers—Design and construction, 1821 Goulbourn (Canada West: Township), 1818–1849.
7. Canals—Maintenance and repair, 1870 Elmsley (Canada West: Township), 1818–1849.
8. Canada—Officials and employees, 1871 John Jones, 1871.
9. Sluices—Design and construction, 1821–1831 Great Britain. Army. Corps of Royal Engineers, 1849–1876.
10. Structural engineering, 1821–1831.

The National Archives of the United Kingdom

* MG12, Admiralty. War Office and Foreign Office Papers; Section A (Admiralty); Section B (War Office); WO55 (Ordnance Miscellanea, 1740–1863)

* MG24, Pre-Confederation Manuscripts. E1, Merritt Papers, 1778–1892; E2, Rideau Canal Lands, 1818–1849; E6, John Mactaggart, 1827–1828; H12 John Burrows.

Library and Archives Canada

* RG1, E, Phillpotts Report, *Report on the Inland Navigation of the Canadas Called in Lord Glenelg's Despatch to the Earl of Durham, 23 August 1838.
* RG7, Governor General's Office, Section G1, Despatches, 1784–1909.
* RG8, British Military and Naval Records, C Series (British Military Records).
* RG11, Department of Public Works. Series I, Lachine Canal Navigation Company, 1819–1821; Commissioners for the Lachine Canal, 1821–1842; H3/312, Lachine Canal, 1828.

McCord Museum—Redpath Papers (PO85)

Archives of Ontario

* C 1 — Thomas Burrowes fonds
* F 4549 — New Edinburgh Mills fonds

General Sources

Bytown Museum
Carleton University Library
City of Ottawa Archives
Upper Canada Land Petitions
Registry Office, City of Ottawa
Ottawa Public Library, Ottawa Room
Queen's University Archives
University of Ottawa Library
McGill University Library and Redpath Library
Heritage Passages: Bytown and the Rideau Canal (VMC)
Bytown.net (Bytown or Bust): A Digital History of Eastern Ontario and Western Quebec, Canada Including the Cities of Ottawa and Hull/Gatineau 1600 to 2015
Dictionary of Canadian Biography Online (DCB)
UK Dictionary of National Biography
Cyclopædia of Canadian Biography (Rose, 1886)
Archives.org

Newspapers

Bytown Gazette, and *Ottawa and Rideau Advertiser, passim*
Bytown Packet (Robert Bell)
Ottawa Citizen (Robert Bell)
Advocate (Ottawa)
Chronicle & Gazette (Kingston)
British Whig (Kingston)
Montreal Gazette
Montreal Witness
Tribune (Ottawa)

Major Works Consulted

Aimers, John. *The Palace on the Rideau*. Bytown Pamphlet Series no. 44. Ottawa: Monarchy Canada. Historical Society of Ottawa, 1996
Andrews, Mark. *For King and Country: Lieutenant Colonel John By, R.E., Indefatigable Civil-Military Engineer*. Merrickville: Heritage Merrickville Foundation, 1998.
Anonymous. *By-Laws of Dalhousie Lodge, of Ancient, Free and Accepted Masons*. Ottawa: Bell and Woodburn, 1868.
Anonymous. *Bytown or Bust, Malaria on the Rideau Canal, Ontario, Canada; Cholera Epidemics in Ottawa/Bytown, 1832, Other 19th Century Diseases*. Ottawa, Online.
Anonymous. *Papers on Subjects Connected with the Duties of the Corps of Royal Engineers (London)*, 1 (1837): 73–102.
Anonymous. *Proceedings of Public Meetings Held at Bytown, October 3rd and 10th, Relative to the St. Lawrence and Lake Champlain Canal*. Bytown, 1849.
Anonymous. "Rideau Hall Reminiscences." *Free Press* (Ottawa), Oct. 21, 1878.
Askwith, John. E. "Recollections of New Edinburgh." Ottawa: typescript, n.d.
Audet, Francis-Joseph. "Rideau Hall and Earnscliffe," *CHA Report*, 1932.
———. "The Honourable Thomas McKay, M. L. C., Founder of New Edinburgh, 1792–1855," *CHA Report*, 1932, 65–79.
———. *Historique des journaux d'Ottawa*. Ottawa: A. Bureau & Frères, 1896.
Baird, David McCurdy. *Guide to the Geology and Scenery of the National Capital Area*. Geological Survey of Canada Miscellaneous Report 15. Ottawa: 1968.
Barker, Edward John. *Observations on the Rideau Canal*. Kingston, 1834.
Barnes, A. S. L, ed. *History of the Rideau Waterway*. Toronto: Conservation Authorities Branch, Department of Energy and Resources Management, 1970.
Blyth, G. R. "Bytown, 1834, to Ottawa, 1854." *Women's Canadian Historical Society of Ottawa, Transactions*, 9 (1925): 5–15.

Bond, Courtney. "Alexander James Christie, Bytown Pioneer: His Life and Times, 1787–1843." *Ontario History* 56 (1964).

Bond, Courtney. "The Canadian Government Comes to Ottawa, 1865–1866." *Ontario History* 55 (1963): 23–34.

Boucher, Louise N. "Chaudière Falls in the Outaouais Region." *The Encyclopedia of French Cultural Heritage in North America.* http://www.ameriquefrancaise.org/en/.

Bouchette, Joseph. *General Report of an Official Tour Through the New Settlements of the Province of Lower Canada.* Québec: Thomas Cary & Co., 1825.

Braid, D. *Nicol Hugh Baird: A Pioneering Scottish Civil Engineer in Early Canada.* Ottawa: Historical Society of Ottawa, 1987.

Brault, Lucien. *Ottawa Old & New.* Ottawa: Ottawa Historical Information Institute, 1946.

———. *Hull 1800–1950.* Ottawa: Les Éditions de l'Université d'Ottawa, 1950.

———. *The Mile of History.* Ottawa: National Capital Commission, 1980.

———. *Parliament Hill.* Ottawa: National Capital Commission, 1981.

———. *The Mile of History.* Ottawa: National Capital Commission, 1981.

Bush, Edward Forbes. *Commercial Navigation on the Rideau Canal, 1832–1861.* History and Archeology Manuscript Report 54. Ottawa: Parks Canada, 1981.

———. *The Builders of the Rideau Canal, 1826–32.* Manuscript Report 185. Ottawa: Parks Canada, 1976. (Digital Edition: Friends of the Rideau, 2009.)

———. "Thomas Coltrin Keefer." *Ontario History* 66 (1974).

Campbell, Robert. *A History of the Scotch Presbyterian Church, St. Gabriel Street.* Montréal, 1887.

Carlos, Ann M., and Frank D. Lewis. "The Creative Financing of an Unprofitable Enterprise: The Grand Trunk Railway of Canada, 1853–1881." *Explorations in Economic History* 32, no. 3 (July 1995): 273–301.

Chalmers, Floyd S. "Thomas Ahearn is Ottawa's Biggest Captain of Industry." *The Financial Post,* August 15, 1924.

Churcher, Colin. *The Railways of Ottawa.* https://churcher.crcml.org/circle/findings.htm.

Cinq-Mars, Ernest E. *Hull : son origine, ses progrès, son avenir.* Hull: Bérubé et Frères, 1908.

Clark, Gregory. *What Were the British Earnings and Prices Then?* (New Series.) Measuring Worth, 2019. http://www.measuringworth.com/ukearncpi/.

Connolly, Thomas William John. *The History of the Corps of Royal Sappers and Miners.* London, 1855.

Cook, Bryan. "Crossing the Chaudière Union Bridges." *HSO Newsletter,* 2017. Historical Society of Ottawa.

Cross, Michael. "Stoney Monday, 1849: The Rebellion Losses Riot in Bytown." *Ontario History* 63 (September 1971): 177–180.

Currie, Archibald William. *The Grand Trunk Railway of Canada.* Toronto: University of Toronto Press, 1957.
Davies, Glyn. *A History of Money: From Ancient Times to the Present Day.* 3rd ed. Cardiff: University of Wales Press, 2002.
De Jonge, James A. *The Military Establishment at Bytown, 1826–1856.* Microfiche Report 109. Ottawa: Parks Canada, 1983.
Denison, Lieutenant W. "Detailed Description of some of the Works on the Rideau Canal, and of the Alterations and Improvements Made Therein Since the Opening of the Navigation." *Papers on Subjects Connected with the Duties of the Corps of Royal Engineers.,* vol. 3. London, 1839, 133–138.
Despatches, Correspondence and Memoranda of Field Marshal Arthur, Duke of Wellington. Vol. 4, 387–397.
Dewar, Anne. *The Last Days of Bytown.* Bytown Pamphlet Series no. 32. Ottawa: Historical Society of Ottawa, 1989.
Drummond, G. P. *Bytown in the Forties with Glimpses of the Thirties.* Ottawa: Historical Society of Ottawa, n.d.
Durnford, Mary. *Family Recollections of Lieut. General Elias Walker Durnford, a Colonel Commandant of the Corps of Royal Engineers.* Montréal, 1863.
Edmond, Martha. *Rockcliffe Park: A History of the Village.* Ottawa: The Friends of the Village of Rockcliffe Park Foundation, 2005.
Elgie, Brian, and Karen Lynn Ouellette. "Notes on the Thomas McKay Family Bible, Found by Brian Elgie at His Church, Chatham." *Historical Society of Ottawa Newsletter,* April 2018. [Bible in the possession of MacKay United Church, 39 Dufferin Rd., Ottawa].
Feltoe, Richard. *A Gentleman of Substance: The Life and Legacy of John Redpath (1796–1869).* Toronto: Natural Heritage/Natural History Inc., 2004.
French, Lieutenant Gershom. *1783 Rideau Survey Report,* Colonial Office, "Q" Series, Governor Haldimand, 1784, National Archives of Canada, Reel-C-11893, MG 11, "Q" Series, vol. 23, 10–23.
Frome, Lieutenant Edward C. "Account of the Causes Which Led to the Construction of the Rideau Canal, Connecting the Waters of Lake Ontario and the Ottawa; the Nature of the Communication Prior to 1827; and a Description of the Works by Means of Which It Is Converted into a Steam-Boat Navigation," in *Papers on Subjects Connected with the Duties of the Corps of Royal Engineers* 1(1837): 73–102.
Gaffield, Chad. *History of the Outaouais.* Québec: Presses de l'Université Laval, 1997.
Gates, David. *The Napoleonic Wars, 1803–1815.* London: Arnold, 1997.
Gelly, Alain, and Yvon Desloges. *The Lachine Canal: Riding the Waves of Industrial and Urban Development.* Montréal: Les éditions du Septentrion, 1958.
Goodenough, Lady Veronica. *Earnscliffe.* Ottawa: Historical Society of Ottawa, 1998.

Gordon, Bruce. "Cpl. Thomas Burrowes (1796–1866)." Toronto: Archives of Ontario, 2017.

Gourlay, John Lowry. *History of the Ottawa Valley: A Collection of Facts, Events and Reminiscences for Over Half a Century*. Ottawa, 1896.

Hansard, passim.

Haig, Robert. *Ottawa, City of the Big Ears: The Intimate Living Story of a City and a Capital*. Ottawa: Haig and Haig Publishing Company, 1970.

Heisler, John P. *The Canals of Canada*. Canadian Historic Sites: Occasional Papers in Archaeology and History No. 8. Ottawa: Parks Canada, n.d.

——. *Financing the Construction of Early Canals in the Canadas, 1779–1841*. The Canals of Canada, Canadian Historic Sites: Occasional Papers in Archaeology and History No. 8. Ottawa: Parks Canada, 1973.

Henderson, Rick. *Walking in the Footsteps of Philemon Wright*. Gatineau, Quebec: Dadson Lane Productions, 2016.

Hendricks, David, and Paul Philpott. *Ottawa Transportation: From Horses to Buses*. Ottawa: Historical Society of Ottawa, 1985.

Hill, Hamnett. *Bytown Election of 1841*. Ottawa: Historical Society of Ottawa, 1986.

——. *The Bytown Gazette: A Pioneer Newspaper*. OH 27 (1931).

——. *The Genesis of our Capital*. Bytown Pamphlet Series, no. 3. Ottawa: Historical Society of Ottawa, 1935 (Reprint).

Hill, Richard. *Prizes of War: Prize Law and the Royal Navy in the Napoleonic Wars 1793–1815*. London: Sutton, 1999.

Hind, Edith J. "Troubles of a Canal-Builder: Lieut.-Col. John By and the Burgess Accusations." *Ontario History* (Journal of the Ontario Historical Society) 57, no. 3 (September 1965): 141–147.

Hirsch, R. Forbes. *The Commissariat: Survivor of the Bytown Era*. Ottawa: Historical Society of Ottawa, 1982.

——. *The Provincial Election of 1848 in Bytown*. Ottawa: Historical Society of Ottawa, 1989.

——. *The Upper Ottawa Valley Timber Trade*. Ottawa: Historical Society of Ottawa, 1985.

Historical Society of Ottawa. *Discoveries Unearthed Prior to the Renovations on Parliament Hill*. 2020. https://www.historicalsocietyottawa.ca/speakers-presentations/discoveries-unearthed-prior-to-the-renovations-on-parliament-hill.

Hope, Doris Grierson. *James Ferguson: A Bytown Pioneer, 1760–1830*. Bytown Pamphlet Series, no. 54. Ottawa: Historical Society of Ottawa, 1996.

Hubbard, R. H. *Rideau Hall: An Illustrated History of Government House, Ottawa; Victorian and Edwardian Times*. Kingston and Montréal: McGill-Queen's University Press, 1967.

Innis, Harold A., and Arthur Lower, eds. *Select Documents in Canadian Economic History 1497–1783*. Toronto: University of Toronto Press, 1929.

Jebb, Lieutenant Joshua. *Report on the Water Communication of the Rideau, 1816.* RG8, 1B, "C" Series, 1915. National Archives of Canada.

Keefer, Robert. *Memoirs of the Keefer Family.* Norwood, Ontario: Norwood Register Press, 1935.

Keefer, Thomas C. "Address of T. C. Keefer, President, Canadian Society of Civil Engineers." Address given at the annual meeting of the Canadian Society of Civil Engineers, 1898.

———. *A Sequel to The Philosophy of Railroads.* Toronto: Lovell & Gibson, 1856.

———. *Canadian Water Power and Its Electrical Product in Relation to Underdeveloped Resources of the Dominion.* Ottawa: Royal Society of Canada, 1900.

———. "Free Trade, Protection and Reciprocity." In *The Canals of Canada.* Montréal, 1876.

———. *Handbook and Official Catalogue of the Canadian Section by Thomas C. Keefer.* London: H.M.S.O., 1878.

———. *Handbook and Official Catalogue of the Canadian Section, Exposition Universelle.* London: Eyre and Spottiswoode, 1857.

———. "Montreal" and "The Ottawa." Two lectures delivered before the Mechanics' Institute of Montreal, January 1853 and 1854.

———. *Philosophy of Railroads and Other Essays.* Edited by H. V. Nelles. Toronto: University of Toronto Press, 1972.

———. *Philosophy of Railroads: Published at the Request of the Directors of the Montreal and Lachine Railroad.* Montréal and Toronto: Armour and Ramsay, 1850.

———. *Report of Thomas C. Keefer. Esq., C.E. of Survey of Georgian Bay Canal Route to Lake Ontario: Accompanied with Maps.* Whitby, Ontario, 1863.

———. *Report of Thomas C. Keefer. Esq., C.E. on the Water Works of the City of Montreal.* Montréal, 1868.

———. *Report of Thomas C. Keefer. Esq., Civil Engineer, on Proposed Water Supply for Dartmouth. N.S.* Dartmouth: Halifax, 1876.

———. *Report on a Survey for the Railway Bridge over the St. Lawrence at Montreal, Surveyed in 1851–52, by Order of the Committee of the Montreal and Kingston Railway, Hon. John Young, Chairman.* Montréal: John Lovell, 1853. https://hdl.handle.net/2027/mdp.39015021228872?urlappend=%3Bseq=3.

———. *Report on the Preliminary Survey of the Kingston and Toronto Section of the Canada Trunk Railway.* Montréal, 1851.

———. *Report on Water Supply for the City of Ottawa.* Ottawa: Bell & Woodburn, 1869.

———. *Specifications & Estimates of the Three Successful Competitors for Premiums Offered by the City Council of Supplying the City with Water: Together with the Report Thereupon of T. C. Keefer, Esquire.* Hamilton: Hamilton Water Works, 1855.

———. *The Canadian Pacific Railway: Address at the Annual Convention at Milwaukee, Wisconsin, June 28.* New York: American Society of Civil Engineers, 1888.

———. *The Canals of Canada.* Montréal, 1850.

———. *The Canals of Canada*. Read before the Royal Society of Canada, Ottawa, 1893.

———. *The Old Welland Canal and the Man Who Made it*. St Catherines: The Print Shop, 1911.

Kemp, Peter. *Prize Money*. London: Gale and Polden, 1946.

Keshen, Jeff, and Nicole St-Onge. *Ottawa—Making a Capital*. Ottawa: University of Ottawa Press, 2001.

Knight, David. "'Boosterism' and Locational Analysis or One Man's Swan is Another Man's Goose." *Urban History Review* 2, no. 3–73 (February 1974): 10–16.

Laberge, Edward P. *Bytown's Own College*. Bytown Pamphlet Series. Ottawa: Historical Society of Ottawa, 1982.

———. *Philemon Wright, a Yankee Who Helped Build Canada*. Bytown Pamphlet Series. Ottawa: The Historical Society of Ottawa, 1989.

———. *The Artistic Legacies of John Burrows and Thomas Burrowes*. Bytown Pamphlet Series. Ottawa: Historical Society of Ottawa, 1987.

Lamoureux, Georgette. *Bytown et ses pionniers canadiens-français, 1826–1855*. Ottawa: G. Lamoureux, 1978.

Latchford, Francis Robert. "Philemon Wright and the Settlement of Hull." In *Women's Canadian Historical Society of Ottawa, Transactions*. Vol. 8. Ottawa, 1921.

Lavallée, Omer. "Historic Review of 'Bytown and Prescott Railway' as Ottawa Observes Centenary [of] First Rail Service." *Spanner*, 1955.

———. "The Rise and Fall of the Provincial Gauge." *Canadian Rail* 143, no. 22 (1963), Canadian Railroad Historical Association.

———. *John By; Builder of the Rideau Canal, Founder of Ottawa*. Ottawa: Historical Society of Ottawa, 1982.

Legget, Robert. *The Jones Falls Dam on the Rideau Canal, Ontario Canada*. National Research Council, Division of Building Research, Tech Paper 128. Ottawa: September, 1961.

———. *Rideau Waterway*. Toronto: University of Toronto Press, 1986. First Edition 1955.

Le Jeune, Louis. *Dictionnaire général de biographie, histoire, littérature, agriculture, commerce, industrie et des arts, sciences, mœurs, coutumes, institutions politiques et religieuses du Canada*. Ottawa: University of Ottawa Press, 1931.

Lett, William Pittman. *Recollections of Old Bytown*. Bytown Series, no. 3. Ottawa: Historical Society of Ottawa, 1979.

Lower, Arthur. *Great Britain's Woodyard*. Kingston and Montréal: McGill-Queen's University Press, 1973.

MacDonald, N. *Canada 1763–1841: Immigration and Settlement*. London, 1939.

Mackey, Frank. *Steamboat Connections: Montreal to Upper Canada, 1816–1843*. Kingston and Montréal: McGill-Queen's University Press, 2003.

MacRae, Marion, and Anthony Adamson. *The Ancestral Roof: Domestic Architecture of Upper Canada*. Toronto: Clarke, Irwin, 1963.

Mactaggart, John. *Three Years in Canada: An Account of the Actual State of the Country in 1826–7–8: Comprehending its Resources, Productions, Improvements, and Capabilities; and Including Sketches of the State of Society, Advice to Emigrants, &c.* 2 vols. London: Henry Colburn, New Burlington Street, 1829.

Malloch, John Glass. *Diary.* MU 842. Archives of Ontario.

Maltby, Janet J. *Archaeological Excavations at the Lock Office, Entrance Valley, Rideau Canal.* Ottawa: Parks Canada, 1988.

Marr, Lucille. *The College and Missions: Jane Drummond Redpath.* Historical Papers 2015: Canadian Society of Church History. Toronto: York University Press, 2015.

McKenna, Katherine M. J., ed. *Labourers on the Rideau Canal, 1826–1832: From Work Site to World Heritage Site.* Ottawa: Borealis Press, 2008.

McNabb, Heather. "Montreal's Scottish Community, 1836–65." Master's thesis, Concordia University, 1999.

Mika, Nick, and Helma. *Bytown: The Early Days of Ottawa.* Belleville: Mika Publishing Company, 1982.

Mills, John. *Canadian Coastal and Inland Steam Vessels 1809–1830.* The Steamship Historical Society of America, Inc., 1979.

Nelles, Mike. *Steamboating on the Rideau Canal.* Bytown Pamphlet Series, no. 71. Ottawa: Historical Society of Ottawa, 2007.

Osborne, B. "The Artist as Historical Commentator: Thomas Burrowes and the Rideau Canal." *Archivaria* 1 (January 1, 1983):17.

Osborne, Brian S. "Thomas Burrowes and the Rideau Corridor." Unpublished. Ottawa: Parks Canada, 1982.

Parent, Jean-Claude. *Profile of Certain Buildings along the Rideau Canal: The Royal Engineers' Office and Commissariat Building in Ottawa, the Landscape at the Ottawa Lock Station, the Railway Tunnel at Ottawa, the Forge at Jones Falls and the Blockhouse.* Ottawa: Parks Canada, 1977.

Parks Canada. *Rideau Hall and Landscaped Grounds National Historic Site of Canada.* Ottawa: Directory of Federal Heritage Designations https://www.pc.gc.ca/apps/dfhd/page_nhs_eng.aspx?id=473.

Passfield, Robert W. "A Wilderness Survey: Laying out the Rideau Canal, 1826–1832." *HSTC Bulletin: Journal of the History of Canadian Science, Technology and Medicine* 7, no. 2 (May 1983): 80–97.

———. *Engineering the Defence of the Canadas: Lt. Col. John By and the Rideau Canal.* Manuscript Report 425. Ottawa: Parks Canada, 1980.

———. *Canal Lock Design and Construction: The Rideau Canal Experience, 1826–1982.* Microfiche Report Series, no. 57. Ottawa: Parks Canada, 1983. (Digital Edition: Friends of the Rideau, 2010).

Patychuk, Dianne L. "Malaria on the Rideau Canal, 1826–32." Bachelor's thesis, Queen's University, 1979.

Pilon, Jean-Luc. *Ancient History of the Lower Ottawa River Valley*. Ottawa River Heritage Designation Committee. Ottawa: Ontario Archaeology, Canadian Museum of Civilization, 2015.

Plousos, Suzanne. *The Evolution of the Landscape at Entrance Valley, Rideau Canal: Results of Archaeological Investigations, 1980–1983*. Ottawa: Parks Canada, 1984.

Potvin, Damase. *Sous le signe du Quartz : histoire romancée des mines du nord-ouest de Québec*. Montréal, 1940.

Powell, James. *A History of the Canadian Dollar*. Ottawa: Bank of Canada, 2005.

Prévost, Michel. *L'Université d'Ottawa depuis 1848 / The University of Ottawa since 1848*. Ottawa: University of Ottawa Press, 2008.

Prévost, Michel. "Ottawa, le choix de la reine / Ottawa: Queen Victoria's Choice." *Tabaret* (Winter 2007): 18; *Le Chaînon* 25, no. 3 (Fall 2007): 19–20.

Price, Karen. *Construction History of the Rideau Canal*. [Manuscript Report 193]. Ottawa: Parks Canada, 1976. (Digital Edition: Friends of the Rideau, 2008.)

Province of Canada. *Enquiry by the Honorable Mr. McKay, in the Legislative Council, and Answer Returned by Government, on the Subject of Laying out the Waste Land Extending from the River Ottawa to Lake Huron*. Printed by order of the Honorable the Legislative Council. Toronto: Queen's Printer, 1852.

Province of Canada. *Resolutions to Be Proposed in the Legislative Council, on the Constitution of that House, by the Honorable Thomas McKay, on Monday, the 18th Day of October, 1852*. Printed by order of the Honorable the Legislative Council. Toronto: Queen's Printer, 1852.

Raudzens, George. *The British Ordnance Department and Canada's Canals, 1815–1855*. Waterloo: Wilfrid Laurier University Press, 1979.

Reddaway, Norman. *Earnscliffe: Home of Canada's First Prime Minister and Since 1930, Residence of High Commissioners for the United Kingdom in Canada*. London, 1955.

Rens, Jean-Guy. *Invisible Empire: A History of the Telecommunications Industry in Canada*. Kingston and Montréal: McGill-Queen's University Press, 2001.

Royer, Martin. "Le dépôt militaire de l'île Sainte-Hélène et les poudrières du complexe militaire de l'Île Sainte-Hélène." PhD diss., OCLC 458753130. Québec: Université Laval, 2009.

Scott, Richard W. *The Choice of a Capital: Reminiscences…* Ottawa: Mortimer Co., 1907.

Sneyd, Robert. "Rideau Canal: Endurance of Its Military Rationale, 1812–1871," *Rideau Reflections*, Fall 2008.

Snyder, Marsha Hay. *Nineteenth Century Industrial Development in the Rideau Corridor to 1920*. Series no. 223 [Microfiche Report]. Ottawa: Parks Canada, 1980.

Sweeny, Alastair. *Fire Along the Frontier: Great Battles of the War of 1812.* Toronto: Dundurn Press, 2012.

———. *George-Étienne Cartier: A Biography.* Toronto: McClelland and Stewart, 1976.

Tassé, Joseph. *Philemon Wright, ou Colonization et Commerce de Bois.* Montréal, 1871.

Taylor, John H. *Ottawa, An Illustrated History.* Toronto: Lorimer, 1986.

Tresham, Linda. *Bytown and the Cholera Epidemic of 1832.* Monarchy Canada. Toronto: Monarchist League of Canada, April 1996.

Tulchinsky, Gerald. "The Construction of the First Lachine Canal, 1815–1826." Master's thesis, McGill University, 1960.

———. *The River Barons: Montreal Businessmen and the Growth of Industry and Transportation, 1837–53.* Toronto: University of Toronto Press, 1977.

Tulloch, Judith. *The Rideau Canal: Defence, Transport and Recreation.* History and Archaeology Series, no. 50. Ottawa: Parks Canada, 1981. (Digital Edition, Friends of the Rideau, 2008.)

United Kingdom. Parliament. *House of Commons, Accounts and Papers,* Session 26 October 1830–22 April, 1831, vol. IX.

United Kingdom. Parliament. *House of Commons, Report from the Select Committee Appointed to Take Into Consideration the Accounts and Papers Relating to the Rideau Canal.* April 22, 1831.

United Kingdom. Treasury. *Copy of Letter from the Secretary of the Ordnance, Transmitting Documents Respecting the Expenditures upon the Works of the Rideau Canal in Canada; Together with a Copy of the Treasury Minute Thereon.* London: House of Commons, June 1, 1832.

Valentine, Jaime. *Supplying the Rideau: Workers, Provisions and Health Care During the Construction of the Rideau Canal, 1826–1832.* Microfiche Report Series, no. 249, Parks Canada, 1985.

Van Cortlandt, Gertrude. "Records of the Rise and Progress of the City of Ottawa from the Foundation of the Rideau Canal to the Present Time." *Ottawa Citizen,* 1858. [The author was 14 years old at the time of writing.]

Walker, Harry and Olive. *Carleton Saga.* Ottawa: Runge Press, 1968.

Walton, Timothy R. *The Spanish Treasure Fleets.* Sarasota: Pineapple Press, 1994.

Watson, Ken W. "A History of the Rideau Lockstations: Jones Falls Locks 39–42." Rideau Canal – National Historic Site/World Heritage Site, 1996–2021. http://www.rideau-info.com/canal/history/locks/h39-42-jonesfalls.html.

———. "A History of the Rideau Lockstations: Malaria — A Rideau Mythconception." Rideau Canal – National Historic Site/World Heritage Site, 2007. http://www.rideau-info.com/canal/articles/malaria.html.

———. "A History of the Rideau Lockstations: Ottawa – Locks 1 to 8." Rideau Canal – National Historic Site/World Heritage Site, 2000. http://www.rideau-info.com/canal/history/locks/h01-08-ottawa.html.

———. "A History of the Rideau Lockstations: Hartwells – Locks 9 and 10." Rideau Canal – National Historic Site/World Heritage Site, 2000. http://www.rideau-info.com/canal/history/locks/h09-10-hartwells.html.

———. *Bye By: The Story of Lieutenant-Colonel John By, R. E. and his fall from grace*. Rideau-info.com. 1996.

———. *Engineered Landscapes: The Rideau Canal's Transformation of a Wilderness Waterway*. Elgin, Ontario: Ken W. Watson, 2006.

———. "The Military Roots of the Rideau Canal." Rideau Canal – National Historic Site/World Heritage Site, Spring 2012. http://www.rideau-info.com/canal/articles/military-roots.html.

———. "The Rideau Canal in Ottawa," *Rideau Reflections*, Fall/Winter 2014. Friends of the Rideau.

———. *The Rideau Route: Exploring the Pre-Canal Waterway*. Elgin: Ontario, 2007.

———. "Washed Away: The Story of the Building of the Hogs Back Dam." Rideau Canal – National Historic Site/World Heritage Site, 1996–2003. http://www.rideau-info.com/canal/tales/hogsback-dam.html.

———. "Women at the Rideau Worksites," *Rideau Reflections*, Spring/Summer 2015. Friends of the Rideau.

Wilson, Andrew. *A History of Old Bytown and Vicinity, Now the City of Ottawa*. Ottawa, 1876.

Wright, Philemon. *An Account of the First Settlement of the Township of Hull on the Ottawa River*. Lower Canada, 1820.

Wylie, William. "Poverty, Distress and Disease, Labour and the Construction of the Rideau Canal 1826–32." *Labour / Le Travail* 11, (Spring 1983): 7–29.

Note on Sources

Images without a source are either Public Domain (PD) or courtesy Mediawiki Commons (MWC), which may or may not have a source. You must verify copyright for anything other than personal use. Virtually all images have been retouched or cropped. Since Library and Archives asks that it be noted if LAC images have been altered, we hereby note blanket use of the credits "detail" or "based on."

Principal Sources

Dictionary of Canadian Biography Online (DCB)
Library and Archives Canada (Library and Archives Canada)
McCord Museum; Notman (McCord)
Ottawa Room; Ottawa Public Library (OPL)
Historical Society of Ottawa (HSO)
Ontario Archives (OA)

Other Sources

Bytown.net (Bytown or Bust)
Mediawiki Commons (MWC)
Bytown Museum (BM)
Bibliothèque et archives nationales du Québec (BANQ)
National Gallery of Canada (@Library and Archives Canada)
National Portrait Gallery (NPG)

Regional Studies

Series Editor: Michel Prévost

The *Regional Studies* series touches on all aspects of the greater Ottawa-Gatineau region, which includes Eastern Ontario and the Outaouais. The series is particularly interested in the history of the Federal Capital from both sides of the river, including the history of the individuals who contributed to its development and the history of its key institutions. It also focuses on the architectural heritage of this symbolic region of the country.

Previous titles in the *Regional Studies* Series

adam p. strömbergsson-denora, *Warring Sovereignties: Church Control and State Pressure at the University of Ottawa*, 2020.

Michelle Guitard, *Le Quartier du Musée : histoire et architecture*, 2018.

Andrew Waldron and Peter Coffman, *Explorer la capitale : guide architectural de la région d'Ottawa-Gatineau*, 2017.

For a complete list of the University of Ottawa Press titles, visit:
www.press.uOttawa.ca

www.ingramcontent.com/pod-product-compliance
Lightning Source LLC
Chambersburg PA
CBHW061342300426
44116CB00011B/1949